WATER RESOURCE MANAGEMENT

WATER RESOURCE MANAGEMENT

Editors

Prof. (Dr.) Sawalia Bihari Verma
Faculty of Commerce, SNS College, Muzaffarpur,
BRA Bihar University, Muzaffarpur
Former Reader, Nagaland (Central) University, Kohima

Dr. Praveen Sahu
Faculty Member,
Prestige Institute of Management, Gwalior
Jiwaji University, Gwalior

Dr. Jawahar Lal
Faculty of Commerce,
B.D. Evening College, Patna
Magadh University, Bodh Gaya, Bihar

PENTAGON PRESS

Water Resource Management

First Edition: 2009

ISBN 978-81-8274-369-4

Published in India by
PENTAGON PRESS
206, Peacock Lane, Shahpur Jat, New Delhi-110049
Phones: 011-64706243, 26491568
Telefax: 011-26490600
email: rajan@pentagon-press.com
website: www.pentagon-press.com

Printed at New Elegant Printers, New Delhi

Preface

What is the most precious and indispensable resource and fundamental to the survival of human beings, livestock and plants? Since the 1970s, the basic needs concept has been a dominating element in the development debate. The Mardel Plata Conference in 1977 focused exclusively on the drinking water and sanitation needs of the poor and vulnerable. This resulted in the designation of the period from 1981 to 1990 as the International Drinking Water Supply and Sanitation Decade (IDWSSD). The Global Water Supply and Sanitation 2000 Assessment (WHO/UNICEF 2000) shows that 1.1 billion people lack access to improved water supply and 2.4 billion to improved sanitation.

The general comment on the right to water adopted by the Convert on Economic, Social and Cultural Rights (CESCR) in November, 2002 recognised water as a fundamental human right and stated that everyone has access to safe and secure drinking water, equitably without discrimination (United Nations, 2003). The judgement delivered by the Supreme Court in the first week of December 2000, held that access to clean drinking water is a fundamental right as enunciated in the right to life under Article 21 of the Constitution of India. The UNDP's Human Development Report, 2000, defined access to safe drinking water as the proportion of the population using any of the following types of water supply for drinking: piped water, public tap, borehole or pump, well (protected and covered) or protected spring.

In fact, great civilizations settled and flourished around water sources and societies evolved their entire cultures and livelihoods based on it. India as a country with an abundance of natural resources is blessed with large resources in terms of water. However, the availability of fresh water varies from place to place based on its geophysical set-up and natural resources in the country.

At present, irrational and unsustainable water withdrawal from groundwater, tanks and reservoirs is on the increase. This water is mainly being used for agriculture and industrial purposes causing drinking water scarcity to human beings. Moreover, water use for drinking and domestic purposes is estimated at around 7 to 9 per cent of the total fresh water.

In mountainous and sub-mountainous areas and in desert and water scarcity rural areas, women and even adult girl travel a long distance to fetch drinking water. This causes a lot of damage to the health of women in general and·pregnant women in particular even resulting in premature delivery and spontaneous abortion. Ironically, it affects largely the education of the girl child in general and those belonging to impoverished families in particular, largely engaging girl children in the collection of water from distant sources.

The present water resources scenario is critical, especially the status of groundwater exploration and availability is causing a lot of concern. The rural areas are most vulnerable to changes in water resources availability, and are least capable in adapting their livelihood to the changes. The water has close linkage with food security and quality of life of the rural people. Water-use and regeneration has to be integrated effectively the way it was done in ancient times as evidenced from 'Varat Samhita' (550 A.D.).

Water management and construction, well organized water pricing system in 400 B.C., and construction of dams, tanks, spillways mentioned in ancient books reveal the significance of water and its management since our hoary past. The traditional wisdom has to be revived if we want our rural communities to lead a productive life. We should accept that when water resources are scarce, they must be conserved and the availability be augmented by minimizing losses and maximizing retention. For this measures like watershed management through rehabilitation of existing systems like tanks, construction of check dams and rain water harvesting needs to be promoted. Above all, promotion of people's participation in implementation and maintenance of water supply sources will lead to sustainability of resources and capacity building of the stakeholders.

Participation has acquired a wider dimension with the assertion of democracy. It is also associated with political liberties and civil consciousness. Local institutions are the major agents of social change and can play an important role in the management of natural resources at the local level Panchayati Raj Institutions (PRIs). Non-Governmental Organisations (NGOs), voluntary organizations like Self-Help Groups (SHGs) and other social organizations are instruments of socio-economic and political change as well as the agents of participatory process in development. A people-centric developmental initiative can be found rooted deep in its mission to ultimately endow the community with greater choices to act *vis-a-vis* the uncertainties in every day life situations.

One can agree with Prof. Ramaswamy when he says, "We must hope that the task force set up as directed by the Supreme Court will consider not merely the 'modalities' of the 'linking of rivers' but also the soundness and wisdom of the idea. Any headlong rush in the pursuit of this will be disastrous. Time well tell whether the proposals in the pipeline for inter-linking rivers hold water."

Inter-basin transfer of river waters, conveying water otherwise going waste to the seas after meeting the needs of their basins and after maintaining a steady, perennial flow through their lengths, is called inter-linking of rivers. The basic concept of this proposal is to transfer surplus waters (after meeting the needs of basins) of the rivers to the deficit ones, and not to link all rivers of India with one another for just the heck of it. One feels that the nomenclature of the concept should be inter-basin transfer of river waters and not inter-linking of rivers.

Rain water harvesting is, of course, a focus area for sustainable agricultural production but attention should also be paid for efficient management of available water resources. There is need to encourage modern techniques of irrigation like drip irrigation; micro-management is also needed for efficient use of irrigation water. Although, rain water harvesting techniques appear to be simple the full benefit could only be gained by adopting a scientific approach of implementation together with community awareness, their involvement and legislative measures for protection of groundwater from over exploitation. Rain is the first form of water in the hydrological cycle. Rainwater offers advantages in water quality both for irrigation and domestic use. It is naturally soft (unlike well water), contains almost no dissolved minerals or salts, is free of chemical treatment and is relatively a reliable source of water for households. It will not only increases the groundwater level but will result in the saving of thousands of mandays which are wasted in bringing water from far flung areas and thus can be more productively used. It not only has the potential to solve water problems of the thirsty millions, but also is environment-friendly. With a little governmental support, problems of famine, food, deforestation and so on, can easily be tackled.

Provision of assuring safe drinking water for all is an arduous task for the government. Therefore, there is need for people's participation for sustainable development of rural India. Bottom-up approach is needed so as to involve local people in the planning, managing, and decision-making processes. The bureaucracy should pay the role of a facilitator. The maximum involvement of people, PRIs, NGOs, SHGs, NRIs, corporate sector, private sector, and other poor social groups besides government should share the burden of the provision, operation and maintenance of safe drinking water sources in the country in general and especially in rural areas. Awareness, education, motivation of the local inhabitants, information, communication, inter-sectoral co-ordination and women empowerment would go a long way in helping the mission to achieve safe drinking water for all in the countryside of India.

Shivpuri, Muzaffarpur

SAWALIA BIHARI VERMA
PRAVEEN SAHU
JAWAHAR LAL

Acknowledgements

These papers have been contributed by distinguished personalities, academicians, social reformers, social scientists and so on. The people who have helped me in shaping this venture and I thank them immensely.

I express my deep sense of gratitude to my father late Baban Pd. Srivastawa and mother late Mrs. Lalmuni, father-in-law late H.N. Verma, Agriculture officer, and my wife Dr. Hema Verma, Deputy Magistrate (Collector) who are not alive but their invisible presence inspired me to complete this venture.

I am thankful to 'Yojana', 'Kurukshetra', 'Employment News', 'Environment and People' and so on for giving permission to reprint the articles published by their journals.

SAWALIA BIHARI VERMA

Contents

PART V
INTERLINKING OF RIVERS: NEED OF THE HOUR

Contributors

Dr. S.D. Sunder Singh: Faculty Member, Tamil Nadu Agricultural University, Coimbatore.

Dr. K. Palanisamy: Faculty Member, Tamil Nadu Agricultural University, Coimbatore.

Sarbeswara Sahoo: Education Officer, Central Board for Workers Education, Orissa.

P. Durga Prasad: Professor and Head, Centre for Human Resource Development, NIRD, Hyderabad.

Dr. N.T.K. Naik: Faculty, S.K. University, Post-Graduate Centre, Kurnool.

Dr. S. Mansoor Rahiman: Faculty, S.K. University, PG Centre, Kurnool.

K. Chinna Venkataswamy: Faculty, Osmania College, Kurnool.

A.R. Patel: Rural Credit Expert and Journalist.

Dinesh Chand: Deputy Advisor, Drinking Water Supply Unit, Ministry of Rural Development, Government of India.

Narayana, K.S.: Faculty, Institute for Social and Economic Change, Bangalore.

T. Manonmani: Reader in Communication, School of Information and Communication Sciences, M.K. University, Madurai.

Dr. A.P.J. Kalam: Former President, Government of India.

K.V. Ramana Rao: Scientist, Soil and Water Conservation Unit, Central Institute of Agricultural Engineering, Nabibagh, Bhopal.

K. Pandimuruga Chinnan: Research Assistant, CAPART Project, Gandhigram, Tamil Nadu.

Dr. B.K. Pattanaik: Faculty Member, Centre for Research in Rural and Industrial Development, Chandigarh.

Privankar Raha: Journalist and Writer.

Manisha Verma: Deputy Secretary, Drinking Water Supply Unit, Ministry of Rural Development, Government of India.

Dr. P. Shiva Ram: Associate Professor, Centre for Human Resource Development, NIRD, Hyderabad.

V. Reddappa Reddy: Professor of Rural Development, S.K. University, Anantapur.

C. Dheeraja: Assistant Professor, National Institute of Rural Development, Hyderabad.

K.V. Raju: Professor of Ecological Economics, Institute of Social and Economic Change, Bangalore.

S. Manasi: Professor of Ecological Economics, Institute of Social and Economic Change, Bangalore.

S. Ponnuraj: Dean, Faculty of Rural Health and Sanitation, Gandhigram Rural Institute, Gandhigram.

P.R. Singh: Faculty Member, Action Programme Division, The Energy and Resource Institute (TERI), New Delhi.

R. Prasad: Faculty Member, Action Programme Division, The Energy and Resource Institute (TERI), New Delhi.

Dr. Sawalia Bihari Verma: Faculty of Commerce, SNS College, Mazaffarpur, BRA Bihar University, Muzaffarpur; Former Reader, Nagaland (Central) University, Kohima.

Anil Joshi: Chairman, Himalayan Environment Studies and Conservation Organisation (HESCO), Dehradun.

Dusmanta Kumar Giri: Faculty Member, Institute of Social Sciences, New Delhi.

Laxmichand Pant: Journalist and Freelance Columnist.

S.S. Khanka: Professor and Dean, School of Management Sciences, Tezpur University, Assam.

Anjan Bhuyan: Head of Department of Business Administration, Tezpur University, Assam.

Dr. Sanjeev Kumar Sharma: Research Fellow, IIHS (UGC Centre of Excellence) Himachal Pradesh University, Shimla.

V.S. Gupta: Senior Media Academic, Former Country Representative, Asia Media Information and Communication Centre, Singapore.

Meenu Arora: Freelance Writer and Journalist, New Delhi.

Sunil K. Agrawal: Scientist, Science and Technology Unit, Government of India, New Delhi.

S.P. Mittal: Principal Scientist, ICAR.

V.P. Rajvedi: Freelance Writer and Journalist.

Harender Raj Gautam: Scientist, Department of Mycology and Plant Pathology, Dr. Y.S. Parmar University of Horticulture and Forestry, Himachal Pradesh.

Rohtashav Kumar: Assistant Scientist, Department of Mycology and Plant Pathology, Dr. Y.S. Parmar University of Horticulture and Forestry, Himachal Pradesh.

Farook Nimbal: Faculty, University of Agricultural Sciences, Dharwad.

Arabinda Ghose: Senior Media Academic, Former Country Representative, Asia Media Information and Communication Centre, Singapore.

M.M.N. Saxena: Deputy Advisor, Water Resources, Planning Commission, Government of India.

Partha J. Shah: Faculty, Centre for Civil Society, New Delhi.

H.B. Soymya: Faculty, Centre for Civil Society, New Delhi.

Udayabhanu, A.K.: Team Leader, Kerala Rural Water Supply and Sanitation Agency, Jalanidhi Project, Calicut, Kerala.

PART I

FRAMEWORK OF WATER RESOURCE MANAGEMENT

1

Water Resources: Issues and Concerns

Dr. S.D. Sundar Singh and Dr. K. Palanisamy

After India's independence, the need for expansion of irrigation facilities was fully recognized for increasing production of food grains to meet the growing requirements of the population. Irrigation has decisively contributed for increased agricultural growth. The irrigation sector is today facing twin issues of sub-optimal sector planning and financial management on the one hand and inadequate water management and maintenance on the other. Even though, during the last fifty years of planned development, agriculture has achieved an impressive success in raising production of food grain increasing income and employment levels and diversifying the cropping pattern and allied activities. The future of agriculture is inextricably interlinked with the development of irrigation.

Water Resources in Tamil Nadu

Among the States in India, Tamil Nadu is one of the water-starved States. The drinking water supply of some of the cities of other states as compared to Tamil Nadu is given in Table 1. The State's endowed irrigation potential in per capita terms is only about 0.08 hectares compared to the All India average of 0.17 hectares. The annual available water resources per capita in Tamil Nadu is estimated at 600 m^3 which is quite small compared to 4000 m^3 of the national average.

Reprinted with permission, *Kisan World*, March 2006, pp. 51-53

Table 1: Drinking Water Supply in some of the Cities in India

S.No.	*City*	*Per day supply (L)*	*Time of supply (Hrs.)*
1.	Ahmedabad	145	2.0
2.	Bangalore	123	2.5
3.	Chandigarh	342	10.0
4.	Goa	341	8.0
5.	Mumbai	240	5.0
6.	Patna	222	10.0
7.	Tamil Nadu	160	—

Source: Mr. John Briscoe, *World Bank Consultant* (2005).

The average annual rainfall of the State is 946 mm received over an area of 13.0 million ha which is accounted to about 12.3 million hectare metres (MHM) per year. But the utilisable runoff is about 2.486 MHM. The working Group on the Estimation of Groundwater Resources had indicated that the utilizable groundwater recharge would be about 2.24 MHM.

Increasing competition for water resources from other user sectors like household and industrial sectors too pose a challenge on the intersectoral allocation of available water. However, the agriculture sector still dominates in using water for irrigation and nearly 85 per cent of water is consumed by this use in the State. The increasing demand for water results in the supply-demand gap for water. The worked out supply-demand gap during the year 2025 will be about 2.12 MHM (44.72 per cent).

The increasing supply-demand gap warrants several strategies to be considered by several agencies for implementation. The supply management strategies include development of new irrigation structures and modernization of the existing structures. The demand management strategies include the use of advanced irrigation methods and techniques such as drip and sprinkler irrigation methods. However, there are related issues and concerns in implementing these strategies.

Issues and Concerns for the Future

Distribution of the available supply between different regions of the country and within the regions raises questions of prioritization among various uses in quantitative and qualitative terms, at different locations and for different groups.

While addressing the issues, there are two major concerns: movement for a transfer of the responsibility for the management of irrigation systems at a certain level to Water Users' Associations (WUAs). However, recent results have shown not much appreciable results.

The second concern relates to traditional community-managed systems of water. In recent years, however, there has been a growing body of opinion in favour of restoring and rehabilitating the old systems and reviving the tradition of community management. Many of the changes that we have referred to in response to issues and concerns will call for a close interaction between the government and the people. *Government functionaries have to work* constructively with the people and with the voluntary agencies engaged in social mobilization. The strategies should be planned in such a way that the results will be certainly achieved. Our past experiences guarantee this. The following are important components in this direction:

1. Planning Reorientation Towards Hydrological Unit

There is now a growing recognition that the planning of individual projects must be a part of, and must derive from, a larger plan for a suitable hydrological unit (a basin or sub-basin); such planning should focus mainly on land and water management; it should be integrated, holistic; 'participatory' and should involve the people at every stage; and it should be inter-disciplinary.

2. Time and Cost Over-runs

In implementation, projects are subject to what are referred to as line and cost over-runs', i.e. unconscionable delays and enormous increases in project costs. There is a serious problem of spreading available resources thinly and therefore, of 'spill-over' of projects over several plan periods. This results in increased capital cost per unit area over years.

3. Inadequate Cost Recovery

Irrigation projects have become poor revenue-earners because of low water rates and still lower collections. Lack of funds, for the construction of new projects and maintenance of existing ones, results in grossly inadequate allocation. Systems built at great cost are allowed to fall into a dilapidated state. Water charge rationalization should be done.

4. Participatory Irrigation Management

The growing feeling is the transfer of the responsibility for the management of irrigation systems at a certain level to Water Users' Associations (WUAs). This has come to be known as Participatory Irrigation Management (PIM) or Irrigation Management Transfer (IMT). The movement is in the early stages in our country, but it is bound to make significant headway in the near future.

5. Minor and Small Irrigation Systems—Water Mining

There are areas where canal irrigation in places well endowed with groundwater has led to a rise in the water table and the emergence of waterlogging and salinity problems. There are other areas where groundwater is being mined, i.e. extracted at a rate exceeding that of recharge, leading to the gradual depletion of the aquifer, and in coastal areas to the incursion of salinity from the sea. In Tamil Nadu State alone, out of 384 blocks, 90 blocks are defined as dark (extraction exceeding 850/0).

6. Minor and Small Irrigation Systems—Problems of Tank Irrigation

Tamil Nadu is known for tank. There are 39,000 tanks. For a number of reasons the physical structures have fallen into disuse and disrepair, and the old traditions and habits of community-management have been almost lost. Restoring and rehabilitating the old systems and reviving the tradition of community management have to be encouraged. Local water-harvesting and watershed development initiatives have intensified.

7. Water and Equity

In the context of large projects there is the question of the inequitable incidence of costs and benefits. One set of people, that is, those in the submergence area bear the social costs of the project and another set of people, those in the command area, enjoy the benefits. Efforts to give the former a share in those benefits and to regard them as 'partners in development' have been inadequate. Secondly, communities living upstream and around reservoir areas also have water and energy needs and are entitled to expect the authorities operating the reservoir and power-station to meet them; but this is not readily recognized.

There are questions of equity amongst the users of reservoir waters between head-reach and tail-end farms, between rich and poor farmers and so on. Another question is that of equity as between those who are served by the canals from a dam and those who are dependent upon river flow downstream of the dam. In relation to groundwater, over exploitation has resulted in well abandonment by many farmers.

8. Water and Quality

There is shocking wastage of water in all uses—agricultural, industrial, municipal, domestic—and the total absence of an awareness of the scarcity of this precious resource. A shift of focus towards water management has been urged and merits serious consideration. The protection of the water sources from pollution hazards is another important concern.

9. Conjunctive Use of Surface and Ground Water

The quantification of water available for conjunctive use is decided by establishing a general groundwater balance in the command area "with and without conjunctive use conditions." The planned quantity of groundwater has to be adjusted in such a manner that neither progressive lowering nor rising of the water table occurs nor is there deterioration of quality. Also conjunctive use helps in increasing the crop and water productivity.

10. Modernization of Existing Irrigation Systems

This programme was initiated in the early 70s by various State Governments. After each modernization project is completed, a performance review should be carried out for all modernization projects which have since been completed.

11. Sewage Irrigation

Waste water should be mainly used for secondary domestic/ municipal purposes such as flushing toilets, watering lawns, air conditioning and cooling, etc. For instance, using treated waste water for irrigation can be a very favourable proposition for releasing fresh water sources for domestic purposes. The quality of industrial and municipal waste water requires to be constantly monitored.

12. Inter-Basin Water Transfer

One of the proposals is to divert a part of the waters of the west-flowing rivers of Kerala to the east for irrigating the drought areas of Tamil Nadu apart from covering new areas in Kerala. The proposed peninsular river development is expected to provide additional irrigation benefits of over 1.3 m.ha. Careful analysis of the water allocation pattern in the country will be helpful for Tamil Nadu, to plan its allocation between different uses where, at present about 85 per cent of the water is utilized for agriculture. Hence the allocation for agriculture will be at least be reduced to about 75 per cent in 2020 by efficient water management practices and techniques after meeting the growing demand for industrial and municipal uses.

13. Implementation of Programmes to Improve the Performance of Rainfed Agriculture

Rainfed agriculture forms a major portion of the cropped area. The following programmes are considered important in this context. These programmes should be properly monitored for better results:

(i) Watershed Programmes (WSP)
(ii) Drought Prone Area Programme (DPAP)
(iii) National Watershed Development Project for Rainfed Areas (NWDPRA)
(iv) Integrated Wastelands Development Project (IWDP)

1. A Water Vision—2025 should be developed exclusively for Water Resources Development and Management.
2. The implementation of the vision strategies should be through participatory misson mode.

2

No Fresh Water—No Future

K. Pandimuruga Chinnan

Water is the most vital resource for the existence of life on earth. It is indispensable for the existence of plant and animal eco-systems and forms an essential element in the development of economic activities. No other natural resource has had such an overwhelming influence on human history. World oceans cover about three-fourths of the earth's surface. However, freshwater constitutes a very small proportion of this enormous quantity. About 2.7 per cent of the total water available on the earth is freshwater of which about 75.2 per cent lies frozen in polar regions and another 22.6 per cent is present as groundwater. The rest is available in lakes, rivers, atmosphere moisture, soil and vegetation. What is effectively available for consumption and other uses is a small proportion of the quantity available in rivers, lakes and groundwater. According to the World Health Organization, less than one per cent of the world's freshwater or 0.007 per cent of all the water on Earth is readily available for human world consumption. As the human population increases the demands on freshwater resources will continue to grow.

No Freshwater—No Future

The world is facing a freshwater crisis. People already use over half the world's accessible freshwater and may use nearly three-quarters by 2025. If per capita consumption of water resource continues to rise at its current rate, humankind could be using over 90 per cent of all available freshwater within 25 years, leaving just 10 per cent for the rest of the world's species. In other words, over 1.5 billion people lack ready access to drinking water and if current consumption patterns continue at least 3.5 billion people—nearly half the world's projected population—will live in water stressed river basins in just 20 years.

On top of this, contamination denies some 3.3 billion people access to clean water and 2.5 billion people have no water sanitation services. In developing countries, an estimated 90 per cent of wastewater is discharged without treatment into rivers and streams. Each year, there are about 250 million cases of water-related diseases with some 5 to 10 million deaths. It is not only people who are threatened by water shortages and pollution, freshwater ecosystems which harbour the world's greatest concentration of species are amongst the most vulnerable on Earth. Half the world's wetlands have been destroyed in the last 100 years. Two-fifths of the world's fish are freshwater species—and of these, 20 per cent are threatened, endangered, or have become extinct in recent decades. In addition to this, freshwater demand will increase greatly during the 21st century, not only because of demographic pressures, but also because of improved living standards, urban and industrial growth.

The world's thirst for water is likely to become one of the most pressing resource issues of the 21st century. Global water consumption rose six-fold between 1990 and 1995—more than double the rate of population growth—and continues to grow rapidly as agricultural, domestic and industrial demand increase. In some areas, water withdrawals are so high relative to supply that surface water supplies are literally shrinking and ground-water reserves are being depleted faster than they can be replenished by precipitation. As a result of over-exploitation of groundwater, water tables are dropping and some rivers often run dry before they reach the sea.

Future Requirements

Freshwater is available as rainfall, atmosphere moisture, surface water and groundwater. All these different forms and locations of water vary over place and time, both seasonally and from year to year. Paucity of funds, over-exploitation of water resources, degradation of water recharge structures, competing demand on the available water resources, depleting water availability due to continuous failure of monsoon are some of the factors that cause concern on the supply front. In addition, on the demand side, factors like growing urbanisation, increase in population, changing lifestyles, inadequate institutional and legislative framework also increase the complexity of the problem. At present, thousands of Indian cities do not have sources of water and in future, it would have to be transported over larger distances as the water sources move much more away from the cities. The country's current and future situation can be gauged by the trend in water availability. Water requirement for different uses in India is projected to the years 2010, 2025 and 2050 respectively in Table 1.

The table implies that irrigation (surface and groundwater) alone accounted for 83 per cent of the total water use in 1997-98 on the demand side and it is likely to slow down to 69.5 per cent by the year 2050 due to the impact of technological advancement in irrigation. In particular, demand for water on domestic, industrial and thermal power generation is expected to increase rather sharply. Demand for industrial uses (surface and groundwater) is likely to go up to 81 km^3 by the year 2050 from 30 km^3 in 1997-98. Water requirement for domestic uses (surface and groundwater) has been estimated to be 111 km^3 in 2050 which is almost three-fold increase on the demand side from 30 km^3 in 1997-98. The dependence is more on groundwater where there is competition on exploitation leading to the depletion of the water and encountering drought situation. The limited groundwater sources have not been able to keep pace with recharge and discharge to renew the balance.

The amount of water available per person in India has decreased steadily from 3450 cm in 1951 to 1250 cm in 1999. According to the Ministry of Water Resources, it is expected to decrease further to 760 cm per person in 2050. It could be predicted with complete certainty that the world in the year 2050 will be largely different from what it is today. The water sector will undergo dramatic changes in the years to come in order to keep up with the advances in technology and burgeoning population. Much of the projected increase in water demand will occur in developing countries where population growth, agricultural and industrial expansion will be greatest. Freshwater will be just the same in the future to a certain extent as in the past and this is precisely the problem for future generations. Therefore, we have no option but to depend on the available sources of water and have the responsibility to save and conserve them without fail.

Table 1: Water Requirement for Different Uses

Sl. No.	*Uses*	*Water Requirement (Quantity Km³)*			
		1997-98	*2010*	*2025*	*2050*
(a) Surface Water					
1.	Irrigation	318	339	366	463
2.	Domestic	17	24	36	65
3.	Industries	21	26	47	57
4.	Power	7	15	26	56
5.	Inland Navigation	—	7	10	15
6.	Environment (Ecology)	—	5	100	—
7.	Evaporation losses	36	42	50	76
	Total	399	458	635	732
(b) Ground Water					
1.	Irrigation	206	218	245	344
2.	Domestic and Municipal	13	19	26	46
3.	Industries	9	11	20	24
4.	Power	2	4	7	14
	Total	230	252	298	428
	Grand Total (a+b)	629	710	933	1160

Water Crisis

Widespread aquifer depletion in the groundwater areas, water logging in the canal regions and soil salinisation due to sea water ingress in the coastal zones are undeniable symptoms of an imminent 'Water Crisis' in India. The water crisis has both quantitative and qualitative dimensions. We have already glaring instances of serious water sharing conflicts not only at the macro-level, i.e., between States but also at the micro-level, i.e., between farmers or other water users. One had not heard of river water disputes till about the middle of the 20th century. Disputes and riots over river water are of a recent origin. And quite possibly, rivers and the distribution of their waters will become one of the most politicised ecological issues in the near future.

Water is scarce even for drinking purposes, not to talk about its availability for agriculture, industries, etc. India already faces an alarming situation. Its fragile water resources are stressed and depleting while various sectoral demands are growing rapidly even as about 200 million people in the country do not have access to safe drinking water and nearly 1.5 million children under five die each year due to water-borne diseases. The drought conditions in several parts of the country like Gujarat, Rajasthan, Orissa and Andhra Pradesh are unfortunately on the rise and disputes over sharing of water resources are becoming grimmer. India will face a severe water crisis if the available fresh water resources are not managed properly. Presently, six of India's 20 major river basins already fall in the water scarce category. By the year 2025, five more river basins are feared to be water scarce. Even Brahmaputra, Barak and west flowing rivers will be water deficient in the times to come. According to estimates, by the year 2025, the country will face a severe water shortage leading to serious struggles and it is also feared that within a few decades availability of water in the country will be about 1700 to 2000 cubic metres per person as against the world average of 5000 to 9000 cubic metres per person.

India is heading towards a freshwater crisis mainly due to improper management of water resources and environmental degradation which has led to a lack of access to safe water supply to millions of people. This freshwater crisis is already evident in many parts of India varying in scale and intensity depending mainly on the time of the year. Groundwater crisis is not the result of natural factors. It has been caused by human action. During the past two decades, the water level in several parts of the country has been falling rapidly due to an increase in extraction. One of the reports blamed the State governments for being a catalyst in accelerating the depletion of water resources by giving farmers free electricity who use it to pump water out of underground aquifers faster than rain that recharges them.

According to estimates, over three billion people of about 65 countries will be affected by the year 2025. India will be one among the water scarce countries. The most tragic part is that water is a finite natural resource and no technology, till date, has successfully contributed to making or producing water for mass consumption. In the context of India, the poverty-stricken regions tend to be in the climatic zones subject to drought and other water problems as they are least able to afford alternative sourcing. The crisis about water resources development and management thus arises because more of the water is not available for use and secondly, it is characterised by its highly uneven spatial distribution. Environmentalists like Sunderlal Bahuguna are not wrong in saying that the acute scarcity of water may force the powerful nations to wage a new global war for the control of depleted sources of water. Such a parallel makes the future picture essentially depressing.

Essential Steps for Tackling Water Crises

The main constraints that are faced in the water sector are inadequate trained personnel, inability to mobilise internal and external resources, inadequate project preparation, un-coordinated development approach, institutional weakness, technological shortcomings, poor quality of water resources itself, water losses through leakage, intermittent services, haphazard garbage collection and disposal systems, inadequate drainage of surface run-off, non-involvement of community in project planning development, operation and maintenance activities, etc. Suggestions for solving the water crisis are given below:

- A large share of water to meet new demands must come by saving water from existing uses through a comprehensive reform of water policy.
- New strategies for water development and management are urgently needed to avert severe national, regional and local water scarcities that will depress agricultural production, damage the environment and escalate water-related health problems.
- Major institutional policy and technological initiatives are required to ensure efficient, socially equitable and environmentally suitable management of water resources.
- In facing the enormous challenge of meeting the requirements of water supply for domestic, irrigation and industrial uses, it is natural to except that the R&D sector should play an important role.
- Since a major portion of water resources are used in agriculture, the farmer's co-operation is a must in the process of water management at all levels. An efficient irrigated cropping system

alone can sustain India's large and expanding population. During the years of poor monsoon, the farmer can go in for crops demanding less irrigation such as gram, barley and mustard during the rabi system.

- Attention should be paid by researchers and extension personnel in increasing the production per unit area/per unit of water in agriculture.
- Water management programmes should be implemented in a systematic way with integrated coordination of all relevant government departments at the State and Central levels. There is a need for revision of water legislation/groundwater control regulation acts to maintain the water table at a reasonable depth for sustainability.
- Clearcut water rights system is indispensable for the sustainability of our agriculture.
- Integrated watershed development actions have to be taken to use rainwater, soil water, groundwater and runoff water to increase production in rainfed areas.
- A data base should be created among all water boards and corporations for effective transfer of best practices.
- Immediate steps should be taken for drastic reduction of wastage of water in all sectors and protection of water sources from industrial pollution.
- The beneficiaries' role should be modified from passive recipients to active participants in water conservation activities. All the matters related to water, participation even from the selection of the site for water projects to maintenance is important.
- Above all, a strong political will of government to frame an appropriate water policy and equally important indomitable conscience of water users to utilize water judiciously are absolutely necessary for sustainable utilization of water.

3

Water Conservation: Need of the Hour

K.V. Ramana Rao

India which has 16 per cent of the world's population, 2.45 per cent of the world's land area and 4 per cent of the world's water resources already has a grave drinking water crisis. A recent study by the World Bank indicates that per capita availability of water, which was in the order of 5000 cubic metres per year at the time of independence, has drastically come down to 2000 cubic metres per year at present. The average annual rainfall of 1100 mm in the country, though fairly high, is marked by wide variations, both spatial and temporal. If water management is not accorded the importance it deserves, the country can very much expect to find itself in troubled waters as the years roll by. Estimates of the Central Ground Water Board are that the reservoirs of underground water will dry up entirely by 2025 in as many as fifteen states in India if the present level of exploitation and misuse of underground water continues. By 2050, when more than 50 per cent of the Indian population is expected to shift to the cities, fresh drinking water is expected to get very scarce. A new category of refugees is expected to emerge around that time: the water migrants. Future wars between or within nations will be fought on the issue of water.

Water is a prime natural measure, a basic human need and a precious national asset. Planning and development of water resources need to be governed by national perspectives. It has been estimated that out of the total precipitation of around 400 million hectare metres in the country, the surface water availability is about 178 million hectare metres. Out of this, about 50 per cent can be put to beneficial use because of topographical and other constraints. In addition there is a groundwater potential of about 42 million hectare metres. The availability of water is highly uneven in both space and time. Precipitation is confined to only about three or four months in the year and varies from 10 cm in the western parts of Rajasthan to over 1000 cm in Meghalaya. Further, water does not respect state boundaries either on surface or in groundwater. One-third of the country is drought prone and according to the National Commission on Floods, the area susceptible to floods is around 40 million hectares.

Rajasthan has adopted the State Water Policy in 1999 to address the problems faced in the water sector. As water is a State subject, each State should formulate its own policies on a national perspective to combat the ever increasing problem of water shortage. Hence, conservation of water at every front is the need of the hour even if it is few litres per day, since drop by drop makes the ocean. It is a matter of serious concern that adequate attention was not paid to handy water management techniques available. There is an urgent need for propagating water harvesting, conservation and recharging on a large scale. If the excess water is managed properly for deficit period, majority of the problems of drought and floods can be minimised.

Water conservation is not just for times of water shortage. Sound water-use practices reduce the amount of stress that we place on our resources, both by limiting water withdrawals and by decreasing wastewater discharges. Conserving water maintains the ecological balance. The Central Ground Water Board has put several programmes into effect aimed at managing water effectively, and developing and implementing an outreach campaign to educate citizens about the importance of water conservation. When people have access to an abundance of water much of the time, the importance of clean water is often overlooked. For most of us, water-use is a habit. We are accustomed to having water available at the twist of a tap. We usually do not think about how much water we waste when we actually use. Apart from use for daily activities by individuals, lot of water is wasted from leaking pipe fittings, taps, etc. Therefore, the objective of water saving and water management should start at the home front first, later in other places. By taking proper care to arrest leakages, water can be saved without requiring changes in personal water use habits. The amount of saving depends on current water consumption habits, water, sewer and energy costs, current flow rates of fixtures and flush volumes of toilets, system pressure, and the amount of water leakage through fittings and toilets. A dripping tap is more than annoying and also it is expensive as it causes wastage of the precious resource. Even small leaks can waste significant amount of water, for example, faucet leaks in toilets (Western style) can waste up to 500 litres of water a day.

The growth process and the expansion of economic activities inevitably lead to increasing demands for water for diverse purposes: domestic, industrial, agricultural, hydro-power, navigation, recreation, etc. So far, the principal consumptive use of water has been for irrigation. While the irrigation potential is estimated to have increased from 19.5 million hectares at the time of Independence to about 76 million hectares, further development of a substantial order is necessary for meeting the essential needs of the growing population. In India, exploitation of groundwater is more and almost 90 per cent of drinking water supplies in rural areas and 40 per cent of the total irrigation potential are to be met from groundwater. At the same time, groundwater is generally widespread and easily available without any restrictions on its use. This has resulted in a rapid expansion in the development of the potential and also exploitation of groundwater in the country. This over-exploitation of groundwater has led to decline of 2 to 4 metres in groundwater levels in many places. The art and science of collecting water where it falls is ancient. Historically, Indians have been the world's greatest water harvesters. Proof of this is reflected in numerous age-old structures like Tankas, Khadins, Johads, Bawaries, etc. found in old forts of India. Even if 5 per cent of annual rainfall is harvested properly, that would produce a substantial quantum of water to the tune of 900 million litres. Presently due to inadequate planning, rainfall excess (run-off) has been getting discharged into the oceans after coursing its way through the drains and rivers. Therefore, it is possible to prevent this wastage of water by storing it during the rainy season for use during the dry season or allowing it to seep underground as a measure of maintaining adequate levels of groundwater. This water can subsequently be 'recharged' or pumped up for irrigation or drinking water purposes.

Therefore, it becomes necessary to examine various options for meeting the basic requirements of safe drinking water to the large rural masses of India. In this regard, one option that is technically feasible, socially accepted and economically viable is rain water harvesting, which is a simple, cost effective and easily adaptable by all. Harvested rain water quantity depends upon frequency, duration and intensity of rainfall, nature of catchment and run-off characteristics.

A water harvesting system may be described as a complete facility for collecting and storing precipitation run-off, comprising a water collecting area, water storage structure and other components like piping and fencing. Water harvesting has certain advantages like optimal use of the scarce resource, easily implementable in all terrains, scope for community participation in construction and maintenance, use of local materials, traditional skills and knowledge besides the option of being eco-friendly. It is well known that rain water is biologically pure, soft in nature and free from organic matter. Specially constructed tanks, cisterns, lined pits and small dams serve as storage reservoirs.

There are different ways in which rainwater can be harvested. One such way is roof water harvesting in which the rainwater from roof tops is collected in built-up tanks. This water can be used later for different purposes including recharging groundwater through simple filtration devices. Studies have proved that groundwater recharge from a house with a 100 sq. metre rooftop will be 55,000 litres in a year.

For achieving the objective of saving the precious natural resource, it is essential to increase mass awareness not only of the criticality of water as a resource, but also of ways and means in which ordinary people can contribute towards its proper utilisation and management. Aspects like water conservation, recharging, efficiency in water-use, water recycling and self-regulation need attention. Some of the State Governments in India are making it mandatory in house construction to have provisions for harvesting rainwater. The Central Government has circulated a Model Bill to all States and Union Territories to enable them to enact suitable legislation for regulation and control of groundwater.

Some of the common methods for conservation of water are:

- Soak pits or recharge pits should be constructed near the house or near the existing bore wells/water supply outlets at a safe distance.
- Provisions for roof water harvesting in the existing as well as in newly constructed houses.
- Judicious use of water in the home as well as in fields.
- Water from kitchens or bathrooms can be safely diverted to kitchen gardens.
- Construction of small tanks for subsequent utilisation of water instead of using running water.

It is man's management of the precipitation available to him that determines whether or not he has both the quantity and the quality of water to meet his needs. Therefore, water which is one of the essential commodities for survival of humankind needs to be managed, since the important civilisations of the world have grown and prospered around perennial rivers. Whatever technology we adopt, it can succeed only if community participation in the programme is amply and adequately ensured. The policies and programmes, which are meant for the masses, can be effectively executed only with their active support and cooperation and participation at every stage, i.e., planning, execution and maintenance. In this regard, the efforts by government alone may not be adequate. Prominent voluntary and Non-Governmental Organisations have a major and crucial role to play for keeping liaison between the State and the community to educate, motivate and to transform water harvesting into a mass movement. All out efforts from each one is required to develop, conserve, utilise and manage this important resource guided by national perspectives.

Courtesy: Employment News, 10-16 May, 2003.

4

Water for Rural Areas

K.V. Raju and S. Manasi

Providing safe and adequate water to the people is one of the several challenges that our country is encountering. The problem is particularly severe in rural areas. Government has been addressing this as a priority issue since the commencement of the First Five Year Plan. An overview of the rural water sector indicates that still a lot needs to be done. The problem is multi-dimensional and area specific in nature. Several factors like increased urbanization, negligence of traditional water resources, poor water management, resource depletion due to over-exploitation of existing resources, lack of co-ordination between departments and poor institutional set-up in addressing the problem have led to the severity of the problem over the years. It is important to understand the existing situation and the complexities in order to address the problem in the context of project design and implementation and factors affecting sustainability of Rural Water Supply (RWS) programmes. Sustainability through water conservation and water management is seen as the best option.

One of the major causes seen is the reversal of environmental quality supply-demand relationships in just a few years. This is mainly due to economic growth accompanied by population increase, over-exploitation and mismanagement of natural resources and urbanization and its cumulative effect resulting in reducing the available supply of clean water and other environmental goods. Access to clean water or better environmental quality has become a scarce or economic good; thereby it has to be proceeded along the general lines of analysis involving the allocation and distribution of scarce goods and services. Water, which was considered as a public good, is now considered a priced good.

With the increase in demand for both water quantity and quality, financial, technical, and environmental constraints join together to limit our capacity to increase water supply as fast as the projected rise in water demand. The competing demands for water for meeting various requirements like domestic use, irrigation, industrial use, etc. are also continuously altering the opportunity cost of water in different sectors. There is a gap between the real economic value of water and the value underlying the irrational use of the resource.

With resource becoming a major constraint, the awakening to water management in a holistic way through water quality maintenance, water allocation to different sectors, decentralization in water allocation, sustainable use of water, improvement of sanitation, water pricing, institutional set-up, technical solutions and education and awareness are being addressed. Conserving water and to use it judiciously has come about only with increasing shortages, depletion of water resources and extremities in weather conditions causing disparity in water availability.

Rainwater harvesting provides a powerful and decentralized solution to the crisis as historical evidences have highlighted the effectiveness of rainwater harvesting (Vishwanath, 2003) at the fort city of Jaisalmer in Rajasthan to the temple town of Melkote in Karnataka. Lately, Anna Hazare's work in Ralegaon Siddhi in Maharashtra and Rajendra Singh's work with Tarun Bharat Sangh in Alwar District in Rajasthan needs special mention. Another most successful rainwater harvesting programme is the one at Mylenahalli in Hassan District by BAIF, Tiptur in Karnataka. But, the key policy message is that water harvesting cannot happen overnight (Sunita Narain, 2003). It involves time and investment to reinvest our rural capital as the aquifers are in deep trouble. Groundwater supplies over 90 per cent of drinking water needs and over 50 per cent of agriculture in the country. Modern borewell technology procures water from deeper ground levels while recharging is totally neglected.

Apart from the various reasons cited above, one of the major causes that have led to the crisis is pointed at implementing agencies that have focused on meeting the increasing demands for water through building supporting infrastructure while the supply aspect has been totally neglected. The consequences of supply driven approach have resulted in over exploitation of water resources, change in cropping systems, negligence of traditional water resources, total dependence on the state and poor cost recovery leading to non-sustainability and inadequate and poor quality service. Hence, the focus has been shifted towards addressing the problem through a demand-based approach in the last few years.

Rural Drinking Water Status

The National Water Policy (1987 and 2003) prioritizes mainly on meeting the drinking water needs. While the Global Water Supply and Sanitation Assessment Report, 2000 targets to reduce the proportion of people without having access to water supply to half by 2015 and provides access to water supply for all by 2025, the Indian Government has aimed at providing safe water by 2004. Importance is given to 'non-covered' and quality affected habitations following which 'partially covered' habitations will be covered.

In India, the State governments are responsible for providing drinking water facilities to rural areas. The Central government provides financial assistance, policy guidance and technological support. Both the Central and State governments have made huge investments through various programmes. The goal of providing adequate water has considerably been achieved in India. However, it does not commensurate with the huge investments made. Rs. 320 billion has been invested on rural drinking water supply in the last 50 years, 86.9 per cent of about 1.4 million rural habitations has been covered. 11.7 per cent habitations are partially covered and 1.4 per cent are yet to be covered. 15 per cent are affected with quality problems like excess flouride, arsenic, iron and nitrate contamination. 3.5 million handpumps and 116,000 piped water supply schemes in different parts of the country have not been able to quench the thirst, particularly during the summer months. Added to this, service levels in this sector need more improvement irrespective of the progress achieved.

Year	*Programme*
1954	Water Supply and Sanitation
1972-73	Accelerated Rural Water Supply Programme
1974-75	Minimum Needs Programme (ARWSP was withdrawn)
1977-78	ARWSP was reintroduced
1986	National Drinking Water Mission (NDWM)
1991	NDWM was renamed as Rajiv Gandhi Drinking Water Mission
1999	Sector Reforms Programme
2002	Swajaldhara

Various Schemes

Priority was given to provide adequate water to the rural areas right from the inception of the Five-Year Plans but the goals have not been achieved completely. A series of programmes have been launched with shift in approaches. In recent years, there have been two important developments in the implementation of rural water supply programmes in India: one, promotion of people's participation in implementation and maintenance of water supply sources and; two, decentralization process leading to involvement of many local organizations at the district level in managing rural water supply.

The Water Supply and Sanitation Programme introduced in 1954 and following years failed to achieve its objectives within the stipulated time frame. It was only in 1972-73 that the Accelerated Rural Water Supply Programme (ARWSP) was introduced. However, with the introduction of the Minimum Needs Programme which incorporated the rural water supply component at the state level, ARWSP was withdrawn. However, ARWSP was reintroduced, as the progress of supply of safe drinking water to identified problem villages was not up to expectations. In 1986, the National Drinking Water Mission was introduced and in 1991 it was renamed as the Rajiv Gandhi Drinking Water Mission (RGDWM) focusing on providing safe water to the problem villages identified as 'No source village' based on a national survey. The survey covered 1,61,722 problem villages in 1990, another survey was conducted in 1993 as the previous survey results were not satisfactory. In 1994, it was estimated to be 1,40,975 non-covered villages, 4,30,377 partially covered habitations/villages and 1.51 lakh habitations/villages suffering from acute water quality problems.

However, again keeping in view the field realities, it was further updated and for the Ninth Plan, the objective was to cover 0.88 lakh non-covered villages and 3.91 lakh partially covered villages.

The Ninth Plan has estimated the required funds to be to the tune of Rs. 4000 crore, inclusive of operation and maintenance and also to control the water quality problems. Six per cent of capital investment is required on an average annually for repairs and maintenance of systems. It is clear that the 10 per cent plan funds from the ARWSP and MNP are inadequate to meet the requirements. Hence, the need for involvement of communities, institutions and private sector is significant.

Sector Reforms Programme

In this context, Sector Reforms Programme, introduced in 1999, is an improvement as it includes community participation, awareness creation, community contribution, and role transformation inclusive of operation and maintenance. Swajaldhara focuses on bringing in all reform initiatives in rural drinking water sector under its comprehensive guidelines. It aims at providing operational flexibility to the State governments and implementation flexibility to the districts and Gram Panchayat level institutions. Community participation, role of Panchayati Raj Institutions and involvement of women have been specifically emphasised.

Issues and Concerns

Policies

The national and state policies place the highest priority on drinking water. Amidst the continuous efforts of various agencies, programmes and schemes, access to safe rural water still remains a serious problem. The coverage of drinking water supply in habitations throughout the country—measured at 40 litres per capita per day—indicates that 86.9 per cent of all habitations are 'fully covered', 11.7 per cent are 'partially covered' and only 1.4 per cent are 'not covered', (Water and Sanitation Programme, 2001).

Many of the schemes concentrated on 'supply driven approach' in which the technical aspects of planning, design and construction are given priority and limited attention is paid to the beneficiaries' needs and preferences and long-term management of the scheme to promote sustainability. It is observed that categorically none can say what the existing situation is regarding issues such as water supply coverage, as there appears to be great disparity between 'official' published figures and the perceptions of certain stakeholder groups in the water sector (Water and Sanitation Programme, 2001).

Deteriorating Water Quality— Serious Cause for Concern

Status of Water Quality

Providing safe water has been one of the major focuses in the recent years with the increasing levels of contamination observed in the groundwater sources. Under the National Drinking Water Mission by the Government of India, a submission on water quality monitoring is integrated as a part of drinking water supply programme. Water quality testing has been conducted in all the rural areas of the state. Major contaminants found are excess fluoride, iron, nitrate and hard water problems. 66 million people in India are estimated to be consuming groundwater with unsafe levels of flouride. Nearly 30 million people in the eastern states are estimated to be at risk of consuming water with higher than acceptable arsenic levels (Kolavalli and K.V. Raju, 2003).

Reasons for Quality Decline

Degradation in water quality has been observed due to various reasons. They include contamination of groundwater sources due to disposal of untreated sewage, disposal of industrial effluents without treatment, disuse of wells, extensive usage of chemical fertilizers, over-exploitation of groundwater and poor sanitation and hygiene.

Additional Costs

The RDPR is burdened with additional costs in tackling this problem. Till today, 99 projects costing Rs. 419.96 crore have been cleared under Sub-Mission programme. Out of these, 45 projects costing Rs. 99.49 crore have been taken up and 9 projects completed while the remaining 36 projects are in various stages of progress. It has been observed that the funds allotted from the Central Government under the ARWSP are inadequate to address quality problems. An additional requirement of Rs. 100.00 crore per year is required for implementation of submission projects for providing safe drinking water to these partially covered and fully covered habitations through distant bore-well sources/surface sources/treatment plants/artificial recharge measures (RDPR, 2003).

It is in this context that rain water harvesting can be tried as an alternative option. The technology is flexible and simple in construction and maintenance apart from meeting the quality (chemical and physical standards) when compared to surface or groundwater. In India, fluoride elimination technologies like Nalagonda technology, Activated Aluminia, Reverse Osmosis and Ion Exchange have not proved to be cost effective and fool proof (Vishwanath S., 2003).

Implications

Inadequate access to safe drinking water results in suffering due to poor public health and energy spent on collecting water. From a recent study conducted by the Department of Mines and Geology, Karnataka, it is observed that Nitrate contamination in water samples in the wells has gone up two-fold within a year. More than 50 per cent of Bangalore district has nitrate in its groundwater. North of Bangalore is more affected with 70 per cent nitrate concentration, more than 45 mg/1 in groundwater compared to 30 per cent in the South. According to the Bureau of India Standards, nitrate in water should not exceed 45 mg/1. Nitrate contamination causes serious health consequences like gastric cancer and affects the central nervous system.

Resource Depletion—An Uncontrolled Arena

The severity of the problem has been felt even in different parts of the globe threatening the world's natural underground reservoirs due to over-exploited aquifers, falling water tables and seawater contamination according to a new United Nations report. However, the trend in groundwater depletion has been there since three decades in Karnataka. The farmers were taking loans for digging wells from the Land Mortgage Bank (presently called the Land Bank) for irrigation, which usually failed leading farmers into a debt trap. It was during the same period that the Karnataka Electricity Board had started energizing irrigation wells to replace manual lifting and using of diesel pumps. A statewide programme launched by the Department of Mines and Geology entrusted geologists to conduct pumping tests to observe the aquifer character below the water table. The scope of groundwater development was established during the same period, 1971-72, when taluk-wise survey on inventory of wells and basic geohydrological mapping was carried out.

While field geologists identified and mapped the prospect areas for development, KEB started energizing wells and Land Banks started their loan schemes. People understood the groundwater prospects and with energization the use of groundwater use increased multifold. The resultant effect was the explosion in the number of wells and more areas were covered by well irrigation and farmers shifted to growing rice and sugarcane (Y. Lingaraju, 2003).

By the end of the 70's, the water table started depleting and the geologists realized the change in the levels of water from three metres in typical hard rock area lowered to 10 metres and beyond. A new concept of drilling from the bottom of the open well came into practice, which also did not sustain as the areas under irrigation borewells increased. More borewells were drilled and open wells neglected. It was during the 80's that the groundwater development was utilized to the maximum and the department classified areas as dark areas where no loans were given but the situation could not be reversed (Y. Lingaraju, 2003).

Status of Groundwater Levels

Groundwater serves 85 per cent of the rural population's requirement of drinking water and nearly half of the urban and industrial requirements in Karnataka. Over the years, groundwater utilization in 21 taluks of the State has exceeded the 85 per cent limit and 22 taluks between 65 to 85 per cent and 29 taluks have exceeded by 50 per cent causing rapid depletion of aquifers. The National Family Health Survey indicates that only 3 per cent of households in 1998-99 made use of surface sources compared with 11 per cent of households in 1992-93.

With no stringent regulations on groundwater, groundwater resources have been over-exploited. As per the Central Water Commission, India has 71 important reservoirs having a total capacity of 133.66 billion cubic metres out of which on May 2, there was 15 per cent of full reservoir level water. With continuous uptake and little recharge, the figure came down to 14 per cent on May 9, 13 per cent on May 19 and 12 per cent on May 23. We are drawing too much compared to natural recharge says Dr. Chander. (*Deccan Herald*, 2003). What complicates the issue is lack of aquifers in the peninsular region; the entire Deccan plateau is a hard rock area where there is hardly any large underground water reservoir says Dr. Subhash Chander, retired hydrologist from IIT, New Delhi. *(Deccan Herald*, June 1, 2003)

The Department of Mines and Geology monitors the groundwater level and quality since 1972. Presently, 1560 observation dug wells and borewells in the state are being monitored. As the monthly water levels recorded does not reflect changes in-between, borewells have been drilled to study the fluctuation in deeper fractured aquifer and digital water level recorders installed to study local short duration changes.

Serious Implications

Severe water scarcity during the dry seasons has led to grave consequences. It is commonly highlighted in the media during the summer seasons on the effects of drought on rural livelihoods. Satellites do not help in picking up early signs of drought either. Theoretically, remote-sensing imageries can pick up soil moisture conditions. But the technique is not operational anywhere in the world and still in the research stage, says Dr. A. Bhattacharaya, Deputy Director at the National Remote Sensing Agency under the Indian Space Research Organization. This year, it was sought to issue water cards for villages, issuing 10 litres of water per day.

Problems associated with over-exploitation are serious resulting in the failure of dug wells countering a loss of Rs. 2000 crore invested by farmers, scarcity of drinking water, increased unit cost of wells, increased energy consumption, drop in efficiency of pumps and productive lands have become fallow. (Dr. Basappa Reddy *et. al.*, 2000).

Groundwater management is a key challenge that requires regulatory and participatory approaches coupled with changes in the demand behaviour of water users. Increase in population and decrease in groundwater quality would bring about pressure in surface water sources for meeting drinking water demands.

Sustainability of Systems

'Sustainability is the most desirable, yet elusive characteristic of a water supply project' (WHO, 1994). However, the nature of water-use, existing quality of the nation's water resources and the implications of different levels of water quality complicates, causing externalities resulting in inefficient allocation of environmental resources even in an ideal market system and the role of government policies to cope with the efficiency and equity problems associated with externalities. Property rights and water law with respect to assigning the full costs or benefits of the use of water are imperfect, significant external diseconomies result from the many competing uses of water. These externalities with the extensive role of water in economic activity imply that important efficiency and equity issues are involved in the use of water resources.

With increasing population, the demands will require more intensive and extensive exploitation of natural resources, particularly water, forests and agricultural lands. The resources have to be increased with careful and sustainable management of those resources that are already in use and reduce the pressure on drawing down new resources.

Three major barriers that have caused improper resource management are—failure to recognize scarcity in the natural world, failure to ensure that the institutions managing natural resources are accountable and failure to mobilize knowledge for managing environmental problems. These issues are to be addressed with a radical transformation through providing accessibility to knowledge and resources and institutions must have a clear legal framework and supporting services and decentralize the responsibilities to individuals and communities where they have to be accountable, using pricing to allocate resources to protect property rights.

Even with decentralized implementation of rural water supply taken up by the state, complexities lie in determining property rights of water resource use, lack of legal policies to control mismanagement and over-exploitation of water resources, lack of finance for operation and maintenance of potable water sources reflecting the inefficiency of the state in mobilizing funds, negligence of traditional water resources, poor supporting services and poor co-ordination between departments in dealing with the problem in a holistic approach. These facts have led to the poor sustainability of rural water supply schemes.

Ninety-seven per cent of rural water supply facilities depend on groundwater sources and continuous decline in groundwater resources have led to malfunctioning of many water supply schemes every year. This will require additional investments to locate fresh sources to meet even minimum requirements of water. The problem is severe during the dry seasons with the groundwater level at the lowest level.

Management, operation and maintenance of the facilities provided is another aspect that needs attention under sustainability. The state's policy so far has been one of providing technical and financial assistance for the maintenance and repair of rural water supply installations with only day-to-day operation and payment of energy charges left to gram panchayats. With the increasing number of installations, the need for role transfer is realized. The World Bank project emphasized on changing the approach in providing rural water supplies, based on the demand-driven approach with complete responsibility of operation and maintenance by the community.

Lack of awareness and responsibility among people in using water carefully also acts as a major constraint in the sustainability of water resources, which adds to serious problems with government drinking water supply schemes (World Bank, 1993). Despite efforts by the government, the number of 'problem villages'—official parlance for villages that do not have water sources—does not seem to be reducing.

Limitations in Adopting Appropriate Technological Measures

Technology is one of the key elements for the successful implementation of the programme. The three main ways of distributing water in the rural areas adopted have been through installing borewells with handpumps, water pumped to small cylindrical shaped tanks fitted with taps under the mini water supply programme and piped water supply is pumped using power pumps, stored in overhead or surface tanks and distributed through public taps. The rural water supply programme is implemented through Zilla Panchayat Engineering Divisions. Villages are chosen based on the extent of water problems faced while the technology is decided based on the population of the village.

The coverage by RDPR is vast and has touched upon every village in the state but people still face acute shortages in drinking water. There are a number of problems encountered at the field level. As there are no groundwater regulations, farmers having lands at an upper level drill borewells affecting drinking water borewells provided by RDPR. With increased number of irrigation borewells, groundwater levels have depleted and the borewells get defunct in many situations. Women find it hard to pump borewells for a long time as the water level has gone down. At the village level, there are no technical persons to do small repairs. For major repairs, the gram panchayats have to depend on the Taluk Panchayat for sanctions.

Erratic power supply and power cuts are among the major causes leading to failure of borewells, frequent repairs due to burning of motors thereby affecting water supply and incurring additional costs. In this context, a success story about Pura Village, Kunigal Taluk, Tumkur district needs special mention as local resources are used to tackle the problem of power, thereby meeting water requirements. Since September 1987, the traditional system of obtaining water, illumination and fertilizer has been replaced by a community biogas plant electricity generation system. It consists of a 3-phase, 3 horsepower submersible pump that generates 6.75 cubic metres of water per hour. The pump is fitted into a bore well and lifts water from a 50-metre depth to an overhead tank. The water is then distributed by gravity through nine street taps located at various sites around the village. The villagers themselves decided the location of the taps; one of the taps is for livestock and one tap is in the biogas plant compound. In addition, since September 1990, there has been growing demand for private water tap connections, and there are now 75 private taps inside households. That is, 85 per cent of households have private water tap connections. When a 24-hour supply of piped water became available through public taps, per capita consumption jumped immediately to 22 litres and then slowly stabilised at 26 litres.

High capital costs have acted as constraints for which community contribution has been compulsory. There have been instances where communities have refused to accept project implementation when approached by the World Bank. Lack of participation in choosing the technology was evident in Karnataka as it was assumed that the villagers needed piped water supply and that this was the best technology, the people were having apprehensions on the dependence on borewells, but the agencies proceeded. Borewells were drilled without forethought on the water table situation thereby leading to defunct borewells. Field observations (e.g., Rajshekar, D. and Veerashekarappa, 2003) have shown that people were not willing to contribute for drilling of borewells as they did not have confidence about its sustainability and finally poor quality of construction of storage tanks, broken pipes reduced the quantity of water supply through PSPs and PHCs.

It has been evident that there are predominant problems in different areas in procuring water resources (like desert area, salinity, hilly area, etc.) and adequate measures have to be taken for the same by methodical steps through identifying problems, identifying sources, water quality monitoring and quantity and quality to be sustained on a long-term basis to ensure ecological stability.

Few other studies on technical aspects highlight the causes of scarcity of drinking water due to indiscriminate drilling of borewells, non-availability of acquifers, water quality problems, non-availability and technical solutions on building artificial recharge structures. Technology-based studies have emphasised on an integrated approach so that conservation and augmentation of water sources would be inter-related with rural water supply schemes to ensure continued availability of safe drinking water.

Institutional Options

Globally, it has been accepted that rural water supply and sanitation services are managed more efficiently at the lowest appropriate level. However, the agreement with respect to the degree of the most appropriate level is still being experimented in India—Functioning of Village Water Supply Committees (VWSC) independent of Gram Panchayat (GP) except as a sub-committee to give it a legal status and the other, gram panchayat as an integral part of implementation.

The results of an exercise conducted to compare the performance of VWSCs and GPs, the main activities on capacity building, planning, implementation, O&M and Monitoring were probed. It was difficult to draw definitive conclusions on perfect institutional models. It was agreed that VWSC has been efficient in the planning and implementation process while the GPs had excelled in accessing engineering skills in post-implementation stages. It was an 'either-or' situation but a 'both together' one. There was no specific model that could be termed as the best one. Rather adopting a 'situational approach' was considered as the best option (Water and Sanitation Programme, 1999).

The organisational structure and implementation arrangements differed across the different programmes. The World Bank programmes created village level organisations under their programmes while local elected bodies represented the line departments at various levels. The organisations were assigned functions and were provided assets to undertake the functions.

Finance

Another important rule promoted financial sustainability by increasing the role of communities in the planning and management of their own facilities and requiring users to pay all operation and maintenance costs and at least 10 per cent of the capital cost. These principles were articulated in the GOI Eighth Five Year Plan (1997-2002) and have helped in formulating the Guidelines for Implementation of the Rural Water Supply Programme. It has been internationally accepted that rural water supply and sanitation services are managed more efficiently at the lowest appropriate level. However, the agreement with respect to the degree of the most appropriate level is still being experimented.

REFERENCES

Kolvalli, Shashi and K.V. Raju (2003), 'Protecting Drinking Water Sources: A Sub-basin View,' Working Paper 126, Institute for Social and Economic Change, Bangalore.

Ministry of Rural Development (2003), 'Guidelines on Swajaladhara'.

Ravichandran, M. and Boopathi, S., 'Economic and Environmental Status of Drinking Water Provision in Rural India', *Journal of Social and Economic Development'*, July-December 2002, Vol. 4, No. 2.

Reddy, Basappa, *et. al.* (2000), 'Groundwater resources in Karnataka and its Management, Ground Works Department, Department of Mines and Geology.

Rural Development and Panchayati Raj Department (2000-05), 'Rural Water Supply and Sanitation in Karnataka—Strategy Paper'.

Saleth, R.M. (1996), 'Water Institutions in India: Economics, Law and Policy', Commonwealth Publishers, New Delhi.

UNDP—World Bank Water and Sanitation Programme, 'Preparing and Implementing Large Scale Rural Water Supply and Sanitation Projects in Asia', Report on regional workshop, Colombo, 27-30, September, 1994.

Vishwanath, S., 'Rainwater Harvesting—Panacea or Mirage?', *Vijay Times*, 29 June, 2003.

Veerashekarappa, 'Community Participation in Rural Drinking Water Supply and Sanitation: A Case study of Karnataka', Working Paper 91, 2001, Institute for Social and Economic Change.

Water and Sanitation Programme, 'Jal Manthan—Launching Sector Reforms', August 2001.

Paper prepared for the workshop on Biogas Technology for China, at the China Centre of Rural Energy Research and Training, Beijing, November, 1994.

Sunita Narain, *The Hindu Magazine*, Sunday, 8 June, 2003, 'A Movement to Value Water'.

5

Managing Water Resources

Sarbeswara Sahoo

Water is the source of life and without this life is unthinkable in our mother earth and that's why it is aptly known as life. Despite its importance water has remained a neglected issue till today. Water as supplied freely by nature is taken for granted in India. This is the reason why in a less than half a century of independent existence, India, a water rich country, has been reduced to a water insecure nation. The acuteness is such that during 2025 there may be a water emergency era where less than 1000 cu.m. of precipitation is considered critical for human survival. This will be clear from the following statistics.

Annual per capita availability of renewable fresh water:

1955—5277 cu.m
1990—2464 cu.m.
2025—1000 cu.m.

India witnessed severe water-related problems during the year 2003 and water became the number one problem. Keeping this fact in mind the present note is an attempt to analyse various issues related to water. Section 1 discusses the contribution of water, the next section will analyse the genesis of the crisis and the last section is devoted to the issue of water management.

Reprinted with permission, *Environment & People*, August 2006, pp. 8-12.

Contributions

The earth is an unique planet in this universe because life is possible here. It is again because of the presence of land, air, water and light. Among all, water is the most important one in making life possible. We can classify the use of water as follows:

User Groups	*Uses*
Plants	Preparation of food (Photo synthesis), habitation
Animals, Reptiles, Birds	Drinking, bathing, habitation
Human Beings	Drinking, preparation of food, bathing, washing, navigation, irrigation, etc.

Among the above users, human beings are important as users as well as managers of water resources and are the major stakeholders and hence our discussion will centre around them on the issue of water resources management, henceforth WRM. Water is in many ways important for bathing and cooking. Without safe water, cooking is not possible and hence food, the entire question of food security depends on availability of sufficient safe water. Second important contribution is its need for bathing and washing. Unsafe and insufficient water is the root cause of many diseases like diarrhoea, fluorosis, cholera, jaundice, chronic acidity and gastric, arsenic poisoning and so on. Regular intake of sufficient safe water will reduce the risk of the above diseases. Further, water is a good stress manager and a deep cool shower or lengthy swim can reduce nervous break down. In brief, a society having plenty of pure water will end up with peace and prosperity.

The second important area where a major chunk of available water is used is irrigation for agricultural growth.

Industries also require water at each stage of production. It also requires power for operation which is further supplied by hydro-electric projects. It is estimated that water requirement will increase with industrial development.

Water consumption in India can be studied from the following table:

Water Consumption in India	*Water Flow (Cu.m)*
Agriculture 90%	Precipitation—4000 cu.m
Industry 6%	Accessible water—1869 cu.m
Domestic 4%	Water used—690 cu.m

The agrarian sector which consumes 90 per cent of water is still the predominant source of livelihood. Industrial requirement which is only 6 per cent is likely to increase in the wake of the industrial revolution. In the case of domestic use its percentage of 4 per cent is however important.

To sum up, the availability of fresh water is not only important for survival but is key to sustainable development and an essential element in poverty reduction. Without adequate supply of safe water all other development efforts are doomed to fail.

Sources

The major source of water is rains which is stored in natural and man-made systems. Natural systems include rivers, rivulets, nallas, lakes, ponds and man-made systems include small, medium and major irrigation projects, tanks and wells.

Crisis

Water, once an abundant resource, became scarce day-by-day and there is a process of desertification in many parts of the country. The year 2003 was the worst not only for excess temperature but also water scarcity. Scarcity of water is the biggest crisis facing India in terms of spread and severely, affecting one in three people of cities and villages. Even in Chennai, Bangalore and Delhi water is rationed. The nightmare has worsened and unless we act now our future is frightening. The crisis will be clear from the following factoids.

Factoids of a Growing Crisis

- Water is now the number one problem in urban India as seen in Aurangabad of Maharashtra where 3 crore or every third person in the state today depends on tankers for their daily need.
- Water tables are plunging in places like Limdi, Surendrangari. Six out of ten borewells dug in North Gujarat, Saurashtra, Kutch

region yield no water even at a depth of 1200 ft. Over 2.5 crore people in Gujarat are in distress.

- Groundwater levels have plunged in 206 districts in the country. Nine states including Gujarat, Rajasthan, Maharashtra, Haryana, Karnataka and Punjab are facing major water deficits where demand exceeds supply.
- As many as 203 of the 401 class II cities in India get less than 100 litres of water per person per day.
- In Rajasthan 10 towns get water once in 3 days and 31 towns once in two days, 12 towns get it from 200 km away.
- Delhi loses 30 per cent or over 800 million litres of water a day due to leakage in the system.
- In one village of Gujarat each of the 200 families has one member suffering from kidney problem because of lack of adequate water.
- India has over 100 million cases of diarrhoea a year and five lakh children die due to this disease.
- 66 million people in 200 districts are at risk of fluoride contamination and 15 million at risk of arsenic poisoning.
- Nearly 2 lakh sq. km. land in eight states including Delhi, Gujarat, Punjab and Haryana have land salinity.
- The four main metros generate over 900 m litres of sewage a day of which 30 per cent is treated.
- Every day four trains fetch 6 million litres of water from Jodhpur for the 4 lakh people of Pali in Rajasthan. These trains are the life line of 12 towns and 128 villages in the desert state.
- Twice a week in Tamil Nadu Soroja Krishna travels 10 km. to her relative's house to.
- 100 million people in 35 big cities take a 30 per cent cut in water supply, 100 million people in 12 cities also thirst for water.
- Over 200 million people residing beside eight river basins are water deficit.

The water problem is on the rise and will worsen in the future. The problem is even worse in rural India where humans and animals face enormous hardship for a few drops of water. There are a large number of unreported deaths due to water scarcity in rural India. Women walk miles to get a bucket of drinking water. A large number of man-days are lost in collecting water for drinking and bathing.

It is due to the above factors that a recent World Water Development report ranked India a lowly 133rd among 180 countries in terms of water availability and 120th among 122 countries in terms of water quality.

Genesis of the Crisis

Dr. A. Vaidyanathan of Madras Institute for Development Studies, argues that water scarcity in India is largely man-made. It is the result of a short-sighted pricing policy that encourages wasteful use of water and makes it difficult to raise resources for upkeep and expansion of systems. Then there is reduced recharge due to the destruction of natural recharge mechanisms. A highly subsidised supply of electricity for pumping ensures unregulated exploitation of groundwater.

Secondly, the spread of HYV seeds which may be profitable but also requires more water and un-regulated groundwater exploitation has aggravated the situation. This exploitation is motivated by considerations of short-term profit rather than a concern for a long-term sustainability. This exploitation in water resources is on because of a highly subsidized system. Water subsidy costs Rs. 6000 crores or barely so.

Increase in Demand

There is talk of family planning and population control during the 1970s which has faded over the years. The root cause of all ills lies in this factor which at present is out of control. Given this situation any development policy is likely to fail. India's population is expected to touch 1650 million by 2050, which will raise the demand for water from 634 billion cubic metre at present to 1447 bcm in 2050. Nearly two-third of this will be for irrigation as India would need to double its food production from the current 200 million metric tons to 450 mmt. The International Food Policy Research Institute projects that India will set up its water demand by 50 per cent over the next 20 years. Most of the increase will go to individual and domestic uses with each projected to quadruple in its current demand.

As cities grew and towns sprouted little thought was paid to the emerging mis-match between demand and supply. In the quest for food security, tapping groundwater was posed as solution. It was quicker, cheaper and profitable. This has led to groundwater depletion.

Other Reasons

- India's water crisis is also the culmination of myopic planning, muddled policies and misguided perceptions. Due to a short-sighted policy for public water supply which encourages wasteful use of water and makes it difficult to raise resources for the upkeep and expansion of the system. This resulted in reduced recharge both due to reduced natural recharge mechanism and ineffective pollution control mechanisms. Further, a highly subsidized supply of electricity for pumping has ensured unregulated exploitation of groundwater. For example, while it costs as much as Rs. 13 to Rs. 17 to supply water the Delhi Government charges only Rs. 0.60 paise per kilolitre.
- A study by the Urban Development Ministry on drinking water subsidy points out that while the average cost of delivering water to metro houses is Rs. 15 per thousand litres, the consumer pays Rs. 1.50 or 10 per cent of the total cost.
- Another reason for the growing water crisis is a decline in public investment in water in recent years. For a country that wants to achieve 8 per cent GDP growth and where 67 per cent of the population is dependent on agriculture, investments in rural infrastructure is pitiful. Public investment in agriculture has gone down from 22.4 per cent in the Ist Five Year Plan to 6 per cent in 2000. As many as 7000 engineers are lying idle without any work. Soil and Water Conservation Department has been virtually closed down. Another factor of the growing crisis is degradation of traditional irrigation systems. As India developed and urbanized traditional systems of water management were dismantled and hence water crisis was aggravated especially in rural India. For example, the erstwhile Mysore had 25,000 tanks and lakes and now it has 10,000 lakes and tanks.

Management

India has 2.45 per cent of the world's land resources and 4 per cent of fresh water resources. India's annual precipitation (snow and rainfall) is 4000 bcm. This translates into 1869 bcm of water in rivers out of which barely 690 bcm is used. In other words, 1179 bcm of water (roughly twice the size of the Brahmaputra flow into the sea. Add 432 bcm of groundwater and the real availability of water at 1122 cm per person in a billion-plus nation.

Theoretically, there should be no shortage of water which largely is man-made and the growing crisis can be solved by the people themselves. There is a growing concern over water. Recent years witnessed large amalgamation of various representatives at Rio, Kyoto and recently at Johannesburg. The Johannesburg summit pointed out 9 groups of stake-holders where the state is still an important agent in managing water. Prof. A. Vaidyanathan of MIDS also suggests the importance of the state where he calls for a concerted effort combining the instruments of sama, dama, danda for fruitful management of water.

SAMA—Sama is required to make the people aware of the magnitude of the problems and to appreciate that competing claims have to be settled on the basis of fair and equitable sharing within the limits of the possible.

DAMA—To set-up transparent and fair mechanisms for regulating, extraction, allocation and use of water and to induce economical and conservative use in the larger long-term social interest.

DANDA—Danda is required for a strict and fair enforcement of the policies by the Government and regulatory agencies.

Till now the state is failing in all these respects and we have many miles to go. For this purpose a rigorous policy on water is needed and to cope with the situation. Only a paradigm shift in policy and proactive approach to implementation can help India skirt the looming crisis. A comprehensive water policy is needed where all the departments of government has to coordinate and work as a team.

National Water Policy

Despite crisis, India till now has no National Water Policy. During drought we dig up many areas under "Food for Work Programme" for storing rain water and then forget about them. Then we come up with ideas like linking of rivers and occasionally we beat our chests for the falling groundwater table. One has been hearing about water harvesting for several years but not much is known as to how much work has been done in this area.

It is therefore essential that the country must have a clear-cut water management policy for the next 50 years. For each district and each village we should have a database on the average annual rainfall requirement and supply of water, number of wells, tanks, ponds, streams, etc. This will help to manage water in a better way. For this purpose a revolution in the field of water is needed.

Blue Water Revolution

- **Bring water policy under one ministry:** Currently there is no coordination among the six ministries including water resources, food and environment. A team work among these ministries is the need of the hour.
- **Transfer water management to the communities:** Scarcity is better handled by communities in managing resources and deciding sustainable crops than by a central fiat.
- **Invest funds in new and existing water schemes:** Investment in irrigation has dropped from 22.4 per cent in the First Five Year Plan to 6 per cent in the year 2000. Therefore, increased investment is urgently needed.
- **Draw up a new crop pattern in tune with water availability:** Certain crops like paddy and sugarcane require a lot of water and it has been observed that poverty is followed in regions growing paddy. According to Prof. M.S. Swaminathan water scarce regions like Andhra Pradesh and Marathwada should not grow paddy and sugarcane but instead concentrate on cotton, groundnut and wheat.
- **Introduce subsidized technology in agriculture:** Measures like drip and micro-irrigation systems which are efficient should be adopted.

Conserving Traditional Irrigation Systems

Anupam Mishra, Secretary, Gandhi Peace Foundation and a staunch supporter of traditional irrigation systems, says that this system preserves surface water efficiently, recharges groundwater and is cheap for which little money is required. Hence step should be taken to preserve this precious resource.

Rain Water Harvesting

There is a hue and cry over rain water harvesting to cope up with water crisis. However, Prof. Vaidyanathan is sceptic about its success. Rain water harvesting is welcome and so are the measures to make it mandatory, but laws are not enough because the enforcement is weak. Besides people are not convinced about the benefits of rain water harvesting. They have a mistaken notion about its cost and there are not enough people to give them proper technical advice.

Privatization

Leaving the harnessing and distribution of water to private enterprise for profit is neither feasible nor desirable. Water provided by nature cannot be commoditised. It is a common property resource whose management must ensure equitable distribution and long-term sustainability. Profit-seeking private enterprises are not interested in either. This does not mean that the present pattern of government ownership is the appropriate solution. We need to create autonomous and decentralized organizations with users' participation, for setting up, financing and managing individual irrigation and domestic water supply systems.

However, there is need for privatization in certain areas. A study by the Urban Development Ministry on drinking water subsidy points out that while the average cost of delivering water to a metro house is Rs. 15 per thousand litres, the consumer pays Rs. 1.50 or 10 per cent of the cost of distributing water. Delhites pay as little as Rs. 0.60 paise. While fixing commercial rates overnight may not be feasible, there is a need to hike it substantially to sustain the system. There is also need to privatize distribution of water to improve efficiency in collection and delivering. Inefficiency in the present system can easily be understood from the following facts. In Mumbai nearly a fifth of the water or around 600 million litres of water per day finds its way to the gutters even before it reaches the consumer. The situation in Delhi is even worse. According to World Bank Assessment Delhi loses 30 per cent or over 800 million litres of water per day through the 8300 kilometre pipeline network.

About River Linking

To solve the problem of water, linking major rivers is coming to the minds of policy-makers and steps are being taken in this regard. Environmentalist Rajendra Singh Rane however is much sceptic about river linking projects. He says river linking in India is not possible and is not a good sign. One should not dare to change the path of nature, it may destroy human civilization. It is because:

- It requires a huge investment amounting a Rs. 5,60,000 crore for which India has to seek World Bank assistance.
- It will be handed over to the private sector.
- It will have a negative impact on nature and environment. We have 80 Agro-Climate Zones and river linking will destroy the bio-diversities in these zones.
- There will be socio-cultural degradation. Ganga, Yamuna, Godavari and Baitarini river will lose their cultural importance.
- There will be pollution linking with river linking. Polluted water of the Yamuna will flow into other rivers.
- There will be displacement of people.

To rush into river linking without addressing the above issues could have disastrous consequences.

Sensitising People

There is an urgent need to change the attitude of the people towards the use of water. As of today people are working and polluting a large amount of water in many ways. The most polluting of them are the city sewage and industrial water discharged into the rivers. Currently only about 10 per cent of the waste water generated is treated. The rest is discharged as it is into our water bodies. Due to this, pollutants enter the groundwater and other water bodies. This water which ultimately ends up in our households is highly contaminated, carrying disease-causing microbes.

The effects of water pollution are not only devastating for people but also to animals, fish and birds. Polluted water is unsuitable for drinking, recreation, agriculture and industry. It diminishes the aesthetic quality of lakes and rivers. More seriously contaminated water destroys aquatic life and reduces its reproduction ability.

Eventually it is a hazard to human health. Nobody can escape the effects of water population.

Therefore, apart from having a national water policy, the government along with NGOs should start a long-term campaign to educate and sensitize the general public about the need to save water and stop its pollution. It should be made a part of the school curriculum.

6

Integrated Water Management—Hunger-Free India

D. Kumara Charyulu, A.V. Ramanjaneyulu and T.L. Neelima

Agriculture, accounting for 23 per cent of the nation's Gross Domestic Product (GDP), 15 per cent of exports and 60 per cent of employment continues to be the mainstay of the Indian economy. Having achieved laudable success in agriculture, India has transformed itself from the pitiable status of a food importing country to a food exporting one. However, currently, the country is facing the problem of sustainability in this era of ever increasing demand for food. Relating to the natural resources and production base, water has emerged as the crucial factor for sustaining the agricultural sector in the coming years. It is said that 'future wars will be fought for water'. Having declared 2007 as 'Year of Water Productivity' and 'Year of Food Processing Industry', this article on Integrated Water Management (IWM) for a hunger-free India has immense importance.

The vulnerability of Indian agriculture is bound to be severe lest the present trend of water-use and management is unchanged. The International Water Management Institute (IWMI) forecasts that by 2025, 33 per cent of India's population will live under absolute water scarcity conditions. The per capita water availability, in terms of average utilizable water resources in the country, has dropped drastically from 6008 M^3 in 1947 to 2200 M^3 now and is expected to

Reprinted with permission, *Kurukshetra*, September 2007, pp. 3-11.

dwindle to 1450 M^3 by 2025. The requirement of water by different sectors by 2025 is estimated to be 105 m.ha.m. but the share of water for agriculture is expected to fall from the present level of 85 per cent to 71 per cent by 2025.

India's water resources are substantial. India is blessed with about 4 per cent of the world's total water resources to support about 16.6 per cent of the world's human population and 15 per cent of animal population with only 2.4 per cent of its geographical area. The average annual rainfall is about 1150 mm but it is unevenly distributed from 100 mm to 11,000 mm. Moreover, most of the rain falls within a period of four months (June to September). On the other hand, the demand for water for agricultural purposes is estimated to increase from 50 m.ha.m in 1985 to 70 m.ha.m in 2050. During the same period, the demand for water for non-agricultural use will multiply four-fold from 7 m.ha.m to 28 m.ha.m. Even if the full irrigation potential is exploited, about 50 per cent of the country's cultivated area will remain unirrigated. Thus, the available and utilizable water resources would not be sufficient to meet the future water demand of all sectors if water continues to be used at the current level of 30-40 per cent efficiency (only).

India's Water Resources and Water Budget

Water covers about three-fourths of the earth's surface and nearly 97.3 per cent of the earth's water is in oceans and seas. Fresh water constitutes only a very small fraction (2.7 per cent). Of this fresh water, 75.2 per cent lies in frozen form in the polar regions and 22.6 per cent as groundwater. That means very little fresh water is effectively available for consumption. India receives only 400 m.ha.m. of rainfall annually, that too irregularly and only during a limited period of two to three months. Out of this, more than three-fourths is lost due to evaporation, deep percolation and seepage to the sea. With the remaining water, we have been able to create irrigation facilities for about 40 per cent of the 142 m.ha. of cultivated land. The main water resources in India include rivers, canals, wells and tanks. According to the World Resources Index (1998-99), India stands seventh in the world and third among Asian countries in annual internal renewable water resources. In annual groundwater recharge, we are fifth in the world and second in Asia.

Need to Protect Available Water Resources

The factors mentioned below force us to protect water resources and promote their judicious use.

(A) Increasing Demand

By 2020, the global population is expected to cross 7.9 billion and half of the world's population will live in countries facing water scarcity. As per the estimates of the Central Ground Water Board, 15 states in India may face severe shortage of groundwater if we continue to exploit it indiscriminately. Now-a-days it is hard to find fresh water due to pollution and ever increasing competition from domestic consumption, industrial use and irrigation. Thus there is a tussle among the three.

In India, only 17.8 m.ha.m. and 40 m.ha.m. of rainfall and snow, respectively is properly trapped by the soil due to inherent topographical problems. India's water consumption is around 20.1 per cent of the world consumption with a per capita consumption of 297.7 cubic metres, which is more than the world average of 287.3 cubic metres. The population of India is expected to stabilize around 1640 million by 2050. As a result, gross per capita availability of water will decline from 1820 m^3 per annum in the year 2001, to as low as 1140 m^3 in 2050. The country's projected water demand for various activities is given in Table 1. The water demand for agricultural irrigation depends upon the requirements of food grains as well as non-food grains. The widening gap between water demand and supply, mismanagement of precious water resources and degradation of water quality are some of the factors that necessitate us to go for efficient use of available water resources.

Table 1: Projected Water Demand for Various Activities in India (billion cu.m.)

Activity	*2010 AD*	*2025 AD*	*2050 AD*
Irrigation	688	910	1072
Drinking	56	73	102
Industrial	12	23	63
Energy	5	15	130
Others	52	72	80
Total	813	1093	1447

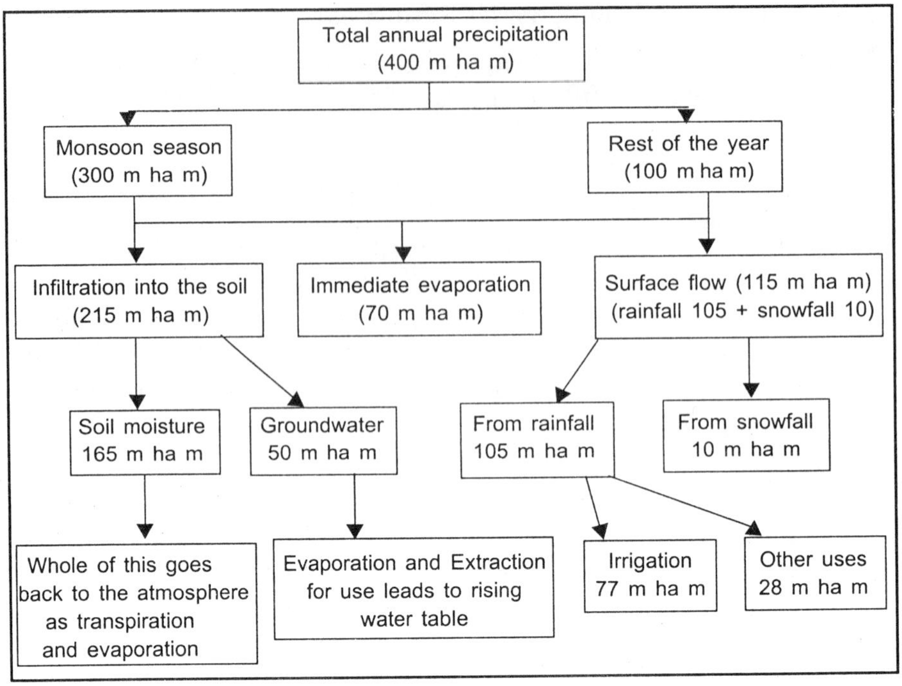

Fig. 1: Annual Water Budget of India

(B) Falling Water Tables

According to state groundwater board officials, the water table is falling by 6 m or more each year. It was learnt that farmers in the country, a generation ago, used bullocks to lift water from shallow wells in leather buckets. But now, they have to draw water from 300 metres below the ground using electric pumps. The pumps powered by heavily subsidized electricity are working day and night to irrigate fields of more water-consuming crops like rice, sugarcane and banana. This massive unregulated expansion of pumps and wells is threatening to suck India dry. Hence, managing water resources should attract due attention.

(C) Weather Abnormalities

The vagaries of the monsoon are late onset, early withdrawal, prolonged dry spells and failure with little showers creating drought and water logging conditions. The distribution of rainfall over different regions varies with highest rainfall in Mawsynaran and least in Western Rajasthan. Due to improper management of water resources, people of Mawsynaran and Cheerapunji also experience water scarcity. Over the years, water abundant regions have become water scarce and water scarce areas face water famines.

(D) High Dependence on Rainfed Agriculture

Rainfed areas occupy 67.5 per cent of the cultivated area, contributing 44 per cent of the food grains and support 40 per cent of population and two-thirds of livestock. In the past decades, the rate of growth of food production has more or less kept pace with the population growth mainly due to the productivity gains from irrigated areas. Even after realizing the complete irrigation potential of the country, half of the cultivated area will continue to remain rain dependent. In the event of plateauing of productivity in irrigated areas, it is inevitable that the next revolution should come from rainfed areas. Currently, the productivity gains from rainfed areas are only 0.7-0.8 t/ha against 2 t/ha from irrigated areas. This means there is a large scope to improve the productivity levels in rainfed areas provided natural resources (water and land) are properly managed and conserved with the application of innovative technologies.

(E) Pollution of Water Bodies

Almost all the water bodies throughout the country including rivers, canals, wetlands and tanks are severely polluted due to release of sewage and sludge, and waste products from industrial units. Thus water is becoming unfit for consumption and irrigation. In some of the dry areas in Rajasthan and Andhra Pradesh (Anathapur, Nalgonda and Khammam), flourosis due to high concentration of fluoride in water is rampant. About 60 per cent of area of Western Rajasthan has chloride higher than 1000 ppm and also the problem of arsenic and selenium in groundwater.

Integrated Water Management Approach

These spatial and temporal variations in water resources availability pose great challenges for storing and regulating the use of the water resources in the country. There is a wide gap between the potential created and the utilization, i.e., more than 10 m.ha. at any point of time. At present, the need of the hour is not only the development of water resources, but also their efficient management in a sustainable manner. The approach of integrated water management to meet the demand of water for agricultural use, drinking and industrial needs, is discussed below.

1. Interlinking of Rivers

It was Sir Arthur Cotton who conceived the idea of networking of rivers two centuries ago. But the idea of interlinking rivers was revived few decades ago independently by M. Visveswarayya, K.L. Rao and D.T. Dastur. Three years back, in response to the order of the Supreme Court of India to complete this mega project costing about Rs. 5.6 lakh crore, the then government appointed a task force of scientists, engineers, economists, biologists and policy-makers to make a detailed project report. The following major benefits may accrue to the country with the completion of the massive project.

- Nearly 35 mha of agricultural land can be brought under irrigation additionally using 173 BCM of additional water thus creating food security.
- Rise in ultimate irrigation potential from 113 million ha to 148-150 million ha.
- Transfer of water from surplus to deficit areas thus mitigating flood and drought problems.
- Production of 34 giga watts of inexpensive and eco-friendly hydropower may be expected.

2. Inter-Basin Transfer

This project was formulated by the National Water Development Agency (NWDA). As per the plan, the project is divided into two broad components.

1. Himalayan component with 14 river links
2. Peninsular component with 16 river links

It is planned to transfer 141 km^3/yr. through peninsular India and 33 km^3/yr. Himalayan links are essentially for redistribution in the Ganga basin and to Western India. Only a small volume of water can be transferred from the Brahmaputra Basin. Thus in totality 1660

km^3/yr. of development water resource can be created which can take care of any exigencies.

3. Methods of Water Harvesting and Groundwater Recharge

"The of collecting the drops of Palar, i.e. of rainfall, are as unending as the names of clouds and drops. The pot like the ocean is filled up drop by drop."

(a) Rooftop Rainwater Harvesting

In this method, the rain from rooftops is fed into tanks through a pipe for meeting domestic needs. The building should be designed for this purpose and the rooftop should be clean and free from dusty pesticides, corrosive materials, etc. The water should go through a pipe into a community sump tank, which should be purified before supply. Harvesting of rooftop rainwater could meet over 60 per cent of domestic water needs. The potential for rooftop rainwater harvesting has been estimated to be 1 km^3/yr.

(b) Water Harvesting

It is the collection and storage of rainfall runoff from any catchment or watershed followed by subsequent use. Rainwater harvesting in a given area depends on topography, soil type, depth and slope, vegetative cover, etc. It largely depends on quantity and distribution of rainfall and will therefore, be more successful in areas where rainfall is sufficient. Recharge of groundwater, which is a concept of rainwater harvesting, utilizes structures like pits, trenches, dug wells, recharge wells/shafts, bore wells, check dams and percolation tanks. The water thus harvested through rainwater harvesting can be used for the following purposes:

- Used primarily for supplemental irrigation during stress periods of crop growth or when there is a long gap between two rainfall events or to meet any other aberrations during the monsoon period allows drought proofing.
- In states like Punjab, Haryana, Himachal Pradesh and the Eastern region, more than 200 water-harvesting dams were already constructed. The harvested rainwater is conveyed to agricultural fields through underground pipelines by gravity,

thus there is no need of electric or diesel engines. One can understand the advantage of such water with a glance at Table 2 given below.

Table 2: Impact of Irrigation Project on Performance of Crops

Particulars	*Wheat*	*Gram*	*Mustard*
Yield before project (q/ha)	8.0	3.9	2.0
Yield after project (q/ha)	27.0	10.2	6.3
Increase in yield (per cent)	237	161	215

- It is an ideal solution of solving water scarcity problem in areas having inadequate water resources. The Centre for Science and Environment (CSE) estimated that even if half of the average annual rainfall of 1190 mm is captured on 1.12 ha of land in each of the country's 5,87,226 villages, 6.57 million litres of rainwater thus collected in each village can meet the annual cooking and drinking needs of an average population of 1200 persons per village.
- Harvested rainwater plays a greater role in sustaining surface water supplies on one hand and recharges aquifers on the other. It prevents the soil erosion.

(c) Watershed Management

An watershed is a natural geo-hydrological unit. It is an area of land and water bounded by a drainage divide within which the surface runoff collects and flows out of the area through a single outlet into a river or other body of water. It must drought proof the rural landscape by capturing each falling raindrop and save crops, human beings and animals.

There are a few successful stories about watershed projects. For instance, Sukhomajri in Haryana and the Ralegaon Sindhi project in Maharashtra have improved socio-economic conditions considerably in a relatively short time. Community participation and equitable distribution of benefits are the reasons behind its success and sustainability. Rajendra Singh of Tarun Bharat Sangh in Rajasthan could make a dead river alive through successful implementation of the watershed concept for which he was awarded the Ramon Magsaysay award. Anna Hazare in Maharashtra is another famous watershed man for his success in water harvesting.

4. Recycling and Reuse of Municipal and Industrial Waste Water

'Recycling' means internal use of water by the original user prior to discharge. While 'Reuse' refers to wastewater that is discharged from municipalities (75 per cent), industries and irrigation are withdrawn by users other than dischargers. After treatment, reclaimed waters are diverted for irrigation. It is clearly evident in big cities like Delhi where the water scarcity is acute; the municipal sewage water is utilized for irrigating vegetable crops. In Tamil Nadu, industrial wastewater is being used for irrigating sugarcane crops.

Water used for domestic purposes (washing, cleaning and bathing, etc.) should be collected, cleaned and recycled for non-drinking domestic and industrial purposes. Near holy places and temple towns, the water that is used for bathing and washing in tanks and ponds should be channelised towards agricultural fields in adjacent areas (e.g. Mahanandi in Kurnool district of Andhra Pradesh). In Israel, water is used 4 to 5 times before it is let off to nature while, it is used only once in India.

As of now, 75 per cent of drinking water is used for non-drinking purposes. It is proposed to supply potable water and non-drinking water separately to ease pressure on the drinking water supply. Besides, water for non-drinking needs could be met by recycling domestic wastewater.

5. Improving Water Use Efficiency (WUE) through Better Technology

The agriculture sector consumes more than 85 per cent of the total water in the country. If we are able to save 7 per cent of it, we will able to meet the domestic and industrial demand. Hence it is imperative to adapt less water consuming or water saving methods of irrigation with an aim of producing more crops per drop (WUE). Such methods include micro-irrigation (drip, sprinkler, bubbler, spray and indigenous drip irrigation) methods. By using these methods, two to three times more area can be brought under irrigation with the same quantity of water besides improving crop quality and doubling productivity. At the same time, increasing salinity and alkalinity problems of irrigation water in coastal areas can be mitigated by using drip irrigation without any adverse effect on crop growth and productivity. Furrow or alternate furrow method of irrigation for wide spaced crops like sugarcane, tomato, maize and tobacco will save nearly 30 per cent of water-use besides reducing crust problem. The basin method of irrigation rather than flooding should be followed for irrigating horticultural crops.

Rice is the most water-consuming crop and 40 per cent of the irrigation water available is used for this crop. Nearly 60 per cent of water applied to rice is lost by deep percolation. This can be substantially reduced by improved puddling through power tillers with cage wheels. As adopted in China and experimentally proved at many places in India, alternate wetting and drying rather than continuous submergence would reduce water requirement by 30 to 50 per cent. The very recent popular method of cultivation of rice under System of Rice Intensification (SRI) saves nearly half the quantity of water compared to traditional submerged rice besides saving other inputs including seed, fertilizer and pesticide. Zero tilled direct seeded rice in heavy soils saves nearly 35 per cent water against puddled transplanted rice. This is true even with zero tilled wheat crop, which is becoming very popular in areas where the rice-wheat cropping system is dominant. On the other hand, rice grown under furrow irrigated raised bed system (FIRBS) was found to save water up to 30 per cent.

In water scarce dry farming areas, peasants should be advised to shift from rice to irrigable dry crops like high value pulses and oilseeds based on agro-ecological conditions and market demand. Swaminathan suggested replacement of double paddy crop by one HYV Paddy followed by cotton as the second crop. This system helps to maintain overall productivity and profitability and also saves an enormous quantity of water. It also avoids salinity and waterlogging. Easy to follow and farmer friendly scientific scheduling of irrigation based on critical stage of crop growth, field modification technique, high seed rate and feel and appearance method should be followed for regulating water-use and avoiding waterlogging problems. Proper levelling of agricultural fields also helps in avoiding waterlogging thus saving water. Scientists should breed HYVs, which are less water consuming, and drought resistant and such seeds should be made available to large sections of the farming community.

6. Reducing Seepage Losses and De-silting of Tanks

Poor maintenance of water bodies encourages water loss through seepage resulting in low water-use efficiency of 25-40 per cent against the target of 65 per cent. Hence, proper lining of water retaining structures should be taken up.

Simply constructing dams across rivers for storing water for subsequent use is not enough, periodical maintenance is also necessary. The main problem that most of them face is silting. Neglect of desilted dams and tanks will drastically reduce their storage capacity. A review of siltation across the country reveals the pitiable condition of these water-storing structures.

- Nizamsagar dam in Andhra Pradesh has lost half its storage capacity due to silting.
- In the first week of May 2005, Parliament was informed that the Tungabhadra Dam has lost 560 million cubic metres (20 TMC) of live storage capacity due to siltation, resulting in reduced capacity utilization.

Table 3 reveals that the dam has lost 20 TMC storage capacity in the last decade (1993 to 2005) against the same level of loss in the past four decades (1953 to 1993). It shows the magnitude of breaching and siltation and also the attention that we are giving it.

Table 3: Change in Storage Capacity of Tungabhadra Dam

Year	*Storage capacity (TMC)*	*Reduction (TMC)*
1953	131	—
1993	111	20
2005	91	20

This is the common problem in most of the Indian dams and canals because of which tail end farmers are not receiving water following reduction in storage capacity. Hence steps should be initiated to desilt these Temples of Modern India. The canal banks and field channels should be provided with cement lining to prevent leakage and seepage, which account for about 30 per cent loss of water. If these measures are initiated, water could be put to better use in all four irrigation systems in India.

7. Arrest Over-Exploitation of Groundwater and Rationalize Water Rates

A few states are providing electricity free of cost to farming community. Even where it is not free, the charge for electricity is a fraction of the average cost, not based on metered use. No or under pricing led to over-exploitation of groundwater and subsequently serious depletion of the water table in many parts of the country. This also leads to inequitable distribution of water between head and tail end areas and big and small farmers. Besides, bore wells have created more havoc. With the mushrooming of bore wells, open wells have dried up. Sometimes, they are dug beyond 500 ft, which affect water structures/aquifers, erode perennial character of streams and reduce surface moisture content. So, banning of bore wells should be given serious thought. In order to reduce wastage, metered water pricing also should be implemented just like in metros (Delhi).

8. Avoid all Forms of Pollution

Industries based on chemicals, fertilizers, garments, skins, leather, textile, liquor, soft drinks, paper, jute, steels, alloys and coal release hot water, coloured water and waste material into nearby surface water bodies like rivers, lakes, ponds, tanks and wetlands thus making them unproductive and non-potable. Such waters will become unfit for further use even after treatment. For instance,

- The great rivers like the Ganga, the Godavari, the Cauvery and the Yamuna have become polluted to a large extent.
- Many of the wetlands across the country have been under threat.
- Industries in Delhi release millions of gallons of waste, polluted and coloured water into the sacred river the Yamuna converting it into a sewage drain.

These can be avoided only when there is political will through formulation and imposition of strict regulations for release of effluents and waste into water. It should be made compulsory for all industries to have their own treatment plants and release effluents only after proper treatment. At the same time, the concerned authority should be empowered to take severe action against those going against rules and regulations. Effective implementation of the Ganga and Yamuna Action Plans will help in cleaning of these sacred water bodies.

9. Revise Warabandi System

In typical canal command areas, the allocation of water on one week fixed rotational system is called Warabandi. This, in its present form, failed to fulfil the objective of equitable distribution of water due to non-consideration of seepage losses between head and tail end of water courses. For this, the warabandi has to be revised by considering actual discharge, after accounting for seepage losses. In order to compensate for the seepage losses in the water courses, the allocation time to tail end farmers is increased and to keep the same volume of water allocation per unit area, the allocation time to head end farmers is decreased (Mandal *et al.*, 2004).

10. DAM Concept

This is known as Deficiencies Allowed by Management (DAM). Generally, whenever there is inadequate water stored in tanks and reservoirs in a bad rainy year, the usual practice is to limit the command area. The better method would be to adopt the 'DAM' concept and irrigate the total command area. This involves supply of reduced amount of water during the non-critical stage of crop growth and supply full requirement of water during the critical flowering and yield formation periods. In this method, yield on individual fields may be less by 5-10 per cent but the overall production in the command area will be more by 50 per cent (Hanumantha Rao, 2001). It was implemented in Andhar Pradesh during 1987-88, the worst drought year since independence. A glance at Table 4 reveals the advantage of the DAM concept.

Table 4: Comparative Water Requirement in DAM Concept and etc. Requirement

Name of the project	*Area irrigated (lakh acres)*	*Water consumed in 1987-88 TMC as per DAM concept*	*Water as per full etc. requirements (in previous years) TMC*
Godavari barrage	9.7	90	130
Krishna barrage	4.0	50	80
Nizamsagar	1.8	12	20
Tungabhadra	0.7	7	12
Total	16.2	159	242

11. Participatory Irrigation Management (PIM)

Despite massive expenditure on canal irrigation over the years, water distribution remained inequitable and inefficient. Recognizing the need for decentralized irrigation management, the first National Water Policy (1987) called for farmers' participation in irrigation management. The AP Farmers' Management of Irrigation Systems Act, 1997 ensures people participation in water conservation activities through watershed committees, Vansamrakshana Samithis and water conservation and utilization committees. The primary task of Water Users' Associations (WUAs) is to manage, operate and maintain water resources. This not only involves raising funds for maintenance but also supervising works, deciding on water allocation and improving services. So far, 10,292 WUAs have been created in Andhra Pradesh.

Steps Initiated by Government

Some of the steps initiated by the government are as follows:

1. Restoration of Water Bodies

A pilot scheme for repair, renovation and restoration of water bodies directly linked to agriculture has been approved by the Government with an outlay of Rs. 300 crore to be implemented during the remaining period of the Tenth Five Year Plan.

2. Flood Management

- A scheme for flood control in the Brahmaputra and Barak valleys of Assam with an estimated cost of Rs. 150 crore has been approved; works have been taken up in Assam, Tripura and Mizoram.
- A Task Force on Flood Management/Erosion Control was constituted for analyzing the problems and suggesting solutions for Assam, North East, Bihar and Eastern Uttar Pradesh.
- Outlay for flood control of the Ministry of Water Resources has been enhanced to Rs. 340 crore during 2005-06, as compared to Rs. 814 crore during the previous year.

3. Accelerated Irrigation Benefits Programme (AIBP)

Under this programme, support is extended to states for completion of incomplete irrigation projects. Eighty major and medium irrigation projects and 3504 minor irrigation projects from 26 states have been provided Central loan assistance. Additional irrigation potential of about 5 lakh ha has been created.

4. Bharath Nirman—A New Deal for Rural India

The Union budget for 2005-06 launched a new scheme 'Bharath Nirman Yojana'—major plan to rebuild rural India. It is a time bound business plan launched for rebuilding rural infrastructure in six areas viz. irrigation, water supply, housing, roads, electrification and telecommunication. It is implemented over a period of four years for building rural infrastructure. The programme is aimed at *inter alia*, to bring an additional one crore acres (2 m ha) under assured irrigation, to provide drinking water to the remaining 74,000 habitations that are uncovered.

5. Water Conservation Mission

The Andhra Pradesh government brought all water conservation activities into a campaign mode for ensuring convergence of the efforts of all water concerned departments in the name of Neeru-Meeru (Water and You) to promote water conservation on a Mission basis. It also envisages creation of awareness amongst people for ensuring their participation in water resource management. Under the programme, water harvesting structures viz. continuous contour trenching/continuous peripheral trenching/staggered trenching on hill slopes, gully control works, check dams and percolation tanks, bunding in farmers' fields, farm ponds, sunken ponds, dug out ponds, rock fill dams, feeder channels, supply channels, de-silting of tanks, restoration of tanks and breach closures were taken up.

Food Security for Hunger Free India

Mahatma Gandhi wrote in 'Young India' in 1920: "We want to organize our national power not by adopting the best method of production only, but by the best method of both production and distribution."

Physical, social, economical, political and ecological access to balanced diets and safe drinking water, so as to enable every individual to lead a productive and healthy life in perpetuity is called food security (Swaminathan, 2002). Food security deals with viz., availability of food, which is a function of production, access to food, which is related to purchasing power, absorption of food in the body, which is determined by the availability of safe drinking water, environmental hygiene, primary health care and primary education, vulnerability to transient hunger, which is related to natural and man-made calamities and disasters, and sustainability of production, which is influenced by the extent of attention given to ecological foundations essential for sustained advances in production. As we witness the problem of food insecurity, malnutrition and hungry India, this is the time for us to usher in a Second Green Revolution, where emphasis should be on soil and water conservation in dry land agriculture, use of micro-irrigation, increased investments in irrigation, organic farming, integrated nutrient, weed, pest and disease management, precision farming, crop diversification, suitable cropping and farming systems based on agro-ecological conditions, cultivation of HYVs resistant to drought, flood, salinity, sodicity, pest and diseases, value addition, food processing, credit to farmers, price stabilization and targeted subsidies.

As Mahatma Gandhi said not only production but also distribution is important. Effective and successful implementation of the Public Distribution System (PDS), National Food for Work Programme (NFWP), National Rural Employment Guarantee (NREG) Scheme, Bharath Nirman and Rajiv Gandhi National Drinking Water Mission (RGNDWM) will ensure better social, physical, economical and environmental accessibility to food. Let us pledge ourselves to work for achieving Millennium Development Goals and Vision 2020 to see fully food secure and hunger free India in the near future.

Conclusion

Every drop of water should be judiciously utilized and its reckless wastage is to be eliminated. Human intervention is called for halting wastage and harness the surplus water to benefit the water-stress regions. Unless the water problem is adequately addressed with sufficient planning and care, the living beings may be threatened in the years to come.

REFERENCES

Narayana, K.S. 2005, 'An Integrated Approach to Water,' *Kurukshetra*, 53(12):48-52.

Srivastava, R.C. and Satpathy, K.K. 2004, 'Getting more from the water and Watersheds: Multiple use of the resources'. Paper presented at ICAR-IWMI-ICRISAT workshop on watershed management, 3-4 November, 2004, New Delhi.

Swaminathan, M.S. 2002, 'Science and our Agriculture, Indian Agriculture, Current status, Prospects and Challenges,' pp. 1-29, 27th convention of Agricultural Universities Association, December 9-11, 2002, Rajendranagar, Hyderabad.

7

Integrated Water Resources Management

Dr. N.T.K. Naik, Dr. S. Mansoor Rahiman and K. Chinna Venkataswamy

Water is a natural resource which is an essential content in every part of life on the earth. Everything originates from water and everything is sustained by it. "Water," said the eminent Greek philosopher Pindar, "is the best of all things." As the twenty-first century dawns, the importance of this statement is becoming evident in many parts of the world, even though Pindar lived some two and a half millennia ago.

Water is the most precious natural resource for the existence of life on earth. Increasing population and higher levels of human activities, including effluent disposals to surface and groundwater sources, have made sustainable management of water resources a very complex task throughout the world. Besides, the per capita demand for water in many countries is steadily increasing and more and more people are achieving higher standards of living and life styles are changing rapidly.

In fact there are no universal solutions for sustainable water management, both geographically and in terms of time. For example, solutions that work in America may not be the appropriate for China or what may work well in China may not prove to be an efficient solution for India, primarily because of the differing economic, social, political, technical and environmental conditions.

Reprinted with permission, *Kisan World*, Feb. 2006, pp. 45-47.

Land of Paradoxes

India is a land of contrasts. But interestingly enough, it is also a land of paradoxes. On one hand, the country is known for its heavy rainfall and the proverbial fury of its monsoons; on the other hand, it is one of the most water-thirsty lands of the world.

News of both floods and famines appear side by side. The toll taken by the two or the miseries caused by such natural phenomena are a constant source of worry in this land where the monsoons are known for their whims and vagaries.

The three regions in Andhra Pradesh State, viz., Andhra, Telangana and Rayalaseema possess distinct characteristic features. Coastal Andhra Region with sufficient irrigational facilities proved as the Rice Bowl of the state and Vijayawada and Visakhapatnam cities emerged as the two prestigious million cities. Telangana Region is backward in the agriculture sector but doing well in industrial and service activities. The credit goes to Hyderabad Mega City which developed as a centre of economic power. But Rayalaseema Region is known as ever drought affected region, or Raalla Seema. Both agriculture and industrial activities in Rayalaseema Region are in doldrums.

Why 'Water Resource Management' ?

Major projects are needed to harness the water flows of the rivers, but they have certain defects. They cost heavily. They cannot be executed quickly. Irrigation potential created by them will not be actually utilized for some time. So, the Planning Commission emphasized the need of keeping a balance between the major and minor schemes of irrigation.

For the above reasons, small and minor irrigation works were given due place in the Five Year Plans. In their case initial outlay is small. They can yield quick results. Moreover, local resources can be mobilised easily for their execution. Thus, it is necessary to give top priority to Micro Level Irrigation Projects which involve a multi-disciplinary interaction to come up with a viable and functional project.

Irrigation Schemes of Rayalaseema Region

Mr. Mackenzie was an eminent British engineer appointed by the

British Government to formulate the irrigation proposals for Rayalaseema Region. He suggested the construction of a major reservoir to Tungabhadra with an integrated canal system linking Krishna Basin with Penna Basin. But after independence the Indian government has forgotten all the proposals made by him.

The provisions in the gentleman's agreement called "Sri Bagh Agreement" between the leaders of Rayalaseema and Coastal Andhra that all major projects on Krishna, Tungabhadra and Penna rivers should aim to irrigate the parched lands of Rayalaseema were given a go-bye by successive governments.

In 1944, the then Madras Government and the Nizam Government agreed to construct the Tungabhadra Project. It was completed in 1956 in a shrunken form ignoring the interest of the Rayalaseema Region.

The composite Madras state government envisaged to construct the Krishna Pennar Project and got the Planning Commission's approval in 1951. This scheme would have irrigated 7.2 lakh acres in Rayalaseema and some areas in present Tamil Nadu. The project was then shelved.

Formation of separate Andhra state in 1953 and Andhra Pradesh State in 1956, did not solve the requirements of irrigation schemes of the people of Rayalaseema.

Integrated Water Resource Development

Rayalaseema comprising Kurnool, Kadapa, Anantapur and Chittoor of Andhra Pradesh State, occupies an area of 75.30 lakh ha. forming 29.86 per cent area of the state. The climate in Rayalaseema is mostly dry. The only major source of water supply to this region is river Krishna. It is the only river that flows through Rayalaseema and 15,040 sq.km of its catchment area is in this region.

The limited groundwater resource is already over-utilised in the region and grey belt areas are increasing year after year. Keeping all these aspects and inherent draw-backs of this area in view, a future strategy has to be worked out for the Integrated Water Resource Development of Rayalaseema Region.

(1) Rain Water

Rainfall is one of the best indicators to examine the viability of agriculture. Rayalaseema Region was found with inadequate and erratic rains which receive less than 700 mm rainfall, with an annual temperature shooting upto 45°C in the summer. In this region while the precipitation is around 20" to 22", evaporation is of the order of 90" to 120".

The period of rainfall is restricted to only four months and the remaining eight months are dry. Even during the monsoon, rainfall is scanty and undependable in many parts of the region. Sometimes the monsoons are delayed considerably while sometimes they cease prematurely. This pushes the region into drought conditions.

Rainfall below 750 mm can be considered as a drought. Due to erratic rainfall in Rayalaseema, drought was found as an uninvited guest in and around its borders. Anantapur is a peculiar district where drought will be always at its doorsteps as a wolf.

There is an urgent need for propagating water harvesting, conservation and recharging on a large scale. Based on "Best Practices" of water harvesting with active community participation by selected individuals and institutions, prospects for large scale advocacy of this people-oriented programme for ensuring sustainability of the source are bright.

(2) Groundwater Development

Groundwater is a precious natural resource that nature has given to human beings. Groundwater has played a prominent role as a primary source of domestic water supplies in rural and urban areas. About 85 per cent of urban population depends on groundwater for day-to-day domestic needs. But the groundwater resources are not scientifically managed. Excessive use often results in declining of groundwater levels, groundwater quality deterioration, enhanced water lifting costs and ultimately groundwater scarcity.

Groundwater and its proper use assume great significance for a region such as Rayalaseema which faces continuous threat of drought and famine. In the early 1960s there has been increasing use of tube wells. Actually it is the groundwater irrigation and not large dams and canals which is the basis of the Green Revolution in our country.

Groundwater development in Andhra Pradesh is about 42 per cent leaving apparently a large potential for future development. Ruthless exploitation of groundwater leads to serious consequences. Since groundwater withdrawal is greater than the recharge, the groundwater table is declining rapidly. Over-exploitation of groundwater can also lead to the intrusion of saline water, making the water unfit for drinking or irrigation. The groundwater table has gone down dramatically in more intensely cropped areas, clearly indicating the need to increase recharges to regulate pumping. In some areas, there is serious pollution danger to groundwater due to industrial wastes.

Concerted efforts have to be put in for safe and optimum utilization of the groundwater resources of the region, based on the principles of techno-economic and ecological efficiency and equity. Rain water harvesting is a suitable situation. It can be taken up on a large scale through involvement of the local population and implementation of simple and friendly techniques like construction of percolation tanks, check-dams, recharge shafts, etc.

(3) Well Irrigation

By the 1980s well irrigation had become the dominant source of irrigation in Rayalaseema Region. The proportion of area under Canal and Tank Irrigation has declined while the importance of well irrigation has gone up substantially. This may be attributed to the decline in public investment in agriculture in recent years. These changes have environmental consequences. The increase in area under well irrigation coupled with the decline in tank irrigation invariably results in over-exploitation of groundwater resulting in environmental problems such as desertification. At present there are 22.23 lakh wells in Andhra Pradesh, out of this 4.71 lakh wells are in Rayalaseema Region i.e., 21 per cent. Further 1.38 lakh wells are estimated to be feasible in this region. With this it is clear that the potentiality for well irrigation is limited in Rayalaseema, due to low level of underground water resources. The construction and maintenance of wells have been, mainly, the work of private landlords, and they vary widely in size and capacity, some irrigating an acre or two and others as many as 150 acres.

In Rayalaseema Region majority of the wells are of 10-20 metre depth. This is reflected in the growth in tube wells in this region. Tube wells tap the sub-soil water resources. They go to a depth of even 500 ft. to fetch the subterranean supplies of water. A tube well irrigates nearly 500 acres. Rayalaseema region has the largest number of tube wells in the state. On the whole, wells are an important source of irrigation, they irrigate about 46 per cent in Rayalaseema Region.

According to the Irrigation Committee, well irrigation is cheaper and suitable for this region. In Rayalaseema Region, still the farmers are expecting more subsidies for inputs. They need the introduction and implementation of modern technology of well irrigation. It can be economically worked if electricity is supplied to the farmers of free of cost.

(4) Tank Irrigation

Rain water is stored by erecting bunds in places which command small catchment areas. Sometimes small streams are dammed to form tanks. In some cases, tanks are fed by canal water brought from elsewhere. Tanks are of different sizes. There are about 70,000 tanks in the state, of which Telengana region has 44 per cent followed by Andhra which has 38 per cent and Rayalaseema with 18 per cent. Interestingly, Rayalaseema region with highest dependence on groundwater has the lowest number of tanks. Effectively only 18 per cent of the tank ayacut is being irrigated. The decline in quantitative as well as qualitative tank irrigation might explain the low feasibility of groundwater development in Rayalaseema Region. The Second Irrigation Commission stated clearly "Dug wells and tanks are, by and large, the most important source in the drought areas."

The policy-maker's fascination with large irrigation projects has led to the neglect of tanks which at one time used to be the traditional and the most common form of irrigation in many parts of the country. Through poor maintenance, tanks were allowed to fall into disuse because of siltation. To the planners and to our bureaucrats, tanks have always meant small technology and their upkeep and maintenance called for people's participation and co-operation, both of which were anathema to them.

It is clear that tanks are important for good water management and are substitutes for canal irrigation in drought-prone areas. They help to reduce and moderate floods, recharge wells and provide drainage in high rainfall periods.

(5) Watershed Development

The rain water flows from the high areas to downward areas through outlets. The flow that takes place from different places to the outlets is treated as 'Watershed'. Watershed Management includes soil and water conservation works such as contour bunds, stone wall pitching, trenches/pits and water resources development include check dams, percolation ponds, wells or spring development, etc., in addition to other income generating activities.

Rayalaseema Region has also adopted the watershed development programmes by strictly adhering to new watershed guidelines since 1995-96. As per the guidelines, implementation of watershed has to be completed in four years covering 500 hectares of area to be treated with an amount of Rs. 20 lakh per watershed i.e., Rs. 4000 per hectare. Anantapur District receives Rs. 22.5 lakh per watershed i.e., Rs. 4500 per hectare, due to its severe agro-climatic conditions. The average area under watershed is about 500 hectares in line with the guidelines. However, there is a gap in terms of amount sanctioned and utilized by the Watershed Committee.

It is clear that a natural bias towards drought-prone districts is shown with regard to watershed development programmes. Out of 3109 watersheds, 1202 watersheds are allotted to Rayalaseema district that is around 39 per cent.

Watershed Development has been identified as a major strategy for integrated development of both arable and non-arable lands in drought-prone regions like Rayalaseema. It is helpful for increasing the level of underground water and stabilising production of crops, forage, fruits, fuel and timber by means of improved soil and moisture conservation measures, better crop and improved technology practices and reforestation.

Conclusion

- There are no major irrigation projects in Rayalaseema region. Now this is the correct time to bring sufficient pressure on the government to complete the Telugu Ganga, Galeru Nagari and Handri Niva irrigation schemes.

- Sufficient financial inputs should be made by the government to arrest desertification conditions. Watershed, Water harvesting and Cloud seeding programmes should be given top priority to arrest drought conditions.
- Research Centres for Underground Water Development should be established in all the four districts of Rayalaseema Region to monitor the situation and improve the level of groundwater.
- Water literacy campaigns should be conducted to create awareness among the people regarding scarce water resources. People should be educated and motivated.
- Universities, Voluntary Organisations, Trade Unions, Student Organisations and Media have to play a key role in bringing mass awareness among the people of Rayalaseema. First we have to fight against factionism in our villages, and have to make efforts to enable the villages to be self-sustainable in all aspects.

8

An Integrated Approach to Water

K.S. Narayana

Water, one of the free gifts of nature, has been sustaining most of the species and the food chain on the planet, since the beginning of creation. Human beings apart, the animals, birds, insects, plants and various species exist due to benevolence of water. This unique gift, exclusive probably to this planet, should be sustained through pragmatism and made best use of, without either polluting or wasting or overdrawing it. It calls for an integrated and scientific approach supplemented by prudence and restraint on its abuse. Rain and both underground and surface water sources should be enriched using human ingenuity. People should not resort to actions that are detrimental but do everything to enrich the perennial character of rivers, lakes, streams, tanks, etc. in many ways as emphasised in the following paragraphs.

Past generations have handed down the water endowments in a healthy status. The present generation has to maintain these endowments as trustees and pass the same on to future generations in a more healthy and enriched form as we have a duty towards posterity. Conservation should be the *mantra*, over-exploitation should be halted and the water sources (perennial and non-perennial surface and underground water endowments) should be enriched. The human and sub-human population has been increasing on this planet, which poses larger demand on water warranting all-out efforts for its sustained use. The task involves a multi-pronged approach to address the water problem effectively.

Reprinted with permission, *Kurukshetra*, October 2005, pp. 49-52.

Conservation

As already mentioned, the increasing population, bovine and other sub-human species pose increasing demand on water. Water saved on agricultural farms could be used for irrigating additional areas or to meet other domestic or industrial water needs. Over-drawing of water may deplete non-perennial water sources, erode underground water sources and pose an additional strain on perennial water sources. Enlarged area under irrigation has become inevitable to meet the food and fodder needs of the increasing human and animal population. While it is so, people should focus on improving yield per hectare rather than enlarging the area under irrigation, through less water-intensive crops and adoption of scientific water management techniques.

Every drop of water should be judiciously utilised and its reckless wastage eliminated. Not all regions are endowed with water sources. There are several zones that are facing severe water stress. However, there are some areas that have surplus water sources. In some areas, lot of water flows into the sea without proper use. At domestic, industrial and on irrigation fields, lot of water is wasted or even polluted. Human intervention is called for to halt wastage and harness surplus water to benefit water-stress regions.

Prudence

Every drop of water should be used and reused (wherever permissible) most judiciously both in off-farm and on-farm activities, i.e. (a) at domestic level, (b) in irrigation, and (c) in industry. As of now, there is large scope for the prudential use of water in all these sectors that are examined here.

At Domestic Level

The traditional way of life is highly water-intensive in nature. The bathing, cleaning and washing practices in vogue in India (both in rural and urban areas) consume a lot of water. Toilet maintenance and flush-type toilets lead to more water wastage. Use of water-tubs or showers are water intensive and hence these should be discouraged. Use of moisture papers as a substitute to traditional bathing practice has immense potential to save water. Promotion of toilet paper has the potential to save water. Kitchen gardens need large quantities of water in the traditional watering method. Better alternative methods to save water need to be evolved and popularised. Use of drip or sprinkler or moisture augmenting practices can save a lot of water in kitchen gardens, parks, front offices and playgrounds. Domestic water instead of being allowed into storm water drains or tanks or rivers should be collected in community water treatment plants for cleaning and recycling.

In rural India, animals are taken to tanks or rivers for bathing. They not only urinate and drop dung in the river but also kick mud and pollute the water. We have also seen that people clean fish and animal skins, intestines, etc. in the tanks/rivers, which too should be avoided for hygienic reasons. This could be done far away from water sources. Similarly, it is observed that trucks, tractors and other motor vehicles are taken into the water for washing. All these practices could be done offshore so that water sources are not polluted.

Rooftop Rainwater Harvesting

Indian villagers have been tapping rainwater at the domestic level to some extent. In northeast India, the rooftop rainwater is fed into a tank through a pipe for meeting domestic needs. Rooftop water harvesting is essential to ease the pressure on piped water supply. The rainwater that goes waste should be channelised, harvested and made use of to meet ever increasing domestic water needs. Buildings should be properly designed for the purpose. The rooftops should be kept clean and freed from dusty pesticides or corrosive materials, etc. The water should go through a pipe into a community sump tank, which should be purified before supply. Harvesting of rooftop rainwater could meet over 60 per cent of domestic water needs. As there is limited scope of exploiting river or tank water for meeting drinking water needs, especially in big towns, it would be inevitable in the near future to properly harvest rooftop rainwater.

Recycling of Domestic Waste Water

Not only should we harvest water in all possible ways, but go beyond it too. Water used for domestic purposes (for washing, cleaning, bathing, etc.) should be collected, cleaned and recycled for non-drinking domestic and industrial purposes. The day is not too far off when we will need to recycle even sewerage water for meeting non-drinking needs. There should be separate water pipes to channelise sewerage water, domestic wastewater and rooftop rainwater. Though these propositions are capital-intensive and need efficient management and maintenance, these measures would become inevitable sooner than later.

In Israel, water is used 4 to 5 times before it is let off into nature. In India the water is used only once. As of now, only drinking water is supplied of which more than 75 per cent is used for non-drinking purposes. It is proposed to supply potable water and non-drinking water separately. This would ease undue pressure on drinking water supply. Besides, water for meeting non-drinking needs could be met by recycling domestic wastewater. Thus, every house should have four separate pipes—one carrying potable drinking water, another carrying water for other purposes, third one carrying rooftop rainwater and domestic wastewater to a community sump tank. The sanitary water should be separately carried to sewerage pits.

Water Management in Irrigation

In the first week of May 2005, Parliament was informed that the Tungabhadra Dam had lost 560 million cubic metres (20 TMC) of live storage capacity due to siltation, resulting in reduced capacity utilisation. As against a live storage capacity of 131 TMC feet as per the first survey in 1953, the storage capacity was 111 TMC feet as per the 1993 survey. No year passes without experiencing a major breach in the TB canal. Similar is the case with the Hemavathy canal, which is expected to supply drinking water to Tumkur. If one goes along the Indira Gandhi Canal in Rajasthan, one would come to know that more than 30 per cent of the land has degraded. In the Malaprabha and Ghataprabha irrigation commands, waterlogging, soil salinity and degradation are major problems. The problem would be more acute in black soil regions. The Hiracud dam also has lost more than 30 per cent of its live storage capacity while in the KRS dam the loss could be above 20 per cent. Thus, due to silt deposit, the dam's live storage capacity has declined drastically. This problem is almost universal in Indian dams and canals. This is the reason why tail-end farmers do not get adequate water. These should be addressed effectively by undertaking de-silting of dams and canals periodically. Canal banks and field channels should be provided with cement lining to prevent leakage and seepage, which account for about 30 per cent loss of water. If these measures are initiated, water could be put to better use in all the four irrigation systems in India.

In paddy cultivation, the wastage is much more which reduces productivity besides making the land uncultivable due to waterlogging and salinity or sterility. In all the command areas, scientific water management coupled with judicious crop mix should be enforced. The flood or flow irrigation method in vogue in paddy cultivation results in more than 50 per cent of water wastage. By avoiding this colossal wastage, India could irrigate atleast 30 per cent of additional area. Agricultural scientists should develop crop varieties that are less water-intensive, high yielding, disease/pest resistant and adaptive to weather fluctuations. The country has invested huge funds in establishing agricultural research stations, agricultural universities, etc. but the outcome from these investments is not satisfactory. Agricultural scientists should develop crop varieties most suitable to agro-climatic regions by taking into account the water intensity, the remunerative capacity and land-safety (certain crops degrade land badly such as tobacco, ginger, turmeric, etc). Mono cropping has caused enormous erosion in bio-diversity. Crop diversity with judicious crop mix should be given due importance. Farmers should employ progressive methods and go in for less-water-intensive varieties and reduce on-field wastage of water.

The returns to investment are eroded, as water cannot be supplied at its full potential. Sugarcane cultivation is also highly water-intensive. There is need to adopt the *warabandi* system (Weekly Rotational Watering System) so that every farmer is assured of water. This could ease the tail-end farmers' problems. Hereafter, per acre productivity should be the focus as there is less scope for enlarging the area under irrigation to meet the food and fodder needs of a growing number of people and animals.

The flood irrigation method in vogue, especially in the area of paddy cultivation, is not very scientific. Overwatering (which is almost inevitable in the flood-irrigation method practised in paddy cultivation) limits the yield level, besides resulting in waterlogging of low-lying areas and thereby making the land unsuitable for cultivation due to soil degradation. In paddy cultivation, about 55 per cent of water goes waste through evaporation, leakage, seepage, etc.

In Tamil Nadu farmers go for a 105 days duration *Kuruvai* paddy crop from June-October; 165 days duration *Thaladi* crop from October-February as the second crop; while a large majority go in for the 180 days duration *Samba* paddy crop from July-January. Swaminathan suggests replacement of double paddy crop by one HYV paddy which would maintain the overall level of paddy production in the delta and cotton can be grown as a second crop more profitably which would help conserve an enormous quantity of water. Krishnaswamy, S.Y. has demonstrated that two crops yield more than one is a misnomer. Single cropped area gives higher yield and therefore returns to investment is higher. He adds that growing a single crop of HYV paddy systematically gives better return than hurriedly grown double crops and therefore suggests that growing of pulses or grams or commercial crops after taking one rice crop would be more profitable and save water significantly. The fact that growing a single HYV paddy crop instead of two crops in vogue in the delta, the production level remained by and large unaltered suggested that such a proposition would save water with the help of which additional area could be irrigated. It reduces soil from the problem of salinity and waterlogging. This situation may apply even in other areas of paddy irrigation.

Optimal Utilization of Groundwater

A UNDP sponsored detailed survey of the groundwater potential was carried out in 1972 in the Tamil Nadu delta. It estimated that about 150 TMC of water could be utilised in the delta since the region is richly endowed with groundwater resources. It has further reported that if the groundwater were not depleted by proper utilisation for irrigation, it would eventually reach the sea. By this, the groundwater gets wasted by flowing into the sea. It would also aggravate water-logging and consequently salinity of the soil affects optimal efficiency of irrigation. By exploiting the groundwater resource, the dependence on surface water could be reduced to a significant extent. Therefore, there is justification to initiate projects for judicious exploitation of groundwater, if the State is interested in solving farmers' water problems on a sustainable basis. The UNDP has estimated that over 88 TMC of surplus water goes into the sea in the Tamil Nadu delta due to the flood irrigation system in vogue; over 55 per cent of water is wasted through evaporation, seepage, leakage, etc. in the flood irrigation method which is highly deplorable.

According to Vohra, surface water used for agriculture through large or medium or small irrigation systems is uneconomical and unproductive. He suggests that storage of water in the form of soil moisture and groundwater within the surface is the ideal form by which water could be conserved and put to better economic advantage. Such a measure would prevent 150 million hectares from soil erosion and facilitate optimal utilisation of water. The loss of land due to waterlogging and sanitation is estimated to cost the economy about Rs. 3000 crore a year.

Tanks Need Facelift

There are about 39,000 tanks in Karnataka. These were meeting both domestic and minor irrigation needs of the people. Our forefathers maintained these tanks for centuries without depending on outside funds by involving local communities annually in desiltation and deweeding tasks. The common land, the catchment area and the basins were protected well.

During the last 30-40 years, the tanks were allowed to slip into disuse. These are in bad shape with silt deposit, weeds and damaged water weirs. The common lands around the tanks have been encroached. The basins and catchment areas are denuded. The borewells that provided drinking water reduced people's dependence on tanks that led to the latter's utter neglect. Now to restore these tanks, the World Bank's assistance of about Rs. 2000 crore was sought. How efficiently these funds would be utilised for the intended purpose would be anybody's guess. There is an acute need to create effective monitoring mechanisms of programmes with accountability, transparency and effective governance. By restoring these tanks, the state's crop productivity could be enhanced significantly. It is a well-known fact that Karnataka's food production has been stagnant for decades.

Watersheds

Watershed construction is gaining momentum recently. This is not a new concept; the tanks and ponds of ancient times were built for similar purposes. In every village, either the existing tank should be restored or a watershed developed. Biomass around the villages should be improved, grazing should be restricted, over-exploitation of water for irrigation should be prevented and felling of trees banned. These would improve water recharge, reduce soil erosion and augment the water table. Watersheds have the potential of creating employment opportunity besides enhancing crop productivity due to assured water. The Panchayati Raj Institutions (PRIs) have been entrusted with the task of constructing micro-watersheds in every block. Though Karnataka has been having PRIs since 1987, they are yet to make a positive impact in tank rejuvenation or watershed construction and management.

Banning of Borewells

Borewells promised to end water problems and, they did help easing the problem to some extent. However, it has inflicted serious problems too. With the advent of borewells, the open wells dried up and depleted the water table. With the mushrooming of borewells, the neighbourhood borewells too have dried up. Irrigation borewells have created more havoc due to over-exploitation of underground water. In some regions, borewells are dug beyond 500 feet which affect water structures/aquifers, erode the perennial character of streams and reduce surface moisture content. Banning of borewells merits serious examination.

At Industrial Level

In industry, not only is a large quantity of water used but is also polluted with effluents. Leather, textile, liquor, soft drinks, paper, jute, steels, alloys and several other industries are water-intensive besides polluting water and environment and thereby pose several health hazards. To manufacture a bottle of liquor, more than 70 litres of water is wasted. Untreated effluent discharge into tanks, storm water drains, rivers and seas are endangering several species. The units that do not have effluent treatment or abatement plants should not be allowed to exist. India is very poor in preventing industrial pollution (air, water and soil). In advanced countries, there are very stringent pollution prevention rules. This is the reason why heavily polluting industries are being shifted to developing countries. It is still fresh in our memory how thousands of people were killed by Union Carbide's poisonous leakage at its plant in Bhopal. Most of the pesticide and chemical manufacturing industries are posing a severe threat to the environment (including water sources). There is need to make environmental pollution prevention law more effective.

Water Table

Increases in human and bovine populations have led to overdrawing of water for domestic, construction, industrial and irrigation purposes. Increased human settlements, roads, dams, and power projects, etc. have displaced forest and common property. Urban areas have displaced many tanks and curtailed the pace of water recharging drastically. The borewells that suck water from greater depth have depleted/eroded water table. Strengthening of biomass and tree cover should receive priority. Ban on felling of trees on common land, community land, forest land and use of alternatives to firewood in a big way, ban on borewells, creation of water structures, roof top rainwater harvesting and many other actions may help in addressing the problem effectively. Strengthening tree cover around human settlements would also help recharging of water. In every locality there should be a micro water-structure (like tanks) and storm water should be fed into it. These measures would improve the groundwater resources considerably.

Strengthening of Forest Cover

The behaviour of the monsson has a positive correlation with land and forest ratio. Besides various other advantages, forests give birth to small streams and rivers besides enhancing their perennial character. As against normative extent of 30 per cent of forest cover, Karnataka has less than 16 per cent and is still less in many other states. If watersheds/tanks should get good water sources, we need a strong forest cover. The forests and mangroves would go a long way in reducing floods and breaching of banks. The catchment forests should be strengthened and a ban imposed on tree felling in these forests. The greatest wealth of this nation has been the biomass, which is unique with vast diversity. Planting of medicinal plants would be a lucrative proposition. Lots of forest and community lands have been grabbed by land-sharks illegally. These lands should be reclaimed and tree cover improved.

Need for a Water Data Bank

Karnataka has been found badly wanting in respect of maintaining proper documentation of area under irrigation (crop-wise), the water needed per crop season, the inflow/outflow data for every reservoir on a daily basis, the rainfall data, the actual impounding capacity of the dams, etc. On this count, the Cauvery River Water Tribunal, the Cauvery Monitoring Committee, the Cauvery River Authority and the Supreme Court have faulted the State machinery on more than one occasion. Yet, it is regrettable that the State is yet to initiate adequate steps in creating a systematic Data Bank. The officials responsible for this state of affairs should be made accountable and punishable for non-performance of the task expected of them. Karnataka being an IT hub should help in evolving a modernised and scientific data bank about water resources, area under cultivation under different crops, water needs of these crops, etc. The information should be disseminated through the electronic media to benefit the farming community. Remote Sensing Data generation, analysis and dissemination should be gainfully utilised. Depending upon the water in the dam the farmers should be advised well in advance as to what crops they can grow and the extent of area that could be irrigated in a given year.

Unless the water problem is adequately addressed with sufficient planning and care, living beings would be threatened in the foreseeable future. Scientists should evolve cost-effective technology to convert seawater into potable water so that it can mitigate to water problem.

9

Integrated Water Mission

A.P.J. Abdul Kalam

There are some who have great expectations about linking of rivers. There are also some others who question whether this programme will be a blessing for the country?

Four aspects will be discussed:

- What is the total requirement of water for our nation for drinking purposes, sanitation, irrigation and other industrial uses and what does the nation get through seasonal inputs (rain and melting of snow)?
- One-third of our population is affected by floods or drought every year.
- Per capita availability of water varies from 10 kilolitres to 50 kilolitres for different seasons and regions.
- What are the optimal ways of meeting the minimum needs of water for the entire population? Assuming a particular population growth rate for the country, by 2020 we have to produce approximately 400 million tons of grain and the water requirement will also go up due to population increase.

India gets approximately 4000 billion Cubic Metres (BCM) of water every year from all natural sources. Out of this 700 BCM are lost in

Based on President's Address at the National Water Convention 2005 on 11 May, 2005 in New Delhi.

evaporation and another 700 are lost during the flow on the ground. Also, a large part of water namely 1500 BCM flows into the sea due to floods. Thus, the remaining available water is only 1100 BCM. Out of this groundwater recharge accounts for 430 BCM per year and the present utilized surface water is 370 BCM. The balance unutilized water which can be harnessed is 300 BCM.

Floods normally affect eight major river valleys spread over 40 million hectares of area in the entire country affecting nearly 260 million people. Similarly, drought affects 86 million people who are spread in 14 states covering a total of 116 districts. Wherefrom does this flood come? It comes from the 1500 BCM of water every year flowing during the monsoon season. If we have to prevent the damage due to the flood and reduce the severity of drought, we have to harness this 1500 BCM of water and distribute it to the drought affected areas. We can also partly store it in a proper storage system so that it can be available during non-monsoon months. If we succeed in doing all these, we will not only save the loss arising out of the damage caused to crops, property and people by the flood to the extent of Rs. 2400 crore on an average per year, we will also save the recurring expenditure of Rs. 1200 crore incurred by the government as short-term relief measures. The questions which arise are how to harness the flood water? And how to regulate the outflow of flood water so that it does not go into the sea and is converted as useful water for mankind.

Harnessing Water

1500 BCM of flood water should be channelised, so that it can be used for drought affected areas and make sufficient water available to the whole country during non-monsoon months through proper linking, storage and distribution. Our plans must consider that presently sanitation facilities are not available in more than 50 per cent of the dwelling units in the country. Planners must take into account this aspect while selecting schemes for harnessing and distributing the water for our growing population. We may have to align our interlinking of rivers project for meeting the growing water demands of the nation by having a hybrid scheme which can harness the additional 300 BCM per year and also the flood water of 1500 BCM.

Flood Control

There is an urgent need to find a long-term solution to control floods, store and utilize the surplus water during drought. In the Gangetic region, I would recommend construction of layered wells in the entry points of the Kosi river. Normally the flood water has certain dynamic flow conditions. The layered wells assist gradual reduction in dynamic flow velocity after filling each storage well. The water thus stored can be useful during shortage period. Similar solution can be found for the north-eastern region. This scheme can be included in the interlinking of rivers programme.

Also the scheme chosen must be such that there is continuous availability of additional water for the growing population and the related needs of the nation by regulating the outflow into the sea.

While working on large schemes, a certain amount of displacement of people is bound to happen. We should aim at minimizing dislocations. We also have to consider the overall impact and benefits of the scheme which in this case is going to benefit nearly 340 million people who are affected constantly by floods or droughts. The Rehabilitation Plan should include area required for providing housing for the affected families which have to be relocated, space required for the livelihood, either agricultural, artisanal or industrial. Adequate funds required should become the component of the mission of "Connecting Water Resources." Also, by learning from the problems of the past, necessary new mechanisms need to be in place to provide facilities to those who are likely to be displaced well in advance. Governance issues connected in these projects are equally important as technologies, project management, finances, etc. The project report should consist of all these components before seeking sanction.

Environmental Upgradation

There are certain apprehensions by environmentalists that the large-scale diversion of water and disturbance to the terrain may endanger or affect the geological and ecological balance. It is therefore essential to find a solution to their concern and build it as a part of the mission of interlinking of rivers. For example, the afforestation area could be increased 10 to 15 per cent from the present forest area designing the river flow management. Therefore, the comprehensive mission planned by the government will have to take into account pooled allocations from the various departments and be closely monitored, as it will have an impact in every field of development programmes of many ministries of state and central governments.

Science and Technology can surely help in executing such missions. India has its own remote sensing satellites and their applications will help in large-scale survey from the source and river flow pattern in various seasons. Optimum water routes and mapping of the environmental profile can be evolved using virtual reality through satellite and aerial imageries. The most important means is to use CARTOSAT-I for getting stereotype pictures on water resources and drought. This should become part of the Water Mission.

Linking Local River Basins

During my address to the Andhra Pradesh Assembly, it was suggested that the Godavari water which flows into the sea to the extent of 2500 tmc during floods and 750 tmc during normal conditions may be diverted into the basin area for irrigation purposes through step dams, irrigation canals and water storage lakes and ponds. This will increase the irrigated area of the Godavari basin by over 30 per cent. The Andhra Pradesh government has agreed to implement this scheme. The Government of Goa has also interlinked the Zuari river with the Kalay river in Mandovi basin through installation of pumps and gravity flow. This has been done to ensure availability of drinking water in this region. Every state should be asked to inter-connect their own rivers on the lines of Goa. This should form part of the state planning. Overall planning of interlinking of rivers has to integrate the state water resource connectivity.

Simultaneously we have to undertake missions for water harvesting, recycling and environmental upgradation, for long-term availability of 800 BCM surface and groundwater. Some examples which have been implemented in different regions are:

Water Harvesting

Water harvesting and water recycling should become mandatory for all the states. To improve the water table we need to build check dams, develop water sheds, desilt ponds and rivers, clear the inlets and outlets to the ponds and water bodies and recharge the wells. If our rural areas are made to have operational clean water bodies, recharging of the wells will take place. These activities will also generate employment. The Tamil Nadu government has taken the lead and made water harvesting a mandatory requirement for all house-holders in the states including rural areas. Studies indicate that this has resulted in considerable improvement in the groundwater level in this season. Recently the permanent housing scheme for tsunami-affected people includes water harvesting in all houses. Some states have taken action to revive lakhs of water bodies of different types. They have also undertaken mini and micro watershed irrigation schemes to improve groundwater level in droughtprone areas to preserve the local rain water for irrigation.

In addition to water harvesting, water recycling is essential for large consumers such as hotels, public institutions and industries. The recycled water must be used for all usages including agricultural needs, except for drinking. This will reduce the per capita requirement of water to nearly 25 per cent of the present consumption and enable a larger number of population to get adequate potable water and for sanitation.

Synergy Mission

The status of environmental cleanliness is one of the indicators of development of a nation. As a nation, we have to keep our environment clean and tidy including all our places of worship and rivers. The Kali Bein rivulet, the place where Gurunanak Devji is said to have received enlightenment, over the years has turned into a weed choked drain. Recently, the river is clean due to the efforts of Baba Balbir Singh Seechewal in partnership with the Punjab State Government. He organized people's participation in stopping the massive flow of sewage into the Bein and cleaned 160 km long polluted and choked rivulet within the last three and a half years by deploying on an average 3000 volunteer pilgrims per day. Today one can feel the flow of fresh water in this rivulet released from the Tarkina Barrage by the government about a year ago. The revival of the rivulet has recharged the water table as the hand pumps that had become dry for the past four decades are now pumping out water.

Let this model spread in all the places of divine worship and inspire the pilgrims to participate in the task of clean environment in water and air. "Thousands of local initiatives will make India green."

Project Siruthuli

This is an initiative started by Coimbatoreans for Coimbatoreans. This ecological project aims to bring back the glory of Coimbatore and its rich heritage. The project is represented by people from all walks of life and is professionally organized. The primary focus is on large-scale rain water harvesting, afforestation, sewage/waste water treatment and solid waste management. They have already standardized five of the nine primary tanks in Coimbatore for large-scale rainwater harvesting. Over 600 saplings have been planted on the bunds of the de-silted tanks and are being maintained. They are moving towards a target of planting 15 lakh trees by the end of 2005. The comprehensive study has indicated an outlet of the city sewage as 10 million litres per day. A pilot plant is being taken up for sewage treatment to treat one million litres per day. The treated water will be sold to agriculturists and industrialists as a revenue earning measure. The garbage and debris to the extent of over 26,000 cubic metres have been removed in one of the city's largest tank. This model can be replicated throughout the country.

Periyar PURA

Over 65 villages near Vallam, Thanjavur district of Tamil Nadu, have been transformed as a PURA cluster. It has a ring road and interconnecting roads covering major villages along with a bus transport system.

They have innovative water management schemes for irrigation and providing potable water for all the village citizens. All 65 Periyar PURA villages are having only rainfed irrigation. Due to shortage of rainfall in that locality, farmers were suffering due to scarcity of water not only for agriculture but also for drinking purposes. Keeping this in mind, Periyar PURA developed six percolation ponds and five check dams to harness the rainwater amounting to 2.73 lakh cubic metre per year. This water is supporting the irrigation of 300 acres of land through recharging their open wells and bore wells. It also supplies drinking water to the people. Periyar PURA has also developed alternate practices such as contour lands, check dams across natural streams for water conservation and developed a model for irrigation for conservation of water. More than 5000 farmers are benefiting from this programme. This example will be useful for water management in PURA complexes.

Our planet will encounter in the next few decades severe shortage of water if we are not careful in conserving and preserving precious water resources. In India, we should have action-oriented plans to foresee the problem and work on a mission mode before the water situation worsens. It is essential to have a water management mission that unfurls our vision for the next two decades, by integrating interlinking of rivers, water harvesting, water recycling, and desalination of sea water using solar energy in specific areas.

The following seven action points are suggested:

- Recommending schemes which will ensure availability of minimum 25 kilolitres of water per year for each citizen in the country.
- The schemes chosen should also ensure the availability of water required for producing four hundred million tonnes of foodgrains per year by 2020. Simultaneously, it is suggested that agricultural scientists need to develop crop varieties, similar to ICRISAT seeds, which will need minimum water.
- Schemes chosen should ensure that no state is affected by flood or drought.
- Water harvesting must be made mandatory for all buildings. Necessary legal provisions may be made in this regard.
- Recommend appropriate legal provisions for making recycling of water mandatory in all buildings particularly large hotels and industries where large amounts of water is consumed.
- Expenditure required for rehabilitation and environmental upgradation should become part of the mission of "connecting water resources." Also a people-oriented governance system should be in place to take care of affected people.
- There are many schemes for interlinking of rivers. The Ministry of Water Resources has to consolidate all the best aspects and bring out a cost effective project report. As a whole, interlinking of rivers has to be a mission mode project.

10

The First and Last Commons

Vandana Shiva

There are two paradigms of water in intense contest—the paradigm of water a commons and the paradigm of water as a commodity.

Water is a commons because it is the ecological basis of all life and because its sustainability and equitable allocation depend on the cooperation between members of a community. Although water has been managed as a commons throughout human history, across diverse cultures, and although most communities manage water resources as common property or have access to water as a commonly shared public good even today, privatization of water resources is gaining momentum.

Prior to the arrival of the British in South India, communities managed water systems collectively through a system called *Kudimaramath* (self repair). Before the advent of corporate rule by the East India Company in the 18th century, a peasant paid 300 out of 1000 units of grain he or she earned to a public fund and 250 of those units stayed in the village for maintenance of commons and public works. By 1830, peasant payments rose to 650 units, out of which 590 units went straight to the East India Company. As a result of increased payments and lost maintenance revenue, the peasants and commons were destroyed. 300,000 water tanks built over centuries in pre-British India were destroyed, affecting agricultural productivity and earnings.

The East India Company was driven out by the first movement for independence in 1857. In 1858, the British passed the Madras

Reprinted with permission, *Kurukshetra*, September 2005, pp 7-10.

Compulsory Labour Act of 1858 popularly known as the *Kudimaramath* Act mandating the peasants to provide labour for the maintenance of the water and irrigation systems. Because *Kudimaramath* was based on self-management and not coercion, the act failed to mobilize community participation and to rebuild the commons.

Self-managed, self-regulating communities have not just been a historical reality; they are also a contemporary fact. State interference and privatization have not wiped them out entirely. In a nationwide survey covering districts in dry tropical regions in seven states, N.S. Jodha finds that most basic fuel and fodder needs of the poor throughout India continue to be satisfied from common property resources. Jodha's studies of commons in the fragile Thar desert also reveal that village community councils still adjudicate grazing rights: institutional rules and regulations, determine periods of restricted grazing, the rotational patterns for grazing, the numbers and types of animals to be grazed, the rights to dung and fuel wood collection and the rules for lopping trees for green fodder. Village councils also appoint their own watchmen to ensure that no community member or outsider breaks the rules. Similar rules exist for maintenance of wells and tanks.

Under conditions of scarcity, sustainable systems of water management evolved from the idea of water as a commons passed on from generation to generation. Labour in conservation and community building became the primary investment in water resources. As Anupam Mishra of the Gandhi Peace Foundation observes,

> The ways of collecting the drops of *Palar,* i.e. of rainfall, are as unending as the names of clouds and drops. The pot like the ocean is filled up drop by drop. These beautiful lessons are not to be found in any textbook but are actually couched in the memory of our society. It is from this memory that the *shrutis* of our oral traditions have come. . . ."
>
> The people of Rajasthan did not entrust the organisation of such a boundless work to either the central or federal government, not even to what in modern parlance is termed as the private sphere. It is the people themselves who in each house, in each village, gave fruition to this structure, maintained it, and further developed it.

The traditional water systems based on local management were also insurance against water scarcity in drought-prone regions of Gujarat. These systems were managed locally by local institutions and mainly by the village communities. In the event of floods, famines and other calamities, the king also helped; the role of a central authority was, therefore, primarily in disaster mitigation. Local institutions in water management included farmers' associations, local irrigation functionaries, the village water associations, and the labour system, maintained by contributions from each family.

In India, farmers' associations for the construction and maintenance of water systems were once widespread. In Karnataka and Maharashtra the associations were known as *panchayats*. In Tamil Nadu, they were called *nattamai, kavai maniyam, nir maniyam, oppidi sangam* or, *eri variyam* (tank committee). Tanks and ponds often serve more than one village and in such cases, representatives from each village or farmers' association ensured democratic control. These committees and associations could also collect tank dues and taxes from users. Lands were also donated, especially for financing capital expenditure on water works.

Village water systems required irrigation functionaries who looked after the day-to-day operation of irrigation systems. In the Himalayas, where *kuhls* serve community irrigation needs, irrigation managers' are called *kohlis*. In Maharashtra, they were known as *patkaris* and *havaldars* and *jogalaya*. In Karnataka and Tamil Nadu, they were known as *nirkatti, nirganti, nirpaychi, niranikkans* and *kamkukatti*.

To ensure neutrality, *nirkattis* were chosen from the landless caste—the Harijans—who were granted autonomy from land owners and caste groups. Only Harijans held the power to close and open the tanks or vents. Once the farmers laid down the rules of distribution, no individual farmer could interfere and those who did could be fined. This protection of the associations from the economically powerful ensured water democracy.

Compensations were based on investments of one's own labour and could not be substituted by capital, or by the others' labour. In South India, collective labour investment was the primary investment in the construction and maintenance of village water systems known as *Kudimaramath*. Each able-bodied person was required to help maintain and clean channels. *Nirkattis* also summoned farmers to clean the supply and field channels. The ancient economic treatise, *Arthashastra* included certain punishments for defaulters from any kind of cooperative construction. Violators were expected to send their servants and bullocks to carry on their work and to share the costs, without laying any claim to the return.

The self-management systems suffered when the government took control over water resources during British rule. Community ownership was further eroded with the emergence of borewells and tubewells, which made individual farmers dependent on capital. Collective water rights were undermined by state intervention, and resource control was transferred to external agencies. Revenues were no longer reinvested in local infrastructure but diverted to government departments.

Community rights are necessary for both ecology and democracy. Bureaucratic control by distant and external agencies and market control by commercial interests and corporations create disincentives for conservation. Local communities do not conserve water or maintain water systems if external agencies—bureaucratic or commercial—are the only beneficiaries of their efforts and resources.

Higher prices under free-market conditions will not lead to conservation. Given the tremendous economic inequalities, there is a great possibility that the economically powerful will waste water while the poor will pay the price. Community rights are a democratic imperative — they hold states and commercial interests accountable and defend people's water rights in the form of decentralized democracy.

Water as a Commodity

Everyone agrees that the world is facing a severe water crisis. Water abundant regions have become water scarce, and water scarce regions face water famines. There are, however, two conflicting paradigms for explaining the water crisis. One is the market paradigm and the other is the ecological paradigm. The market paradigm sees water scarcity as a crisis resulting from absence of water trade. If water could be moved and distributed freely through free markets, it would be transferred to regions of scarcity and that higher prices would lead to conservation. As Anderson and Snyder state, "At higher prices people tend to consume less of a commodity and search for alternative means of achieving their desired ends. Water is no exception."

Market assumptions are blind to the ecological limits set by the water cycle and the economic limits set by poverty. Over-exploitation of water, and disruption of the water cycle create absolute scarcity that markets cannot substitute with other commodities. The assumption of substitution is in fact central to the logic of commodification. Such abstract arguments miss the most crucial point—when water disappears, there is no alternative. For example, Hirshleifee and his colleague state:

> This is not to deny that as a commodity, water has its special features, for example, its supply is provided by nature partly as a store and partly as a flow, and it is available without cost in some locations but rather expensive to transport to others. Whatever reason we cite, however, the alleged unique importance of water disappears upon analysis.

Such abstract arguments miss the most crucial point—when water disappears, there is no alternative. For Third World women, water scarcity means longer distances in search of water. For peasants, it means starvation and destitution as drought wipes out their crops. For children, it means dehydration and death. There is simply no substitute for this precious liquid, necessary for the biological survival of animals and plants.

The water crisis is an ecological crisis with commercial causes, but no market solutions. Market solutions destroy the earth and aggravate inequality. The solution to an ecological crisis is ecological, and the solution for injustice is democracy. Ending the water crisis requires rejuvenating ecological democracy.

11

Communication Strategy for Water Management

T. Manonmani

Communication is an inevitable input for human development. Every citizen should be in a position to choose for himself a better way of life without anyone's interference and influence. To do this, he must be adequately informed, educated and empowered on matters that have a bearing on food, water, health, environment and every aspect of human life. Thus, communication and its technology in the 21st century has become the fulcrum for research and development as an ally in the social movement. This study pleads a strategy harnessing the power of New Information and Communication Technology for water management and development.

Communication Strategy

Water scarcity due to diminishing water resources is an issue of the highest contemporary centrality. Although there have been sizeable budget allocations for water management in the successive five-year plans and sufficient natural resources found in and around India, water is still expected to be at the core of this country's concern. According to the World Resource Index (1998-99), India stands 7th in the world and 3rd among Asian Countries in annual internal renewable water resources. In annual groundwater recharge, India stands 5th in the world and 2nd among Asian nations, that is, next to China. In this context, it needs to search the ground realities to frame the appropriate communication strategy for future planning and development.

The inferences from various case studies reveal the following inappropriate plans and policies, which led to mismanagement of water in the country.

1. Water governance in India adopts an excessively centralised top-down, linear approach. For instance, the large irrigation systems managed by bureaucrats bosses over the community organisations. In the past, farmers would collectively maintain traditional water sharing but they were sidelined by workers of irrigation authorities who built new channels and dictated the release and termination of water supply. When the irrigation channels eventually broke down, the farmers just waited for the same works to turn for repair rather than to fix the problems by themselves. Problems related to this in-appropriate plan of controlled irrigation range from seepage in the canal system to excessive irrigation. This causes salinity, waterlogging, reducing aeration and percolation of applied fertilizers below the root system. Finally, it leads to groundwater scarcity. Logically, irrigation system has led to benign neglect of both contextually relevant social institutions and traditional technology. Moreover, it is an onslaught of formal structures of representative democracy. In short, the scheme has failed to realize the appropriation of a bottom-up, participatory and empowerment method of action.

2. For too long, the Government and techno-centric policy-makers have responded to water scarcity through grandiose ideas of big structures, linking waters and creating mega reservoirs, but not through renovating community water banks, a fertile source for recharging groundwater.

3. Previous water policies have focused practically exclusively on augmenting supply thus paying little heed to conservation and more optimal utilisation. The policy has no provision for creating awareness on the multi-dimensional nature of water-use and also for disseminating information and education on promotion of retention of soil moisture, the cultivation of higher value but low water requiring crops like pulses, oil seeds and some herbal plants. If only 7 per cent of water saved in the agricultural sector (Totally 93 per cent of water is used for agri purposes), that would be sufficient to meet the entire domestic and industrial demand.

4. Negation of inclusion of targeted groups in planning and decision-making in terms of participatory and partnership methodology. Most of the studies emphasise on blending the institutional and technical approaches to water management. Technology is not made synonymous with either techno-centric or mega scale projects. There are numerous illustrations of the ways in which water can be more effectively utilised in large parts by involving users themselves. Effective participation of the priority target groups in the decision-making process from the very start is the only way to divert thinking and planning from mere supply augmentation without enough attention to its deleterious consequences.

5. User's ignorance and inadequate knowledge on water management is a matter of serious concern.

The problems associated with unscientific and unregulated development of groundwater are over-exploitation of resources leading to a fall/tube well deepening of the structure, resulting in higher cost of pumping.

6. Lack of provisions to frame communication strategies for conflict resolution and management to overcome water disputes between international, inter-state, inter-district and even inter-block agencies. Many international experiences like Rhine research project have proved useful in arriving at solutions based on negotiation, bargaining and co-operation.

7. Lacunae in legal framework and legal literacy:

(i) Need to redefine the relationship between water and land rights, specially in the case of groundwater. Many studies make out a strong case for prescribing and enforcing legal limits to groundwater exploitation.

(ii) Need to modify irrigation legislation provisions for dispute settlement.

(iii) Present legal framework is gender-insensitive. As ownership of land and water provide the basis for immense power under existing Indian conditions, it needs an explicit recognition of the gender and class character of access to water.

(iv) Finally, the law should also hold the state accountable for failure to develop legal literacy among the targeted groups. This is the only way that the resource poor not only get their legal rights but are also able to claim the rights they already have.

8. Above all, the water management projects adopt the injecting model (Needle theory) and imposing methodology for implementation. An instance is the Tamil Nadu Government's scheme on Rain Water Harvesting. Although rainwater harvesting is economically cheap, technically simple and an easy method of conservation of both surface and groundwater, the scheme has failed to attain its goal, just because of the Government's imposing attitude.

From the above discussion, it is evident that one of the missing links in the Indian water management efforts has been information, education and communication. Communication support has remained the weakest link in the process as the policy-makers and development managers have underestimated the communication part. The information and knowledge on water management were just disseminated through all kinds of popular media and enhanced people's compliance with authorities. So, it is not enough to simply make services available to the targets. It involves initiating and sustaining fundamental behavioural changes at individual and social levels. Individuals need to be shaped to translate the messages into personal behaviour and life style for better development.

The much needed breakthrough in the programme will not come merely from additional infrastructure or repeating or intensifying the same old communication strategy. One should understand that communication strategy does not mean mere supply of media and other infrastructure, but it is a formula for changing the behaviour of individuals and systems based on communication theories that provide a framework for designing and implementing communication interventions. The communication interventions must extend beyond information dissemination and should deal with the issues of community participation and partnership. An effective strategy to mobilise the public for collective action should use three necessary components:

- Participation by the targeted group,
- Partnership with the targeted group, and
- Empowerment of the targeted group.

Functional Strategy

The strategy to be designed is to empower the targets with new knowledge and skills on water management. The first step to take in bringing such empowerment is the initiation of a knowledge revolution in rural India through effective and meaningful use of modern information and communication technology.

The two revolutions of the third millennium, namely, the Information and Communication Technology (ICT) and the Self-Help Revolution are capable of being adopted for empowerment methodology. ICT can play a role in bringing people together by the establishment of networks based on an integrated application of Satellite, Cable TV, Wireless Telephony and Internet which is offering multimedia capabilities with human touch like integrated live-voice, video conferencing and data services not just on PCs or TVs, but also on mobile phones, set-top boxes, web pages, etc. The integration of these technologies again with the community radio and language press can become effective instruments for harnessing the power of participation of user groups (mainly farmers, womenfolk and the industrial public) and partnership with professionals, political leaders, public policy-makers, technocrats, NGOs, etc. Such partnership alone can help to bridge the growing divide between scientific know-how and field level know how.

The self-help revolution based on micro-credit (now it has been expanded into the community owned and managed micro-enterprise) is an opportunity to enhance participation and partnership in the empowerment process. The experiences gained from pilot projects on "Rural Knowledge Centres" managed by Self-Help Women groups with the motto of "think globally, act locally" can be of help to horizontal linkages with related national and international resource agencies. The emphasis in the formula is standardisation of delivery systems ensuring social inclusion in terms of access to relevant technologies and knowledge. Moreover, the micro-level knowledge centres are able to convert generic information into location specific and *vice-versa*. The diffusion of traditional knowledge and regional grassroot innovations beyond their boundaries also gets equal importance in the network because sharing experiences, information and knowledge is recognised as the fundamental building blocks of developmental options for disadvantaged communities around the world. Sharing across the block level can improve collective planning and productivity.

Virtual Design

The resource centres to be designed can be linked together in the form of structured organisation as Virtual Academy for water management like the following Virtual Universities:

- Virtual University for Agrarian Prosperity in Maharashtra.
- Virtual University for the Semi-Arid Tropics set-up by the International Crops Research Institute for Semi-Arid Tropics, Hyderabad.
- Virtual University for Agricultural Trade in Kerala.
- Virtual Academy for Rural Prosperity in Tamil Nadu to be set up.

The proposed model should have the following linkages for effectiveness as advocated by M.S. Swaminathan in his model.

(a) Lab to Lab: This will involve organising a consortium of scientific institutions and data providers at national and international levels.

(b) Lab to Land: This will involve symbiotic linkages between the providers of information and the beneficiaries so that the information dissemination is relevant to the life and work of user groups.

(c) Land to Lab: There is considerable traditional knowledge and wisdom among rural and tribal families concerning the sustainable management of natural resources, particularly water. Therefore technical experts should not only learn from traditional knowledge and experience but also take steps to conserve for posterity.

(d) Land to Land: There is scope for lateral learning among local user groups. Such learning has high credibility because the knowledge coming from a fellow user would have been subjected to an impact analysis from the point of its social relevance to population.

All aspects of water conservation and sustainable use should be dealt with in the model since the academy will function as a resource centre. Data on the profile at community water banks, rural low water demonstration parks, training manual to promote the retention of soil moisture, rain water harvesting, efficient use of rain, surface and groundwater, cultivation of high value but low water requiring crops like pulses and oil seeds, short, medium and long-range weather forecasting, information received from space to create land records, natural resources, pin-point suitable sites to obtain drinking water, locate watershed areas that can recharge groundwater aquifers and find suitable tracts of waste land that can be reclaimed for cultivation and up-to-date climate data for a region along with weather forecasts and disaster management should be available and accessible easily. Education on water and land rights, bio-diversity and eco-system is also an ally in the process. The data generators will manage the data base.

Operational Technical Design

For the selection of appropriate technology, the factors to be considered are geographical location, its remoteness from the switching centre (Main Hub), anticipated traffic volume and operational cost. A network up to the grassroot level with data bases, knowledge systems and decision support system will have to be developed. Any kind of technical design proposed should be of international standard in micro-planning and efficient delivery. So, cost effective appropriate media integration should be developed. A three-tier structure that is a main hub at the switching centre, block level hubs and facilitation booths/ centres providing connectivity down to the village level will be used. The village level facilitation centres will have access to the block level hubs as well as main hub through a dial-up network. To provide reliable network, a high speed wireless LAN will be provided at the block level centres. The VSAT network will work with the shared hub in the mainland. A high speed IPA VSAT is connected for Internet access. Web-based server will be installed to host web-based applications.

The main hub will be structured with multimedia video conferencing system and a number of tools for imparting interactive educating data provider to remote receiving end. The multi point conferencing unit and IP-based VSAT system will be used. All the village centres will have interactive multi-casting, voice-over IP, external data sharing and internet access on local area network (LAN). The selected useful message could reach selective user groups and in turn user groups can also respond to certain messages, among themselves. If people can come together with the help of SHGs themselves (through collectivism) to the computer centre, they can also communicate to other groups in other villages through the Net.

Local village radio (FM radio) can also be networked with the internet in such a way as to create information seekers from the state of mere receivers. Thus, the centres will create "Cyber Groups" everywhere to share their experiences. The design might prove that the ICT and other media could be integrated which would be cheaper than other forms of broadcasting or narrow casting practices.

The technical constraints will be removed with the help of Wireless Local Loop Technology (WLL) introduced by HT, Chennai as telephone connections are not satisfactory. The solar power also can be harnessed when supply of power is irregular. This approach should be based on the principle that there is an implementable solution for every problem.

REFERENCE

Bhatnagar, Subhash and Schware, Robert (Eds.), (2000), *Information and Communication Technology in Development; Cases from India*, Sage Publications, New Delhi.

Part II

DRINKING WATER MANAGEMENT STRATEGIES

12

Drinking Water Management Strategies

P. Durgaprasad

The Indian population clock in New Delhi has been relentlessly ticking on and on over a base population of one thousand million plus. Amongst others, the unquenching needs of these growing millions and the availability and quality of drinking water is a major problem. This paper highlights key policy issues and operational strategies, even while reviewing the achievements and underscoring the problems of drinking water in the country.

Declining Water Sources

The annual per capita availability of freshwater in 1951 was 5177 cubic metres, that declined to 1869 cubic metres in 2001. It is likely to fall further to 1341 cubic metres in 2025, and in 2050, it will be 1140 cubic metres. It is generally presumed that if per capita level falls to 1000 cubic metres, it could seriously affect the health and economic activity of the entire country. At this level, water crisis will be seen in 25 per cent of India's geographical area, affecting 21 per cent of the total population. Already, 5.5 per cent of the country's geographical area and 7.6 per cent of the population are facing acute water shortage, with availability less than 500 cubic metres.

The competitive and at times conflicting demands of irrigation water and drinking water often cause avoidable community stress and ecological disturbances. The agricultural sector alone consumes over three-fourth of all fresh water. Table 1 details the current water requirements as also projects the demand for water in the years 2010 and 2025. (Manjeshwar, 2003).

Table 1: Water Requirements

(Figures in billion cubic metres)

Use	*2000*	*2010*	2025
Domestic	30	56	73
Irrigation	501	688	910
Industry	20	12	23
Energy	20	5	15
Other	34	52	72

Source: Manjeshwar, Nandu, *Swagath Magazine,* July 2003.

Excessive Dependence on Groundwater

It is in this context that one needs to evaluate the past experiences of over-dependence on groundwater even while exploring new sources of surface water and rejuvenating the dormant rivers and lakes as has been done in Rajasthan, for example by the Tarun Bharat Sangh. This would (also) entail development of freshwater resources and transfer of water from surplus to deficit basins (Goswami, 2003). Groundwater is a major contributor in many States, ironically even in those States that have several rivers. Some of the states depend upwards of 50 per cent on groundwater, while the all-India average itself is 45.78 per cent (Table 2).

Table 2: Dependence on Groundwater

(Based on ultimate irrigation potential)

States Heavily Dependent on Groundwater	
Manipur	61.09%
Uttar Pradesh	55.08%
Madhya Pradesh	54.27%
Jammu & Kashmir	52.13%
Tamil Nadu	51.19%
Punjab	48.80%
All-India	45.78%

Source: MoWR, *Annual Report,* 2002-03.

Unrestricted exploitation of groundwater has other manifestations. In West Bengal, almost 5,00,000 people are affected by arsenic through groundwater. Increased salinity in Gujarat, Haryana, Karnataka, Punjab, Rajasthan and Tamil Nadu as well as high fluoride levels in peninsular India and western parts of the country affect nearly 14 million people. The solution lies in recharging of aquifers to stabilise the flow as well as arrest contamination. To check the depletion of groundwater aquifers, a regulatory mechanism needs to be created and rigorously implemented (Radha Singh, 2003).

State Interventions

The Rajiv Gandhi National Drinking Water Mission (RGNDWM), Government of India (GOI), strategy to achieve the objective of securing safe drinking water to all rural habitations revolves around the following three distinct but inter-related issues: (i) Accelerating the coverage of all rural habitations, especially to reach the un-reached with access to safe drinking water; (ii) To promote sustainability of the systems and sources to ensure continued supply of safe drinking water in the covered habitations, and (iii) To tackle the problems of water quality in affected habitations, and to institutionalise water quality monitoring and surveillance systems.

The following norms have been adopted for providing safe drinking water to rural population in the habitations:

(a) 40 litres of safe drinking water per capita per day (Ipcd) for human beings.
(b) 30 Ipcd additional for cattle in the Desert Development Programme Areas.
(c) One hand-pump or stand post for every 250 persons.
(d) The water source should exist within the habitation or within 1.6 km in the plains and within 100 mtrs. elevation in the hilly areas.

According to the Government of India reports* of 2002, over 90 per cent of all rural habitations in the country have been covered. Also, it has set the objective to provide potable drinking water to all

* Report presented at the All-India Conference of State Ministers of Rural Drinking Water Supply, Vigyan Bhavan, 5 December, 2002, MoRD, GOI, New Delhi.

rural habitations in the country by the year 2004. The coverage data (Table 3) shown here are based on the nation-wide habitation survey conducted through State Governments in 1991, revalidated in 1994, and updated in 1997 and 2002.

Table 3: Current Status (2002) of Coverage of Habitations in the Country

Type of coverage	*No. of habitations*	*Per cent*
Total	1422664	100.00
Fully Covered (FC)	1284203	90.27
Partially Covered (PC)	123359	8.67
Not Covered (NC)	15102	1.06

The national and state governments face the challenge of providing the poor with efficient services and substantially increased access to sufficient quantity and quality of water and sanitation services. The positive synergistic relationship between drinking water, sanitation and health needs no further emphasis.

Shortcomings of the Mission

Notwithstanding the achievements outlined above, the relative inability of the Mission, among other factors, is amply illustrated by the following summary of the 'Report of the Expert Committee on Rural Water Supply Programme':

> "The Mission mode strategy followed was *ad hoc* and has not been institutionalised. The programmes could not achieve the integration of services and resources from different sectoral agencies to ensure sustainability. Also, the Mission mode of functioning has not provided the desired level of flexibility to enable quick decision-making. Right from the sanctioning stage of the scheme, important software aspects like training, awareness building, community participation and micro-level ecological planning were not accorded due priority. The scientific source finding method alone appears to have succeeded and all other aspects of sustainability relating to water conservation and water recharging have been neglected. The traditional technologies and systems have not been well integrated into rural water supply systems.

The Mini-Missions and Sub-Missions have not attempted to develop appropriate operation and maintenance models to suit varied hydro-geological, agro-climatic, techno-economic conditions and societal perceptions in rural areas. The operation and maintenance of rural water supply systems continue to be weak. Community participation has not been given the importance it deserves and the involvement of NGOs has only been marginal. The pioneering experiment of district level water quality testing labs has succeeded in bringing out the relevance of the quality aspects of rural water supply. However, the establishment and functioning of the laboratories has not been instrumental in evolving a functional water quality surveillance programme.

The Sub-Missions have not succeeded in tackling the quality problems in a systematic manner except in the case of guinea worm eradication, which stands out as an example of a well-coordinated programme. In deflouridation, the Fill and Draw type of plants appear to have been acceptable at the community level. However, the Hand pump attached Defluoridation and Iron Removal Plants have been failures due to inappropriate technology, unsuited to community perceptions and community involvement.

The Human Resource Development activities too, have been of marginal impact. The monitoring and evaluation of the whole programme has been routine. Adequate collection, collation and analysis of information and data from the field level have not been made such as to facilitate any mid-course correction."

Therefore, the Rajiv Gandhi National Drinking Water Mission (RGNDWM), GOI has embarked on a nationwide programme of 'sector reforms' in rural water supply both to remedy problems that have been cited by the Sudersan Committee in as much as streamlining the current drinking water management systems.

Sector Reforms in Water Supply

Owing to the problems of centralised management of drinking water systems, the GOI has introduced a national policy that promotes the financing and management of rural drinking water and sanitation services at a decentralized level through local governments and communities. Key principles of the reform agenda, written into The Kochi Declaration are:

- adopting demand-responsive approaches and the use of participatory processes;
- changing the role of the government from provider to facilitator;
- establishing financial viability and sustainability of rural water supply services; and
- promoting integrated water resource management.

The GOI has demonstrated its intention of revamping its approach to providing water through centralized State Water Boards by sanctioning Rs. 2500 crore over three years for piloting water and sanitation reforms in 63 districts in 25 states across India. Twenty per cent of the Accelerated Rural Water Supply Programme of the Government of India and the Restructured Centrally Sponsored Scheme for Sanitation is dedicated to fund the reform pilots in 63 districts of the country. Both the programmes advocate an increased role of communities in the planning and management of their own facilities. They envisage a shift in the role of government from provider to facilitator, promote participatory management and increased cost recovery from users (at least 10 per cent capital cost and 100 per cent operation and maintenance contribution) as being critical in order to ensure good quality and sustainable services. Under these programmes, the fiscal transfer from the national government is directly made to a dedicated district unit that, in turn, acts as a facilitator of these programmes with the involvement of local government and community groups.

As institutional change of this magnitude has to be supplemented with adequate capacity, a third of the national funds are earmarked for capacity building of the local government and communities. This is a unique scheme to pilot a reform process in Rural Water Supply and Sanitation (RWSS). The nature and scale of the reform process being unprecedented (target population of about 50 million), it requires focused intervention to catalyze the capacity fund to make the reforms more effective. This programme would increase the access of the poor to safe and sustainable water and sanitation services.

Encouraged by the early success of the pilot reform projects, the Government of India has extended the sector reform package to all the districts in the country through a national programme of drinking water programme called 'Swajaladhara' in 2003.

Capacity Building

Networking

Regular exchange of ideas among implementators of reforms through direct personal and electronic interaction in the form of rural think tanks, networking of training centres, electronic discussions and posting of best practices, providing technical assistance and access to expertise, training manuals, etc. is in process.

Supply

Creation of market-based capacity-building consortiums at national, regional and state levels would act as a resource base, prepare HRD and IEC materials, provide training at national, state, district and gram panchayat levels, liaise and assist governments on reforms, etc. and aim at providing solid software.

Demand

Setting up a fund as well as a network of experts in the reform districts so that they can access additional funds and capacities.

Box I: Swajaladhara Project—A Success Story of Community Participation

The World Bank aided SWAJAL Project in UP aims to:

- improve sustainability by adopting a demand responsive approach which introduces partial recovery of capital costs and full recovery of operation and maintenance (O&M) costs;
- develop community participation so that communities play a major role in identifying, planning, building and operating and maintaining their water supply and sanitation schemes; and
- create institutional structures to facilitate decentralised decision-making and in co-doing to test an alternative to the supply driven approach to service delivery.

For O&M, mere handing over of assets to panchayats may be counter-productive, unless the panchayats/water user groups are adequately trained and prepared to take on the O&M. The project emphasises community involvement from the very beginning even in planning and design and in the choice of technology. The village community is involved with the help of NGOs and CBOs from concept to commissioning and its O&M.

Other features of the project are:

- Establish one NGO/CBO for 5-10 villages;
- Heavy emphasis on promoting off-farm activities through training;
- 10% capital cost and 100% O&M cost to be borne by the community;
- A minimum of 22 months of preparatory activity for mobilising community support; and
- Village committee decides technology and places order.

The community analyses needs, problems, solutions, technology options and costs to come up with tentative "Feasible Technical Plan." The NGOs and the CBOs, then give technical inputs to come up with cost and final technical plan. By this time, there is a strong sense of ownership, which is further strengthened with the community being involved with implementation and nominal cost sharing and the community becomes ready to take up O&M, when the time comes.

The committee for village Kamtoli consists only of women. When the time came for procurement of pipes, the chairperson and the treasurer travelled 350 km. from the hills of Pithoragarh to the outskirts of Delhi with the engineer of the SO (NGO support organisation) and after careful scrutiny and weighing of all the pipes took the goods back with them in a truck. As for the fittings, taps and specials, they opened the gunnysacks containing them and checked each item. When they found any item without the ISI mark, she insisted on a replacement.

Source: Swajal Information Brochure, 2001.

Box II: Partners in Development: Integrated Rural Water Supply and Environmental Sanitation Project, Mysore, Karnataka

This is a unique multipurpose project in Karnataka that receives its strength from partnership-based endeavours involving the Government of Karnataka, the World Bank, the Drinking Water and Sanitation User Groups, NGOs and Panchayats. It is being implemented in 110 selected villages of Mysore district, Karnataka.

- The project is being jointly managed by the Project Planning and Management Unit (PPMU), the District Project Unit (DPU) and the Village Water Supply and Sanitation Committees (VWSCs). The community plays an active role throughout the project-cycle, i.e., planning and implementation of project activities, operation and maintenance of water systems, environmental sanitation and habitat development facilities. The NGOs are made partners in planning and implementation of the environmental sanitation and health communication components of the project.

- The lesson learnt from this project is that where there is effective partnership of institutions, the drinking water and sanitation projects are bound to be successful.

NGO's Partnerships in Software Activities

- Mysore Resettlement and Development Agency (MYRADA) was commissioned to facilitate social mobilisation, community participation and awareness of the linkages between safe water, health, sanitation and well-being.
- Symbiosis of Technological Environmental Management (STEM) was made a partner in preparation of IEC materials, awareness creation among the villagers towards health education and sanitation to impart training to the health facilitators.
- Jagadguru Sri Sivaratreswara Swamy (JSS) was given the job of imparting training to technicians, masons and secretaries of GPs for operation and maintenance.

NGO's Partnerships in Hardware Activities

- Globe Consultants were responsible for identification of water sources, construction of overhead tanks, laying of pipelines, creation of stand posts and drainage systems in the villages.
- National Industrial Development Corporation (NIDC), Inter-continental consultants, and Technocrats Pvt. Ltd. (ICPL) were asked to oversee the implementation of all the schemes in the project.

Partnership endeavours of the project are analysed through a SWOT analysis.

Strengths

- Water supply, Environmental Sanitation and Health Communication have been integrated in one investment package.
- Community Participation was one of the in-built systems in the project. Women's participation was greater in the project villages.
- The Information, Education and Communication (IEC) components are strong in the project villages.
- Training of local youth for O&M was an in-built component of the project. People's participation through O&M and training of local youth was ensured for better management.

Weaknesses

- People's participation was inadequate in some project villages.

- The NGOs have failed to create awareness for 30 per cent contribution. Their partnership (software) was very limited and confined to the initial stages of the project.
- Irregular supply of power is a very crucial problem in the project villages.

Opportunities

- The success of this partnership would help replicate the project in other uncovered problem villages/districts within and outside the state.
- The project would help reduce school dropouts and increase the literacy level, especially of the girl child.

Threats

- Sustainability of the project in the long-run is a big threat.
- No financial provision/reserve fund exists to meet repair costs of motor and pipeline systems.

Thus, more intensive awareness building efforts need to be made to promote hygienic practices of handling water. Women and children should be specially educated and urged to devote special care in accessing, storing and handling water. Special attention is to be given for water conservation/harvesting strategies for sustainability of the project by dovetailing drinking water projects with watershed and irrigation projects.

Source: Partners in Development—A Case Study of Integrated Rural Water Supply and Environmental Sanitation Project, Mysore, P. Durgaprasad, Research Study, 2002, P. Sivaram, MJ. Mohan Rao.

Other Challenges

While focusing on capacity support for the pilot districts, all the implementing agencies should constantly address the second generation issues in RWSS. Some of these include:

- Scaling up of reforms at national and state levels.
- Assist state governments that wish to restructure their water boards/departments.
- Address issues of fiscal reforms to build sustainable mechanisms of RWSS delivery by local governments.
- Institutional innovation for multi-village schemes.

- Assist local governments with capacity-building to finance, design and manage their own RWSS schemes.
- Prioritizing hygiene and sanitation.

People's Participation

Field research has shown that stakeholders are involved in Operation and Maintenance (O&M) only when they pay for it; when they are certain that they will control the funds, which are collected from O&M, and the water supply would be dependable. However, except in a few projects (such as the World Bank projects in Uttar Pradesh Box item-I and Karnataka Box item-II), beneficiaries have not been made aware of the technology aspects or given the choice between different technologies and the right to know the details of expenditure on the project including user costs.

Non-involvement of people in the design and execution of project leads to sub-standard quality of materials used, poor workmanship and insufficient maintenance. If these problems are not addressed, the sustainability of the project itself will be under a big question mark. On the other hand, if the entire community is involved in decision-making, it may even be advisable to directly transfer funds to the user committees or panchayats, which may be asked to procure materials, install the operating systems and manage the same.

The cost sharing arrangement would ensure involvement of the users and the supporting agencies like Panchayati Raj Institutions to own, operate and manage the drinking water supply programme. Arguments are generally advanced that people in the rural areas, especially the poor, cannot afford to share the cost involved in capital investment and the operation and maintenance of the systems. However, various field level studies indicate that the operation and maintenance cost per handpump/surface water per person per year works out to meagre amounts (Durgaprasad *el. al.*, 2002).

It is, therefore, clear that operation and maintenance cost and replacement cost is within the reach of a vast majority of the rural population. It is also possible for the beneficiaries to share at least a portion of the capital cost (as in the Swajaldhara Programme of RGNDWM), which would also inculcate a sense of ownership of the system among the stakeholders. The experiences of World Bank assisted projects in Karnataka, Maharashtra and Uttar Pradesh show that it is possible and desirable to decentralise community-based rural drinking water supply programmes.

Water Quality

Lack of reliable data, however, makes it difficult to appreciate the magnitude and impact of crippling and incurable diseases like fluorosis and arsenical dermatitis. Fluoride contamination affects districts in 15 states and excess arsenic affects eight districts of West Bengal. Fluoride levels are high in Andhra Pradesh, Gujarat, Haryana, Karnataka, Punjab, Rajasthan, Tamil Nadu and U.P. and iron levels are high in the north-eastern and eastern part of the country. Similarly, salinity is high in Gujarat, Haryana, Karnataka, Punjab, Rajasthan and Tamil Nadu. The number of quality affected habitations with excess fluoride/arsenic/salinity/iron, etc. is about 1.54 lakh.

Towards following up the quality problems as outlined, a large number of district water testing laboratories have been established in Panchayat Raj Engineering Departments in different States under an elaborate action plan of the RGNDWM. In the present socio-economic condition, reaching the vast rural areas of the country with decentralized water quality-monitoring programme is an almost impossible task and the formidable problem is to bring water samples from the remote parts of the districts to the labs. Although samples may be collected and brought to the labs for examination, pooling them at one place for subsequent transportation is extremely difficult. Also, to collect and bring samples regularly for chemical/bacteriological quality assessment has also not been easy because of storage problems.

Therefore, there is need for introducing simple bacteriological quality assessment tests such as the H2S Strip test, which can be done by the people themselves. Routine quality assessment (both chemical and bacteriological) can be done in the local field labs that may be established in schools or PHCs.

Research studies in 144 countries by Esrey and Nookes (1992-93) show that interventions like Safe Disposal of Excreta, Household and Personal Hygiene, Quantity and Quality of Water can make significant difference in the overall health and quality of life of people, especially that of children.

REFERENCES

Annual Report, 2002-03, Ministry of Water Resources, GOI.

Manjeshwar, Nandu (2003), 'Swagat', July 2003.

Marielle Snel, *et. al.* (2002), IRC Technical Paper Series No 39: School Sanitation and Hygiene Education in India, UNICEF documents on School Health and Sanitation, 2002-03.

13

Community Managed Rural Water Supply

Dinesh Chand

Water is an essential prerequisite for development and growth. In fact, all civilisations have evolved around water. The world has entered the 21st century with an enormous challenge—safe drinking water for all. As per Global Water Supply and Sanitation Assessment Report—2000 (GWSS Assessment Report—2000) prepared by UNICEF-WHO-WSSCC, over one billion people across the world do not have access to adequate and safe drinking water facilities. It is also predicted that it would be about three-fold within the next two decades (generations). Most of these people live in Asia, Africa and Latin America. Nearly 3.4 million people in the world, most of them children, die every year from diseases associated with lack of safe drinking water, inadequate sanitation and poor hygiene. Water is fast becoming a scarce resource and in many regions of the world lack of fresh water has already reached a stage of crisis.

In many parts of the world drinking water has been acknowledged as a fundamental right. However, the poor continue to be the most vulnerable to changes in water resource availability, and are the least capable in adapting their livelihood to the changes. They will be the worst victims if an effective solution to water resource management is not found.

The Indian scenario of the drinking water sector is no different. There is a global desire to surge ahead and achieve the goal of reaching the un-reached. India being on the same policy frame has accorded the highest priority for rural drinking water to ensure universal access. The National Water Policy, 1987, clearly states that "drinking water needs to human beings and animals should be the first charge on any available water."

The GWSS Assessment Report—2000 has set the target to halve the proportion of people without access to water supply by 2015 and to provide access to water supply for all by the year 2025. However, the Government of India has set the goal to provide safe drinking water to all in rural areas by the year 2004. In India the State Governments are responsible for providing drinking water facilities to rural habitations. The Centre through the Department of Drinking Water Supply supplements their efforts by providing financial assistance, policy guidance and technological support. The only source of funding in the sector has been government investment without any private sector investment. Over the decades massive financial and technical inputs into the rural water supply programme have come from both the Central and the State Governments.

In 1986, the Government of India created a National Drinking Water Mission, which in 1991 has been named as Rajiv Gandhi National Drinking Water Mission, with the mandate to provide financial, policy and technological support, and develop a multi-pronged approach relating to the rural water supply sector.

India has achieved considerable coverage of the drinking water needs of the rural population. Yet, the results have not been commensurate with the huge investments made in this sector. With an investment of about Rs. 380 billion of rural drinking water supply in the last fifty years, it has been possible to fully cover 86.9 per cent of about 1.4 million rural habitations with drinking water facilities, about 11.7 per cent partially covered and about 1.4 per cent yet to be covered. The latest report indicates that about 15 per cent of the total rural habitations of the country are facing water quality problems, mainly due to excess of fluoride, arsenic, iron, nitrate contamination and salinity. Despite this impressive coverage with installation of more than 3.5 million hand-pumps and over 116 thousand piped water supply schemes, in many parts of the country especially during summer months, water scarcity still persists.

Now, Government has concluded that systems are failing to sustain even after the huge investments. Systems often fail due to poor Operation and Maintenance (O&M). This is due to the perception of the rural people that water is a social good to be provided free of cost by the government, rather than a scarce resource that should be managed by the community, through local level institutions, as an economic asset. The 'dependency culture' among the rural people has also been responsible for it. From various studies, it has become clear that while managing these systems, the local community should be involved, not only in O&M of the systems created, but also in implementation of the project.

The rural water supply programme has so far been driven by a lop-sided top to bottom approach, entirely managed by government agencies like PHED/Water Boards in the form of purely engineering-based solutions. There has been lack of involvement of communities, the primary stakeholder, in the planning, choice of technologies, construction and management of the systems resulting in lack of ownership by the community towards the systems. In addition to this, the linkages with other potential partners, viz. local bodies, private sector, NGOs, local entrepreneurs, etc. have also been almost non-existent.

It has been estimated that to provide safe drinking water to all rural habitations in the country with a minimum satisfactory level of service would require a further investment of about Rs. 450 billion. In view of increasing constraints, it would be a difficult task for the government to alone mobilize such huge investment single handedly. Therefore, a productive and proactive involvement of user community and other stakeholders in resource mobilization and community participation in the implementation as well as the O&M of the systems has become imperative. To translate the above strategy into practice, it requires massive efforts to transform the prevailing mindset of the major partners—the users, community, local government, government agencies, NGOs, etc.

In the words of President K.R. Narayanan, "India today needs a people's movement to meet its water needs and to protect its water resources—encouraging a people's movement means a redefinition of everybody's role." With this in view, the Government of India redefined the strategy in the drinking water supply sector and recognized it for reform to adopt community participation in the rural water supply programme and launched sector reform projects in the country on a pilot basis.

Community-Based Approach: Paradigm Shift

These systems were conceived and designed by a government department and were imposed on the end-users. These systems were generally executed with limited evaluation of the local requirements, preference of technology, its affordability and willingness to pay for the service. As such, planning and design of the water supply schemes did not take care of the financial aspect of the proposed system in terms of capital cost and recurring cost.

Acknowledging the necessity to involve the local community for sustainability of the system, the following elements are necessary:

- Community mobilization and capacity building,
- Community share in the capital investment,
- Community ownership and control,
- O&M and management by the community, and
- Dependable water source to meet community needs.

Field studies have shown that when users are involved in operation and maintenance of the systems, they are likely to be willing to pay for it. When they are certain that they will control the funds, which are collected for O&M and that water supply will be dependable, they participate in the process. In traditional government programmes, people are neither aware of the technological aspects nor are given any choice between different technologies. Non-involvement of people in the design and execution of projects often leads to use of sub-standard quality of materials, poor workmanship and inadequate maintenance.

Most of the sector constraints identified by GWSS Assessment Report—2000, viz., (i) financial difficulties, (ii) institutional problems, (iii) inadequate human resources, (iv) lack of sector coordination, (v) lack of political commitment, (vi) insufficient community involvement, (vii) inadequate operation and maintenance, (viii) lack of hygiene education, (ix) poor water quality, and (x) insufficient information and communication, are equally applicable to India.

Launch of Sector Reform Project

After the Seventy-third Amendment to the Constitution of India, the subject of rural water supply was placed under the Panchayati Raj Institutions (PRIs—rural local bodies) making them responsible for it in their respective areas. The Government of India is supporting the process of empowerment and capacity building of the PRIs to enable them to discharge their responsibilities. In every village, Gram-Sabha, the general constitutional body of the village having all adult villagers as members, has to be fully involved in reviewing the implementation and management of drinking water systems and sources.

In order to achieve the desired goal, the Government of India has brought about policy changes by introducing reforms in the rural drinking water supply sector in 1999. A paradigm shift has been evolved in the sector, where the emphasis is on demand responsive approach, empowerment of local communities and ensuring their participation in the planning, choice of technological options, implementation, O&M and management of drinking water supply schemes.

The efforts are focused on creation of awareness amongst the people to ensure their participation in the programme. The community should be willing to manage and operate the drinking water supply schemes for which they should have a feeling of ownership. A part of the capital cost (10 per cent) and full O&M cost is to be borne by the community. In this new approach, the Government's role is primarily that of a *facilitator* rather than a *provider.*

Funds for sector reform projects have been released directly to the District Water and Sanitation Mission (DWSM) which is a multi-disciplinary body and registered as a society which has been especially created for the purpose of implementation of the project works under the control, supervision and guidance of district level Panchayati Raj Institutions (PRI). In some districts, where the PRIs are fairly active and well entrenched, they are themselves implementing the projects directly instead of the DWSM. It has been planned that after gaining experience in the first phase, the sector reform approach would be further improved and replicated in the remaining districts of the country.

Institutional Arrangement

At the national level, there is a national body which has members from various fields and acts as a National Scheme Sanctioning Committee (NSCC) with the Secretary, Department of Drinking Water Supply (DWS) as Chairman. This body is responsible for overall coordination and guidance. At the state level, the existing institutional set-up or a specially constituted State Water and Sanitation Mission (SWSM) is responsible for overall policy guidance, coordination with Central Government as well as with other State departments and sector partners, monitoring and evaluation of the project implementation, auditing, etc. The DWSM District or PRI itself implements the project and would be responsible for decision-making, formulation and management of the project, receipt and accounting of central funds, selection of private sector partners, NGOs, sensitization of PRI functionaries/government officials/opinion-makers, formation of Village Water and Sanitation Committees (VWSC), community mobilization, IEC campaigns, capacity building, implementation of project activities, post-project O&M, etc.

Project Operation Process

Under the pilot project, in each village, after the sensitization, awareness campaign and capacity building, demands have been generated, VWSC would be constituted for the purpose of actual planning, implementation and O&M of the system. This would be a sub-committee of the Gram Panchayat (GP), which is the grass-root level body of the three-tier PRI. The VWSC is regulated by a set of bylaws under the state Panchayati Raj Act/Rules. This body is in overall charge of the implementation of the scheme(s) and is the backbone of the reform process. In this committee, adequate representation is given to women, members of weaker sections of society and provision is also made for the cooperation of other stakeholders, NGOs, subject matter specialists, etc.

Project Cycle

Under the project, the cycle is envisaged to be about 36 months, consisting of: (i) Institutionalizing phase (3 months); (ii) Sensitization and identification phase (12 months); (iii) RWS Scheme/System planning phase (9 months); and (iv) Implementation and commissioning phase (12 months). Under the project concurrent activities like institutionalization of community-based water quality monitoring and surveillance, monitoring and evaluation of various aspects of the project/schemes and other associated activities are also proposed to be taken up for implementation.

Conclusion

Having achieved appreciable physical coverage through the normal supply-based programme with 100 per cent government funding, it is now envisaged that these programmes should be reoriented towards community-based demand-responsive approach as soon as possible. This transformation would depend on the time taken by the sector reform pilot projects to gain success and for replicable models to emerge. It is envisaged that sector reform pilot projects would go a long way to improving the quality of life of the common man, especially the rural poor. It would empower them to shoulder the responsibilities of taking up other community-based rural development programmes and revolutionize the total developmental activities on a long-term and sustainable basis.

Once the area specific models are developed through these pilot projects, it would be replicated throughout the country with constructive efforts by not only the Government, but also the people, their political representatives, NGOs, media and the private sector. However, the sector reform pilot projects are very complex in nature and quite large in magnitude, and implementation of 63 pilot projects itself would be a challenging task.

REFERENCES

Government of India (1987): *The National Water Policy,* Ministry of Water Resources, New Delhi.

WHO-UNICEF-WSSCC (2000): *Global Water Supply and Sanitation Assessment—2000,* Report.

Government of India (2000): *Guidelines for the Implementation of Rural Water Supply Programme,* New Delhi.

Tripathi, S.K. & Kumar, Anil (2000): Rural Water Supply Programme in India: People's participation in drinking water supply; Sector Reforms: the emerging scenario, Government of India, New Delhi.

Government of Uttar Pradesh (2000): *Report on Uttar Pradesh Rural Water Supply and Environmental Sanitation (Swajal) Project,* Lucknow.

14

Safe Drinking Water For All

Dr. B.K. Pattanaik

Since the 1970's, the basic needs concept has been a dominating element in the development debate. The Mar del Plata Conference in 1977 focused exclusively on the drinking water and sanitation needs of the poor and vulnerable. This resulted in the designation of the period from 1981 to 1990 as the International Drinking Water Supply and Sanitation Decade (IDWSSD). The Global Water Supply and Sanitation 2000 Assessment (WHO/UNICEF, 2000) shows that 1.1 billion people lack access to improved water supply and 2.4 billion to improved sanitation.

The report mentioned that if improved water supply and basic sanitation facilities were extended to the present day 'unserved', the burden of infectious diahorrea would be reduced by some 17 per cent. If universal piped and well-regulated water supply is ensured and full sanitation is achieved, this would reduce the burden by some 70 per cent. The UNFPA's State on World Population 2004 envisaged that as recently as 2000, 1.1 billion people did not have reasonable access to safe drinking water and 2.4 billion people worldwide lived without basic sanitation. Lack of access to clean water and sanitation in the developing world led to 1.7 million deaths in 2000. The 2000 World Summit for Sustainable Development (WSSD) set the goal to achieve access to drinking water by the year 2015.

Water is the most precious and indispensable resource and fundamental to the survival of human beings, livestock and plants.

Reprinted with permission, *Kurukshetra*, October 2005, pp. 53-57.

Worldwide agriculture use 69 per cent of the total water available, 23 per cent is used by industries and 8 per cent is utilized domestically. Water, which is essential for life, growth and health, can also be a source of spread of disease and cause of ill-health, if contaminated or improperly handled and stored. Safe drinking water plays a major role in the overall well-being of the people, with a significant bearing on infant mortality rate, longevity and productivity (Economic Survey, 2003-04). The World Bank and the World Health Organization (1993) have estimated that in India 21 per cent of all communicable diseases (11.5 per cent of all diseases) are water-related. Every year, 1.5 million children under five years of age die of water-related diseases and the country loses 1800 million person hours (over 200 million man-days) each year due to these diseases (Ministry of Rural Development, 1993). The UNICEF has warned that 44 million people in the country suffer the consequences of drinking contaminated water, thereby, seriously affecting the health of future generations who are growing up with bouts of debilitating diarrhoeal diseases. The diseases, which are spread through the microbial contamination of water, are those caused by enteric bacteria and viruses like cholera, acute gastro-enteritis, diarrhoea, dysentery, typhoid, viral hepatitis A and E and poliomyelitis.

The General Comment on the right to water adopted by the Convent on Economic Social and Cultural Rights (CESCR) in November, 2002 recognized water as a fundamental human right and stated that "everyone has access to safe and secure drinking water, equitably without discrimination (United Nations, 2003). The judgement delivered by the Supreme Court in the first week of December, 2000, that access to clean drinking water is a fundamental right as enunciated in the right to life under Article 21 of the Constitution of India. The UNDP's Human Development Report—2000, defined access to safe drinking water as the proportion of the population using any of the following types of water supply for drinking: piped water, public tap, borehole or pump, well (protected or covered) or protected spring.

As per the Census of India 2001 figures, the coverage of households having water was 77.9 per cent comprising 90 per cent of urban households and around 73 per cent rural households. The NSSO report (1999) has revealed that the percentage of households using tap water in the urban areas is 70.1 per cent, considerably higher than the rural areas, 18.7 per cent. The National Family Health Survey II (1998-99) found that 39 per cent of households in India use piped water comprising 25 per cent in rural areas and 74.5 per cent in urban areas. The report also envisages that the median time to get drinking water is five minutes in rural areas, whereas in urban areas the majority of households do not have any travel time to their source of drinking water. As per Census of India, 2001, the coverage of households having access to safe drinking water was 77.9 per cent comprising 90 per cent of urban households and around 73 per cent of rural households.

There are still many villages in the country without safe drinking water facility. In mountainous and sub-mountainous areas and in desert and water scarcity rural areas, women and even adult girls travel a long distance to fetch drinking water. This causes a lot of damage to the health of women in general and pregnant women in particular even resulting in premature delivery and spontaneous abortion. Ironically, it affects largely the education of the girl child in general and those belonging to impoverished families in particular, largely engaging girl children in the collection of water from distant sources. A problem village is one where drinking water is not available within a radius of 1.6 km or in hilly regions, within 100 m-elevation difference. Besides the lack of access to safe drinking water, some areas of the country are affected by excessive salinity, fluoride, and nitrate arsenic in groundwater making it unfit for human consumption.

To achieve the objective of providing safe drinking water in all rural habitations, programmes like the Accelerated Rural Water Supply Programme (ARWSP) and the Pradhan Mantri Gramodaya Yojana—Rural Drinking Water (PMGY-RDW) are being implemented. The ARWSP is currently implemented through the Rajiv Gandhi National Drinking Water Mission by the Department of Drinking Water Supply.

Public and Private Partnership

Provision of assuring safe drinking water for all is an arduous task for the government. Therefore, besides the government, private sector, corporate sector, NRIs, NGOs, etc. should share the burden of the provision, operation and maintenance of safe drinking water sources in the country in general and in rural areas in particular. For example in Punjab, NRIs are providing financial help to panchayats, for the provision of safe drinking water in NRI funded model villages. The

Table 1: Sources of Drinking Water

Source India (in %age)	*Urban*	*Rural*	*Rural-Urban Difference*
Tap	70.1	18.7	51.4
Tubewell/Hand pump	21.3	50.1	-28.8
Well water	6.7	25.8	-19.1
Tank/Pond reserved for drinking	0.2	1.3	-1.1
Other tank/pond	0.1	0.6	-0.5
River/canal/lake	0.2	1.3	-1.1
Spring	0.1	1.7	-1.6
Tanker	1.0	0.2	0.80
Other	0.1	0.2	-0.1

Source: NSS, Report No. 449, July 1999.

Table 2: Distribution of Households on the Basis of Distance from Safe Drinking Water, 1999

Safe Source	*Rural*				*Urban*			
	I	*II*	*III*	*IV*	*I*	*II*	*III*	*IV*
Tap	19.1	22.0	55.9	2.9	45.8	25.3	27.1	1.8
Tubewell	14.9	19.3	59.8	5.9	29.8	29.1	37.7	3.4
Well	0	22.7	66.4	10.8	0	10.1	46.9	5.8
Tanker	0	22.6	71.0	6.5	—	7.5	76.8	15.8

Notes: I: Within dwelling; II: Outside dwelling but within premises; III: Outside premises at a distance of less than 200 metres; and IV: Outside premises at a distance of beyond 200 metres.

Source: NSS Report No. 449, July 1999.

Table 3: Access to Safe Drinking Water of Different Communities

Categories	*Protected Water*	*Piped Water*
Scheduled Tribes	61.6	17.2
Scheduled Castes	72.8	22.6
Hindus	71.1	25.3
Muslims	78.1	19.4
Christians	64.7	27.8
Others	83.2	20.6

Source: Indian Human Development Report, 1999, NCAER, New Delhi.

New National Water Policy—2000 calls for private sector participation in the planning, development and management of water sources projects, on the ground that this may introduce innovative ideas, generate financial resource, introduce corporate management and improve service efficiency, etc. The levy of user charges on the users would raise community responsibility and promote economic utilization of piped water. One of the exponents from the Kerala experience viewed that with water becoming a scarce commodity and the government unable to provide funds for water supply schemes, it has become imperative for small communities to establish and operate their own water supply schemes.

Community Participation

It is a well-established fact that the government alone cannot take up the responsibility of meeting the heavy cost of operation and maintenance and therefore people's participation is *sine-qua-non* for all such projects. Involvement of people would not only enhance the economic viability of operation and maintenance, but would lead to better upkeep and increase the life span of the system created (Economic Survey, 2003-04). In recent years, under the provision of the 73rd and 74th Constitutional Amendments, state governments are delegating the responsibility of operation and maintenance of water supply projects constructed by the government to panchayats. However, since panchayats are not involved during the formulation and implementation stages of the projects, they are reluctant to shoulder the onus of operation and maintenance of various water supply schemes, one of the reasons being that without involvement and formulation of Water Management Committees during the pre-projects, the abrupt levying and collection of charges from the households by the panchayats would create a tussle between the community and the panchayats. Thus, community participation at all stages of water supply projects such as formulation, construction, operation and maintenance is a *sine-qua-non*. The Tenth Five Year Plan (2002-07) document has also realized that presently water supply projects are designed and executed by the implementing department and passed on to the end-users. *Panchayats are unwilling to shoulder the responsibilities for operating and maintaining these projects. Therefore, emphasis must be laid on the participation of stakeholders at all levels, from planning, designing and location to implementation and management.* The management of the stand posts and public hand pumps and collection of user charges should be done by the water management committees in coordination with government.

Information, Education and Communication (IEC)

Educating the community about safe drinking water practices is key to the provision of safe drinking water for all. Most of the people particularly the illiterate and those who are living in the rural and urban slum areas are not aware about the safe drinking water practices resulting in outbreak of water borne diseases in certain seasons. The civil society members, i.e. (i) Panchayat Members; (ii) Youth Club Members; (iii) Mahila Mandal Members; and Women Self Help Group members; (iv) Retired Servicemen and other members of civil society need to be inculcated about safe drinking water, the chlorination of water sources and chlorination of household drinking water. The health worker must impart education to school children by organizing health camps in schools from time to time.

Inter-Sectoral Coordination

The lack of inter-sectoral coordination is perceived as one of the important reasons for the poor operation and management of safe water sources. There is lack of coordination among various departments dealing with different aspects of water supply. For example, the construction of water supply scheme lies with the Public Health Department, while the operation and maintenance is with the rural development and panchayati raj department; whereas the matter of educating people about safe drinking water is thrust on the health and family welfare department. The Village Safe Drinking Water Management Committees (VSDWMC) need to be formulated with the following members: personnel from public health department; water pump operator; panchayat members at least one of them being a woman; Health Worker; Aanganwadi worker; school teacher and; one member each from Scheduled Castes, Scheduled Tribes and OBCs. The main activities of the committee would be to oversee operation and maintenance of water supply schemes and water sources such as wells, tube-wells and hand pumps; management of stand-post at public places such as in schools, community houses, common places and in backward clusters, etc. checking quality of water and status of chlorination; management of water borne diseases and epidemics;

IEC (Information, Education and Communication) on safe drinking water.

Better Deal for Disadvantaged

The percentage of disadvantaged groups of the population such as scheduled castes, scheduled tribes, economically backward and dalit minorities having access to safe drinking water is lower than their counterparts. Besides, they are also not adequately knowledgeable about the sources of safe drinking water, economical use of water, prevention of wastage, methods of purification, water borne diseases, etc.

Women Empowerment

Women are the prime players in the field of drinking water. They fetch water and serve water to the household members. However, colossal percentages of them particularly the illiterates in rural areas are not aware about what is safe drinking water? How to purify water and make it safe for drinking purposes? Moreover, drinking of contaminated water especially by pregnant women would expose them to worm infections and consequently make them anaemic. Therefore, there is need for training of women in general and those of Manila Mandal members, women panchayat members, SHG members and other women group members in particular.

Conclusion

Water is life and is a basic need for human beings. The prime responsibility of a nation is to ensure safe drinking water to all its citizens. Access to safe drinking water in both quantity and quality should be treated as a fundamental right of the individual. The endeavour of every nation is to provide "Safe Drinking Water for All." The promotion of community participation, involvement of panchayat, public-private partnership, IEC (Information, Education and Communication), inter-sectoral coordination and women empowerment would go a long way in helping the mission of achieving *Safe Drinking Water for All in the countryside of India.*

15

Safe Drinking Water

Privankar Raha

It is commonly understood that safe drinking water is a vital link between life and death. A recent report by the Washington-based World Watch Institute has concluded, "one of the first and foremost basic changes that lengthens life-expectancy is the supply of clean water."

There are several categories of natural water. They are based on different approaches to the problems.

- By its origin, water is classified as atmospheric (precipitation, subterranean (springs, wells) surface water (rivers, lakes, seas) and groundwater.
- By the amount and character of impurities, water is divided into fresh, salt, soft, hard, clear, colourless, opalescent, turbid, coloured, etc.
- By its use, water is classified as potable (cooking and drinking purpose), domestic, technical (industrial), cooling, medicinal, etc.

Every Indian faces everyday the problem of obtaining safe, potable water. In a tropical elimate like ours, one needs about two litres of drinking water daily. This water should be fit for drinking, meaning it should be free from disease-causing micro-organisms and chemicals that are deleterious to health. At the same time, other factors such as objectionable taste, odour and colour must also be absent.

The impurities or contaminants that occur in natural water can be broadly classified into three groups.

Non-biological contaminants: Non-biological impurities can be classified into three groups.

(i) *Soluble contaminants:* These are substances which completely dissolve in water. They are present in water as separate molecules or ions. This water cannot be distinguished from absolutely pure water. The presence of impurities can only be detected by chemical analysis or by taste. Dissolved impurities are not retained by sand, paper or any of the common filters.

Examples: Soluble gases (H_2S, CO_2) etc. soluble salts (Na, K, Ca, NH_4 + Mg, Al, Fe, Mn, etc.)

Industrial heavy metals (Cu, Pb, Mn, Hg, As, Ni, Cd, etc.), organic substances such as phenols, formaldehyde and suchlike.

(ii) *Colloidal systems:* Impurities belonging to this group form colloidal systems with water. Colloidal systems are formed from substances practically insoluble in a given liquid. Colloidal particles are so small that they can only be seen with an electron or ultramicroscope. These fine particles are not retained by sand in settling tanks or by paper filters. But they are held by membranes of bovine bladder collodion.

Examples: Substances of mineral origin (SiO_2, $Al(OH)_3$, $Fe(OH)_3$, organic substance (humins or fulvic acid).

(iii) *Suspensions:* The third group of pollutants form suspensions in water. These are particles of sand, clay and organic matter which are washed off from the soil by rain water, thawing snow and ice and other run-off. Pollutants of this kind settle on standing. They are retained by paper and partly by sand filters.

Biological pollutants/contaminants: Natural waters are rich in bacteria, algae, protozoa, worms and other organisms. The most frequently occurring micro-organisms are bacteria which take an active part in the formation of all aquatic populations.

Oil pollution of water: The greatest damage to water is inflicted by petroleum and its products. According to Thor Heyerdahi, more than 100,000 tonnes of oil is annually discharged into the Mediterranean Sea. The odour of petroleum in drinking water is a typical problem in the coastal belts of Bengal and Tamil Nadu.

Most of our urban population gets treated surface water from rivers and lakes. The treatment process covers the following operations:

- Sedimentation or settling
- Coagulation or flocculation
- Filtration
- Disinfection

The rural folk, on the other hand, draw water largely untreated from both the surface and ground sources. Almost 70 per cent of water available in the country is not potable causing various illnesses.

Sedimentation: Coarse particles suspended in water can be removed by settling. This method is used as an independent part of water purification.

In order to accelerate settling, water is first passed through a filter packed with sand, keramzit, anthracite and other filtering agents. When water is passed through a granular filter, the suspended matter is absorbed physically.

Coagulation: Fine dispersed particles (humins, clay, silica, etc.) are removed from water by coagulation, that is, by treating the water with special reagents (i.e. $Al_2(SO_4)_3$, and $FeCl_3$, Aluminium Sulphate, Ferric Chloride) which enlarge particles to promote their precipitation.

In the rural areas of our country, the traditional wisdom of purifying water by using coagulants like Nirmali seeds (*Strychnes potaterum*) is a very common practice. The Nagpur-based National Environment Engineering Research Institute (NEERI) has scientifically established that the seeds of the Nirmali tree cleanse muddy water by coagulating the suspended impurities. Similarly, cardamom leaves, drumstick (*Moringa oleifera*) seeds and many other herbs and roots, which are locally available, have been traditionally in use for ages.

Disinfection of water. Coagulation and filtering purify water from suspended solids and partly decrease its bacteriological contamination. Complete disinfection is attained by chemical reagents (Chlorination, iodine, O_3), physical treatment (UV radiation, and ultra sound, etc.).

(i) *Disinfection with chlorine and chlorine compounds*: Chlorination is the most important process for production of drinking water. Chlorine acts through hypochlorous acid ($Cl_2 + H_2O \leftrightarrows HCl + HClO$) which is formed when chlorine reacts with water. The acid further decomposes into (nascent) oxygen, a strong oxidizing agent. Chlorine destroys pathogens fairly quickly and is cheap, but some viruses are resistant to chlorination. At the dosage normally employed, chlorination is ineffective against certain parasites.

For domestic use and for use during travel, chlorine tablets (bleaching powder) or chlorine ampoules are convenient. The former contain bleaching powder [$2CaCl_2O + 2H_2O$, $CaCl_2 + Ca(OH)_2 + 2HOCl$], the latter sodium hypochlorite [$NaOCl + H_2O = NaOH + HOCl$] which releases chlorine on dissolving. About 15 years ago, a product, 'steritabs' containing sodium dichloroisocyanate as chlorine-releasing agent was marketed in India. A similar proprietary preparation 'Puritabs' was used by the British army. Inexpensive technologies for the production of chlorine tablets and ampoules have been developed by the National Environment Engineering Research Institute at Nagpur.

The action of chlorine is affected by the presence of suspended solids and organic matter as well as ammonium ions. It is, therefore, very necessary to maintain a residual concentration of free chlorine after all micro-organisms and dissolved matter have been saturated with chlorine. A residual chlorine of 0.2 to 1.0 mg/litre of treated water is regarded as adequate chlorine for water treatment.

(ii) *Disinfection by iodine:* Iodine, another favourite disinfectant, is a germicide much more effective than chlorine. Iodine can kill bacteria and some viruses, too. It is, however, not used for large-scale disinfection of water. For domestic purposes, a triiodide resin in a styrene matrix having polyiodide (a patented technology) is used in online water purifiers such as Zero-B. A small amount of iodine leaches out with flow of water, and its cumulative effect on ingestion is a matter of concern to persons such as hyperthyroidism patients for whom excess iodine could be troublesome.

(iii) *Disinfection by ozone:* Ozone is considered an alternative to chlorine and is used as a primary disinfectant in Europe, USA and Canada since large scale ozone production is well established there. Ozone is a strong oxidizing agent and reacts rapidly with most organic molecules. It has a disinfecting power similar to chlorine but is more expensive. However, it has a decided advantage over chlorine in that no after taste is produced in the treated water. But its short half life in water, approximately 10-30 minutes, leaves no residual effect to protect it from reinfection.

(iv) *Disinfection by silver ion:* The bactericidal action of silver has been known since time immemorial. Water and wine used to be kept in silver vessels in order to retain their quality over a long period of time. Thus water can be disinfected with silver metal. The silver ion concentration grows if the contact surface increases. In order to ensure the maximum surface of silver with the least possible expenditure of metal, it is precipitated in a thin layer onto a material in a form with a well-developed surface such as sand, rings, beads and candles through which water is passed.

A popular household purification method is the use of 'candle' filters. These are hollow tubes made of unglazed porcelain designed to prevent passage of contaminating micro-organisms. If the pores in them are larger than the bacteria or if the pores increase in size after use and frequent brushing the effectiveness of the filter is reduced. Ordinary candle filter cannot make the water 'germ-free' since viruses and bacteriophages can pass their pores.

The relevant Indian Standard Specification for Filter for Drinking Water Purpose (IS:7402-1986) prescribes that the candles should contain fine metallic silver embedded in their body in order to give bacteria-free water. This is an essential requirement for filters to yield potable water. Otherwise, they merely remove suspended impurities from the water, at least in the long-run. Competitive testing of water filters by the Consumer Guidance Society of India, Mumbai, showed that some brands do fail to restrict passage of bacterial organisms.

(v) *Disinfection with ultraviolet radiation:* Ultraviolet (UV) water purifiers have been in the Indian market since 1984. This method of purifying water is nearly always a supplementary measure to other methods like chlorination and is seldom used as the sole method of purification though UV light actively kills bacteria when applied properly. It has very slight powers of penetration, and therefore exposure of water to radiation must be direct, intense and sufficiently prolonged. In other words, the water should flow in a thin layer and must not be turbid or discoloured to enable unhindered transmission of the UV rays. For this reason, the water to be purified by UV radiation is first filtered and passed through activated carbon to rid it of organic contaminants.

Short wave UV radiation (254 nm) is known to destroy all water-borne micro-organisms provided sufficient UV energy is used. High pressure (400-800 mm Hg) mercury lamp of 15-20 cm long manufactured of quartz or uviol glass is used as the source of ultraviolet radiation. With the application of an electric current, mercury vapour emits a bright greenish-white luminous flux rich in ulraviolet rays. The pre-treatment filter is made of ceramic or synthetic material, followed by a carbon bed, maybe with granulated silver. For optimum efficacy, correct UV output must be ensured. For this purpose, the radiation source must be cleaned regularly. Irradiance of UV lamps decreases over time and needs to be replaced after some time. The average life of the germicidal lamp fitted in water purifiers is about 2500 burning hours.

(vi) *Disinfection with ultrasound:* Oscillations at frequencies over 20,000 Hz not usually perceived by a human are called ultrasound. Ultrasound kills animal and plant cells, protozoa and micro-organisms. The vital function of the cells are disrupted mainly by the decomposition of the proteinous substances of the protoplasm. It has been established that ultrasound destroys larger organisms which are especially detrimental to the drinking water supply. Laboratory experiments show that ultrasound has a bactericidal effect on dysentery bacilli, typhus virus, etc. Milk can be sterilized by ultrasound.

(vii) *Thermal disinfection:* The most common method of disinfecting water that has been known from time immemorial is boiling. But the method is expensive, it requires large vessels for boiling and is not, therefore, used even in minor water supply systems. Furthermore, the thermal method fails to kill spores and water taken from dubious sources will not necessarily be disinfected by boiling.

(viii) *Traditional method of disinfection of water.* Scientific studies have proved that simply leaving water in a clean glass container out in the sun for two days makes it fit for drinking. The UV exposure that water receives kills more than 90 per cent of the germs present. Camphor and Tulsi leaves are used for disinfection of water by village people. A lot of people, particularly while going on long journeys, buy bottled drinking water. The water is labelled as 'pure' or 'mineral'. Mineral water is distinguished from ordinary water by its content of certain mineral salts and other constituents. Mineral water is classified as 'natural' and 'fortified', the former obtained directly from natural sources such as springs or wells. The latter is any potable water artificially blended with mineral salts. The Prevention of Food Adulteration Act, 1994, which brought mineral water too within its ambit, does not specify minimum levels of mineral salts to qualify as mineral water. Only maximum concentration of mineral constituents are prescribed. Although these minerals are essential to the human body, drinking water is not the major source of them. People buy bottled water, not for its mineral content, but to save themselves from water-borne diseases. In fact, tests have shown that so-called mineral water is often plain municipal tap water, though disinfected by suitable means. Often, chlorination which is not a preferred method for disinfection of mineral water is used for this purpose.

A number of diseases, bacterial and viral, are transmitted by contaminated water. According to the Bureau of Indian Standards, if enterovirus—the most resistant organism to chlorination — is absent from chlorination of water, it can be assumed that the water is safe to drink. Reinfection by ingress of sewage or polluted water into the distribution system is a serious matter of common occurrence in most places. Five minutes of actual boiling is a sure method of killing pathogens in water. A longer period, about 10 to 15 minutes, may be necessary if a resistant virus like hepatitis B is present.

In communities without safe drinking water, proper latrines and appropriate refuse disposal, it is not possible to check the spread of diseases. Diarrhoea, for instance, kills one and a half million children annually in India. The result of unclean water and poor hygiene, this disease is a major cause of malnutrition among children of all age-groups, culminating in dehydration and finally death.

Fluoride Concentration

Another problem of vital concern in many states of India is the presence of high level fluoride in groundwater. There are 8700 villages in India which suffer from excessive fluoride in water affecting nearly 25 million inhabitants. The maximum desirable limit for fluoride is 1.0 mg per litre of water, an outside limit in the absence of an alternative source is 1.5 mg per litre as per the guidelines of the World Health Organization and the Water Technology Mission, Government of India. High concentration of fluoride in drinking water causes dental and skeletal fluorosis. The *Nalgonda technique* developed by the National Environmental Engineering Research Institute (NEERI) is designed to bring down the level of fluoride to the acceptable limit of 1.0 mg per litre. Several defluoridation plants based on this technique have been installed in the affected areas.

Arsenic Content

A situation of similar dimension occurs in parts of West Bengal where the arsenic content of well water has risen to alarming levels, very much higher than the maximum allowable limit of 0.0 mg per litre. Chronic arsenic poisoning results in various skin ailments, liver inflammation and degeneration of liver and kidneys. Over-exploitation of groundwater at greater depths has resulted in high toxic levels of mineral impurities naturally present in the soil bed in the drawn water. It is unfortunate that groundwater, a gift of nature, too, turns out to be a man-made curse.

16

Rural Drinking Water Supply: Ensuring Safe Source for All

Manisha Verma

Provision of safe drinking water is considered today as fundamental to good governance to promote good health and welfare of the people. The States/UTs strive to resolve the issue involved in making safe drinking water accessible to all and to tackle the ever increasing concerns of depletion of groundwater tables and quality problems that affect its sources. As such, primarily it is the responsibility of the State governments to provide drinking water facilities to the rural population by ensuring supply of adequate potable drinking water from a source available at a reasonable distance from the rural habitation. However, considering the magnitude of the problem, the Central Government had to intervene to supplement the efforts of the State Governments.

ARWSP Component

To ensure that different aspects of Rural Drinking Water Supply are adequately taken care of, the funds budgeted for rural drinking water supply under the centrally sponsored scheme—ARWSP—are bifurcated in different components. The criteria for bifurcation of funds under different components and the funding pattern for these components have been indicated below:

- Upto 20 per cent funds are kept for reform process, i.e. Sector

Reprinted with permission, *Kurukshetra*, October 2006, pp. 21-26.

Reforms introduced in 1999 in selected districts and later scaled up in the entire country through Swajaldhara.—90 per cent GOI share, 10 per cent Community Contribution.

- 5 per cent funds are kept for States under Desert Development Programme—100 per cent GOI funding, no State share.
- 5 per cent funds are kept aside for meeting contingencies arising out of natural calamities—100 per cent GOI funding, no State share.
- The remaining funds are allocated to the States as per a laid down criteria. They are also required to provide matching share under State resources. States can utilize 15 per cent of the said funds for O&M. States can utilize upto 20 per cent of their annual allocation for taking up projects for sub-mission projects. The existing sub-missions are on control of Arsenic, Fluoride, Brackishness and Iron, besides Sustainability. 15 per cent of the ARWSP funds are to be utilized on water quality and 5 per cent on sustainability. The funding pattern for sub-mission projects is 75:25 between Centre and State.

Criteria for Allocation of ARWSP Funds

The criteria for allocation of ARWSP funds to the States being followed with effect from the current financial year is as under:

	Weightage for	*Percentage (%)*
1.	Rural population	40
2.	States under DDP, DPAP, HADP and special category hill States in terms of rural areas	35
3.	NC/PC villages (at 2:1 ratio between NC and PC)	15
4.	Quality affected villages (40:40:15:5)*	10
	Total	100

*Keeping in view the differential impact of chemicals such as Fluoride, Arsenic, Brackishness and Iron on human health, higher weightage have been given to Fluoride (40%) and Arsenic (40%) affected habitations which have serious health problems when compared to Brackishness (15%) and Iron (5%) while arriving at quality parameters.

Norms

Under ARWSP, the following norms are adopted for providing drinking water to the rural population in habitations:

(a) *40 litres* per capita per day (Ipcd) of safe drinking water for human beings.
(b) *30 Ipcd* additional for cattle in the Desert Development Programme Areas.
(c) One hand-pump or stand post for every 250 persons.
(d) The water source should exist within the habitation/within 1.6 km in the plains and within 100 mtrs. elevation in the hilly areas.

[Water is defined as safe if it is free from biological contamination (cholera, typhoid, etc.) and chemical contamination (excess fluoride, brackishness, iron, arsenic, and nitrates]

Financial Progress

Component-wise Release of Funds during the Tenth Plan

(Rs. in lakhs)

Release of funds under different components of ARWSP

S.N.	*Component*	*2001-02*	*2002-03*	*2003-04*	*2004-05*	*2005-06*
1.	ARWSP (Normal)	163010.62	174158.31	143967.46	175441.59	322288.09
2.	ARWSP (DDP)	9300.00	8032.84	9985.63	12407.00	19262.00
3.	ARWSP (SRP/Swajaldhara)	11188.90	15027.39	52102.23	49240.07	49043.76
4.	ARWSP (PM Programme)	0.00	0.00	31007.15	38784.22	
5.	ARWSP (Calamity Relief)	0.00	7773.01	10676.25	13939.25	10620.55
6.	ARWSP (HRD & IEC)	2071.74	663.40	423.72	810.00	2005.03
7.	ARWSP (R&D)	80.00	58.40	65.58	4.77	9.30
8.	ARWSP (Others)	8654.22	4356.83	8262.12	2452.01	6574.72
	Total	194305.48	210070.18	256490.14	293078.91	409803.45

Definition of Not Covered (NC) and Partially Covered (PC) Habitations

Habitations which have a safe drinking water source (either private or public) within 1.6 km in plains and 100 metres in hill areas but where the capacity of the system ranges between 10 Ipcd to 40 Ipcd, are categorized as Partially Covered (PC) and those having less than 10 Ipcd are categorized as Not Covered (NC).

Rural Water Coverage Status

A survey of drinking water supply in rural habitations was conducted in 1991, which was validated in 1994. A Comprehensive

Action Plan, 1999 (CAP 99) was prepared by updating the habitation survey results validated in 1994. The coverage position as on 1.4.99 at the time of formulation of CAP 99 was as under:

Category	*Number of Habitations*
Fully covered	1116103
Partially Covered	268496
Not Covered	38065
Total	1422664

It was envisaged in the Tenth Plan that during the first two years of the Plan, i.e. 2002-03 and 2003-04, the emphasis would be to cover the remaining 'NC' and the 'PC' habitations of CAP 99. As a result of these efforts, 96.13 per cent habitations have become fully covered, 3.55 per cent are partially covered; and the NC habitations are 0.32 per cent. In absolute terms, the coverage status as on 1.4.2005 is as under:

Category	*Number of Habitations*
Fully Covered	1367216
Partially Covered	50479
Not Covered	4588
Uninhabited/Urbanized, etc.	381
Total	1422664

A fresh habitation survey has been conducted in 2003 and the results of the same are being validated at present. The Tenth Plan Working Group has estimated the number of slipped back habitations as 2.8 lakh. It is proposed to cover the slipped back habitations on the basis of list of habitations to be provided by the State governments which would be a web-enabled computerized list.

Coverage of habitations is a dynamic concept and the reasons for fully covered habitations slipping back into NC/PC may be due to a number of factors like:

- Sources going dry or lowering of the groundwater table.
- Sources becoming quality affected.
- Systems outliving their lives.

- Systems working below rated capacity due to poor operation and maintenance.
- Increase in population resulting in lower per capita availability.
- Emergence of new habitations.

Bharat Nirman

Drinking water supply is one of the six components of Bharat Nirman, which has been conceived as a plan to be implemented in four years, from 2005-06 to 2008-09 for building rural infrastructure.

The proposed strategy for coverage in respect of rural drinking water supply under Bharat Nirman is as follows:

Year	*Activity*
2005-06 to 2008-09	Coverage of 55,067 uncovered habitations of Comprehensive Action Plan 1999 (CAP 99)
2005-06 to 2008-09	Coverage of water quality affected habitations
2005-06 to 2008-09	Coverage of slipped back habitations based on 2003 survey with priority to tackling problems of arsenic, fluoride and salinity.

Uncovered Habitations of CAP 99

As on 1.4.2005, there are 55067 NC/PC habitations of CAP 99 spread over 16 States and 4 Union Territories which are yet to be covered. These habitations are targeted to be covered during the Bharat Nirman period from 2005-06 to 2008-09.

Water Quality Affected Habitations

Rural drinking water supply is, to a large extent, depends on groundwater (85%). Though groundwater is less susceptible to pollution, the quality problem in groundwater is inherent in the form of contamination caused by the very nature of geological formation, viz. excess fluoride, arsenic, brackishness, iron, etc. The reasons for chemical and bacteriological contamination are: poor hygienic conditions around the water sources, improper disposal of sewage and industrial waste water, callous disposal of solid waste, indiscriminate use of chemical fertilizers having high quantity of nitrates used in the agricultural sector, pollution from industrial effluents (untreated), over-exploitation leading to quality degradation, pollution of the source due to ignorance of the people, over-population and lack of public awareness. The groundwater level has depleted resulting in surfacing of quality problems due to higher concentration of the contaminants in the depleted sources of water. Inadequate recharging also aggravates the problem of chemical contamination.

For ascertaining the magnitude of the quality problem, a survey of drinking water problem habitations was undertaken in 2000. As per data received from the State governments 2,16,968 habitations are affected due to a variety of water quality problems in their drinking water sources with following break-up: Excess fluoride: 31306; excess arsenic: 5029; excess salinity: 23495; excess iron: 118088; excess nitrate: 13958 and multiple quality problems: 25092.

Emphasis is being given on tackling water quality schemes relating to arsenic, fluoride, nitrate and salinity.

It is proposed to tackle the quality problems within the four-year period 2005-06 to 2008-09, i.e. the Bharat Nirman period.

Coverage of Slipped Back Habitations

States/UTs have been requested to furnish list of habitations to be covered and it is proposed to cover the slipped back habitations during the Bharat Nirman period 2005-06 to 2008-09. Priority is proposed to be given as follows:

- Newly emerged NC habitations/slipped back to NC category.
- Second priority to slipped back PC habitations.

Action Plan for Bharat Nirman

The States and Union Territories have been requested to furnish Action Plans along with list of habitations to be covered during the 4-year period of Bharat Nirman. This will facilitate preparation of a road map for achieving the goal set up under Bharat Nirman for rural drinking water supply by 2008-09.

Strategy

- Supplementing with new schemes for the habitations served by outlived schemes.
- Rejuvenation of the outlived schemes which are functioning below their rated capacity.

- Providing regional schemes from alternative safe sources by extending new pipelines.
- Providing rainwater-harvesting structures.
- Reviving the traditional sources.
- Utilizing low cost technology for mitigation of quality affected habitations.
- Providing water supply from alternate sources for coverage of habitations with no safe source.

Sustainability of Rural Water Supply Sources

- For sustainability of systems, the Department has undertaken extensive exercise for institutionalization of community participation in O&M of rural drinking water infrastructure.
- Low-cost technologies are being promoted not only for meeting drinking water requirements, but also for re-charging of the water table.
- Source strengthening measures proposed to be made an integral part of all Rural Water Supply schemes.

Targets and Achievements during 2005-06

	Uncovered habitations of CAP 99			*Slipped Back habitations*			*Quality affected habitations*	*Total*
	NC	*PC*	*Total*	*NC*	*PC*	*Total*		
Target	3522	8375	11897	16468	17905	34373	10000	56270
Achievement	1523	11563	13086	27097	52447	79544	4531	97161

- Convergence of efforts of all departments in watershed development and management would go a long way in meeting the drinking water needs.

Policy and Implementation Measures

- Intensive interaction with States for firming up the Action Plan for Bharat Nirman.
- Collecting locational details, technology options and fund requirement from States.
- Sorting out administrative and technical problems in poorly performing States on a case-to-case basis, e.g., in sanction of schemes, in procurement machinery and equipment.

- Commitment of States for providing matching or higher State share for coverage of NC/PC/quality affected habitations.
- Focused funding for tackling water quality problems, particularly those relating to Arsenic/Fluoride/Salinity.
- Identifying and preparing standardized low-cost technologies for tackling water quality problems.
- Involvement of scientific institutions.
- Sustainability measures such as involvement of PRIs/VWSCs in Operation and Maintenance of assets created in the past. In addition, some contribution towards capital cost of new assets to be created for generating sense of ownership among local community.
- Need for a system of incentives for PRIs/VWSCs for ensuring village level O&M of assets.
- Capacity building of PRIs/VWSCs.
- Sustainability of sources by creating re-charging structures and regulating over-exploitation of underground water.
- Compilation and circulation of best practices in the Drinking Water Sector.
- Strengthening of the Technical Wing of the Department of Drinking Water Supply for better planning and monitoring of quality affected and inaccessible habitations.

Monitoring

(i) Regular monitoring, concurrent evaluation/social audit of Bharat Nirman Drinking Water Schemes by lead NGOs/ academic and research institutions, reputed social workers, professional experts.

(ii) Obtaining monthly reports regarding the implementation of schemes from the District officers/State Governments.

(iii) Taking feedback regarding implementation of schemes from District Vigilance and Monitoring Committees which include elected representatives.

(iv) Involving community and local institutions in water quality monitoring and surveillance.

(v) Monitoring by State/District/Village Water and Sanitation Committees.

(vi) Creation of awareness and publicity of the schemes through mass media.

(vii) The Department/State/District website to contain information of habitations to be covered as per the Action Plan and the up-to-date progress.

(viii) Display of information of details and progress of the project in the Panchayat Ghars.

Sustainability

While active participation of stakeholders ensures system sustainability, scientific management of water resources particularly groundwater resources, contribute towards source sustainability.

Source Sustainability

The primary responsibility of ensuring the sustainability of the water sources available in the country and coordinating with various departments/agencies to achieve this rests with the Ministry of Water Resources. However, being one of the users of the water resources, the Department of Drinking Water Supply would also initiate action to supplement the efforts of the nodal ministry.

Almost 85 per cent of the drinking water needs are met from groundwater. Only 5 per cent of total groundwater extraction are used for domestic drinking water supply. Irrigation accounts for 85 per cent of all groundwater extraction. The remaining 10 per cent of the groundwater extraction is utilized by other sectors including industries. The rapid development of groundwater-based irrigation in many States has caused groundwater depletion. This affects the drinking water supply source adversely. Further, during summer months groundwater depletion affects drinking water supply in rural areas.

It has been noticed that groundwater depletion has aggravated water quality problems due to excess fluoride, arsenic and brackishness, in certain areas. This gets manifested in the form of various diseases like fluorosis and arsenical dermatitis, which has forced the State governments to abandon low-cost hand pumps preferring costly piped water supply schemes.

For the reasons stated above, there is a need to regulate the extraction of groundwater. A model bill to regulate and control the development of groundwater drafted by the Ministry of Water Resources has been circulated to all the State governments for enactment by their respective State Legislative Assemblies.

Attempts are also made to tackle the problem of sustainability through Sub-Missions on Sustainability by taking up projects for conservation of water and rain water harvesting. Out of Sub-Mission project funds 25 per cent is to be utilized for schemes on sustainability. Further, the following action has also been taken by the Department of Drinking Water Supply to promote Rain Water Harvesting:

- Ministry of Urban Development has been requested to make rainwater-harvesting structures mandatory for urban constructions.
- Ministry of Water Resources has been requested to promote water-harvesting measures.
- All MPs have been requested to encourage/take up water harvesting schemes from their Local Area Development Fund.
- Technical Manual on Water Harvesting and Artificial Recharge has been finalized.
- Different models of rainwater harvesting available in the country have been collected and a CD showing different models has been circulated to the States.

17

Government Initiatives in Rural Water Supply

Dr. P. Siva Ram

Water is important for human life. Safe drinking water influences the quality of health and productivity. Water is called as *'Indrajal'* in mythology—nature's gift through rainfall, it not only satisfies the thirst of human beings but also gives food and sustains life of human beings, plants and animals. In fact, great civilizations settled and flourished around water sources and societies evolved their entire cultures and livelihoods based on it.

India as a country with abundance of natural resources is blessed with large resources in terms of water. However, the availability of fresh water varies from place to place based on its geo-physical set-up and natural resources in the country. At present, irrational and unsustainable water withdrawal from groundwater, tanks and reservoirs is on the increase. This water is mainly being used for agriculture and industrial purposes causing drinking water scarcity to human beings. Moreover, water use for drinking and domestic purposes is estimated around 7 to 9 per cent of the total fresh water in India. As per the estimates of the National Water Commission, the total water requirement of India in the year 2050 will be about 973 billion cubic metres depending on its population growth.

This paper attempts to study and analyze the government initiatives in rural water supply, particularly its programmes and reforms. Also, it analyses the strategies and achievements in rural water supply under Bharat Nirman.

Reprinted with permission, *Kurukshetra*, October 2006, pp. 27-35.

Government Initiatives

Drinking water supply and sanitation are the subjects of State governments. These are included in the Eleventh Schedule of the Constitution of India among the subjects that are entrusted to Panchayats by the States. Since, the First Five Year Plan, both the Government of India and the State Governments have substantially invested about Rs. 55,000 crore in the rural water supply sector for providing potable water to the rural people. As a result, more than 37 lakh hand pumps and 1,73,000 piped water supply outlets have been installed to provide access to potable drinking water, crediting the country with one of the largest rural drinking water supply networks in the world.

Coverage of Rural Habitations

During 2005-06, the status of coverage of rural habitations with drinking water facilities is presented in Table 1. It indicates that more than 95 per cent of habitations have been 'fully covered' with one or two water systems. The 'Partially Covered' habitations are 3.13 per cent followed by 'Not Covered' habitations, which are negligible. However, a large number of habitations, which are fully covered earlier, have slipped back as 'Not Covered'/'Partially Covered' due to the following factors—sources are becoming dry because of over exploitation of groundwater, in turn the groundwater table is depleting day-by-day; water sources are affected with quality problems; water systems are working below rated capacity due to poor O&M; increasing population results in lower per capita availability of drinking water.

Table 1: Distribution of Coverage of Rural Habitations—All India

Type of Coverage	*Number of Habitations*	*Total Percentage*
Fully Covered (FC)	13,73,827	96.56
Partially Covered (PC)	44,521	3.13
Not Covered (NC)	3,935	0.28
Uninhabited/Urbanized	381	0.03
Total	14,22,664	100

Source: Annual Report—2005-06, Ministry of Rural Development, Government of India.

Water Quality Problem

A large number of habitations (2,16,794 habitations) are affected with water quality problems (Table 2). A programme for water quality monitoring and surveillance developed in consultation with the Ministry of Health and Family Welfare, Government of India, is contemplated through National Level and State Level Referral Institutions. The National Institute of Communicable Diseases (NICD) is acting as National Level Water Quality Referral Institution. Also, a Manual on Catchment Area Approach is on the anvil.

Despite respectable coverage in terms of access to drinking water, proper upkeep of water supply schemes has been a problem. Many factors like sources going dry, increase in quality problems, systems becoming defunct due to poor maintenance, demand from other competing sectors like agriculture, industry etc., pose a threat to sustainability of drinking water supply schemes. Putting in cost of O&M of the water supply networks created so far is estimated at Rs. 6750 per annum, whereas the total fund for O&M purposes under ARWSP is grossly inadequate.

Table 2: Water Quality Affected Habitations—All India

Type of Water Quality Problem	*Number of Affected Habitations*
Excess Fluoride	36,988,
Excess Arsenic	3,136
Excess Salinity	32,597
Excess Iron	1,38,670
Excess Nitrate	4,003
Other Problems	1,400
Total	2,16,794

Source: Annual Report—2003-04, Ministry of Rural Development.

Accelerated Rural Water Supply Programme (ARWSP)

A national water supply programme was introduced in the social sector in 1954. The Government of India provided assistance to the States establishing special investigation divisions in the Fourth Five Year Plan to carry out identification of drinking problem villages. Taking into account the magnitude of the problem, and accelerate the pace of coverage of problem villages, the Central Government has introduced the ARWSP in 1972-73 to assist the States and Union Territories with 100 per cent grants-in-aid to implement drinking water supply schemes in such villages. The entire programme called the National Drinking Water Mission (NDWM) was introduced as one of the five Missions in the social sector in 1986. NDWM was renamed as Rajiv Gandhi National Drinking Water Mission (RGNDWM) in 1991. The objectives of ARWSP are as follows—

Objectives

- To ensure coverage of all rural habitations with access to safe drinking water.
- To ensure sustainability of drinking water systems and sources.
- To tackle drinking water quality affected habitations.
- To institutionalize the reforms initiatives in the rural drinking water supply sector.

Norms for Coverage

- 40 litres per capita per day (LPCD) of drinking water for human beings.
- 30 LPCD of additional water for cattle in areas under the Desert Development Programme (DDP).
- One hand pump or stand post for every 250 persons.
- Availability of water source within 1.6 km in plains and 100 metres elevation in hilly areas.

Funding Pattern

- Under ARWSP, funds are provided to States for making provision of safe drinking water in rural habitations. 15 per cent of these funds can be spent on O&M of the existing drinking water systems and sources. The State Governments should release the matching grants on 1:1 basis.
- Up to 20 per cent of the funds can be utilized by the State Governments to take up projects under the Sub-Mission programme for tackling water quality problems like excess fluoride, excess iron, arsenic, brackishness, etc., and to ensure source sustainability by conserving water, recharging aquifer etc. Out of 20 per cent funds, 15 per cent of the funds are

allocated for water quality projects and 5 per cent of the funds for sustainability of sources. Funding is done in the ratio of 75:25 between Central and State Governments.

- 20 per cent of the annual outlay of ARWSP has been earmarked for implementation of Swajaldhara and Sector Reform projects. The funding pattern for these projects is 90 per cent from Government of India and 10 per cent by way of community contributions.
- About five per cent of the annual allocation is also earmarked to the States covered by DDP under ARWSP. For DDP districts, 100 per cent central grant is allocated to the states.
- Further, five per cent of ARWSP allocation is earmarked to meet the contingencies arising due to natural calamities and emergent situation. For this, 100 per cent grant is provided by the Central Government.

Implementation of ARWSP

The State Governments are implementing ARWSP through their departments, namely, Public Health Engineering Department (PHED), Panchayat Raj Engineering Department (PRED), Rural Development and Panchayat Raj Department. In some states, Government boards/ Nigams, for example, Gujarat Water Supply and Sewerage Board, Uttar Pradesh Jal Nigam and Tamil Nadu Water and Drainage Board are implementing ARWSP.

Financial Investment

The Central outlay for the rural water supply (2005-06) is Rs. 4050 crore. ARWSP allocation of funds and releases to all the State Governments are made under ARWSP (Normal), ARWSP (DDP) and ARWSP (calamities).

Role of PRIs and Village Water and Sanitation Committees (VWSCs)

As per the 73rd Amendment to the Constitution of India, the subject of rural water supply vests with PRIs. The PRIs and VWSCs are playing a pivotal role in providing safe drinking water and managing the water systems in rural areas. They are also involved in implementation of schemes, particularly, in selecting the location of hand pumps, stand-posts and spot sources; in O&M, etc. The Government of India has laid emphasis on empowering and capacity building of the PRIs and VWSCs to enable them discharge their responsibilities in drinking water supply.

Management Information System (MIS)

This system (MIS) is extremely important for planning and effective monitoring and implementation of the main components of the programme. A quick to and fro exchange of information between the Mission and States is ensured by using the state of the art Information Technology (IT). The public can access the habitation-wise data through the NICNET. The MIS project consists of Selection of Hardware, Selection of Operating System, Preparation of Software Requirement Specifications Document, and Development of Customized Application Software.

Documentation and Information Centre (DIC)

To shoulder the enormous task of documenting and monitoring the drinking water supply and sanitation programme implementation, the Department of Drinking Water Supply, Ministry of Rural Development, envisages dissemination of and access to information about issues related to the sector. Therefore, it has entrusted the responsibility of setting up a documentation centre on drinking water and sanitation to the Indian National Scientific Documentation Centre (INSDOC), under the Council of Scientific and Industrial Research (CSIR). Facilities are also being created to store data on CDs and disseminate information to various organizations.

Human Resource Development (HRD)

A National Human Resource Development Programme (NHRDP) was launched in 1994. Its primary focus is to build-up the capacity of users for effective community participation and also enhancing the performance and productivity levels of water sector professionals. This would ensure sustainability of water supply schemes. The programme has now been revamped by introducing the concept of Communication and Capacity Development Unit (CCDU). At present, each state is having CCDUs.

Gender Concerns

Gender considerations are at the heart of providing, managing and conserving our finite water resources and safeguarding health through proper sanitation and hygiene. The importance of involving both women and men in the management of drinking water and sanitation was recognized at the global level in the 1977 UN Water Conference held at Mar del Plata and also during the observance of the International Drinking Water Supply and Sanitation Decade 1981-90.

Since the collection of drinking water in villages is primarily done by women, they need to be actively involved in planning, choice of technologies, location of systems, implementation, and O&M of water supply schemes. Towards this end, at least 1/3rd members of the VWSCs are women and they should get preference in training for repair of hand pumps, etc. Formation of users' groups exclusively of women in villages should also be promoted. Additionally, women are also to be involved in the implementation of the programme in the following manner:

- At least 30 per cent of hand pump mechanics under NHRD and other training schemes should be through women of the local areas/habitations.
- There should be women caretakers for hand pumps in the habitations.
- Certificate about satisfactory completion of the schemes should be obtained from women groups in the habitations.
- Prominent women from the habitation should be given representation on the village level water monitoring committees.

Sector Reforms in Rural Water Supply Programme

The Sector Reforms Project (SRP) in Rural Water Supply Programme of the Ministry of Rural Development, Government of India, was introduced in April, 1999. The main aim of the SRP is to replace the government-oriented, centralized, supply-driven RWS programme by a people-centred, decentralized, demand-driven and community-based programme. The project strategy and components include adoption of a demand-driven approach based on empowerment of villagers to ensure their full participation in preplanning, planning and implementation; decision-making in the choice of scheme design, technology and management systems; shift in government's role from *'provider to facilitator'*; focus on village level capacity building; ensuring an integrated service delivery mechanism by streamlining the functions of the agencies involved in project implementation; 10 per cent capital cost sharing by users, cent per cent O&M by users and emphasis on conservation measures for sustained supply of water through surface water, rain water, groundwater source sustainability and augmentation and conservation of water are considered equally important.

Swajaldhara

The SRP initiative was scaled up throughout the country by launching 'Swajaldhara' in December 2002. All the States across the country are now implementing the Swajaldhara schemes. In fact, under the SRP and Swajaldhara framework, individual water supply schemes are expected to be planned, designed, implemented, operated and maintained by the community through VWSCs. Unlike the SRP, which had the district as the unit for implementation, the User Groups such as PRIs, NGOs, can implement the Swajaldhara schemes. A major thrust of the reforms initiative is on empowerment of the PRIs not only for operating and maintaining the drinking water schemes but also to manage the entire rural water supply sector.

State Governments make a decision on the implementing agencies for the Swajaldhara programme. The agencies include the Public Health and Engineering/Irrigation Department as in Himachal Pradesh or Rural development in Orissa or Government Boards/ Nigams as in Gujarat (Gujarat Water Supply and Sewerage Board), Jal Nigam as in Uttar Pradesh or TWAD Board as in Tamil Nadu.

Micro Level Reform Initiatives and Community Participation

The cost recovery status of rural projects funded by international donors and NGOs is also relatively better compared to other areas. In these cases, the general acceptability of revised charges also indicates that the users are willing to pay higher charges for improved and more reliable services. Interestingly, such willingness is observed across all social-economic groups dispelling the widely held view that poor groups are unwilling to pay higher water charges (Saleth and Sastry, 2004)

Since the government-dominated and supply-driven approach is identified as one of the major causes for both the poor financial and operational performance of the sector, the role of user groups and community organizations is now receiving higher priority both in policy discourse as well as in programme implementation. Community participation is recognized now as the main vehicle for instituting the operation of the demand-driven approach within a decentralized institutional framework. Most recent experiments with community participation in the water supply and sanitation sector provide strong evidence for their critical role in improving the financial and operational performance of the sector through their contributions to better cost recovery, infrastructure maintenance and service provision (Sivaram *et. al.*, 2002)

Empirical Evidences from Sector Reform Project

Presented here are selected findings and recommendations relating to a set of field studies that have been conducted by NIRD in the WATSAN sector.

Main Findings and Recommendations
Dakshina Kannada District in Karnataka

- There is a high level of community participation in planning and implementation of SRP in the sample villages. The participation of women in social mobilisation and awareness activities is evidently high.
- The scarcity/problem of drinking water has been solved to a large extent both from the view point of quantity, quality and drudgery. Depending on the type of drinking water distribution system and its capacity, the VWSCs have extended the facility of household drinking water tap connections irrespective of income and caste groups.
- The VWSCs are very active in the sample villages but their tenure is only 20 months. It was found that the majority of VWSC members in the district were going to complete their terms within three months. If the newly elected VWSCs are not as enthusiastic in performing their responsibilities as the present

ones, then there will be a problem of quality of work and delays in completion of the project.

- The Support Organisation (SO), namely, the Zilla Parishad Engineering Wing (ZPEW) conducted village level meetings and briefed the people on the benefits of the project as well as the responsibilities assigned under the project including cost-sharing and O&M. The ZPEW convinced the people and helped in the formation of VWSCs and collection of 10 per cent capital cost.
- The VWSCs did not insist on uniform cost sharing by all the stakeholders. Instead they collected the amount as per affordability of the households. On the whole, higher income groups contributed a major amount towards 10 per cent capital cost without insisting on the concept of equal sharing by all.
- The members of VWSCs unanimously expressed that they were given the full liberty by the SO in respect of choice of water system and purchase of material; selection of masons for construction; freedom in formation of VWSCs and their office-bearers and selection of pump operator for O&M and fixation of water charges. However, the VWSC members said that even though the SO was given the necessary guidelines in technical aspects of the project, they failed in respect of software which was an important component of SRP.
- The villagers fully acquainted themselves with the project thus indicating the faith of the project authorities that community ownership of the project is a prerequisite for its sustainability. The VWSCs had rationally fixed water metres for household tap connections based on the extent of utilisation of water. The minimum water charge was fixed at Rs. 50-70 per month. This amount was being used for meeting the O&M costs of water systems.
- There were no water quality problems as such, except for occasional bacteriological problems in the open wells. The health workers under the supervision of ANMs were regularly chlorinating the cisterns as well as the open wells and water tanks.
- The VWSCs were implementing activities like tendering, purchase of materials like pipes, cement, etc., under the

guidance of the support organisations such as ZP and GP. The VWSCs issued cheques to contractors only after completion of works under the joint signatures of VWSC President and Secretary of GP.

- The IEC campaigns with focus on linkages between water, sanitation, health and development were meaningfully carried out as was evident from the depth and quality of responses given by the respondents. However, it was found that compared to IEC campaigns on water, the sanitation campaigns were weak.
- Training programmes for DWSC and VWSC members were conducted effectively as evident by the quality of their understanding of the objectives of the Sector Reforms Project.
- The tap water emerged as a predominant source of drinking water in the sample villages. The respondents appreciated the PR functionaries for their active participation in the SRP.
- There was an attitudinal change among the villagers towards open defecation after the implementation of the Total Sanitation Campaigns under this project.

Chittoor District, Andhra Pradesh

- The Drinking Water and Sanitation Sector Reforms Project in Chittoor is named as 'Maa Neeru' (meaning 'our water') and the implementing agency are the Chittoor Water and Sanitation Society (CWSS). In the first phase, the society has identified 417 habitations. However, the project was initiated only in 21 habitations as a pilot project. The villagers have contributed 10 per cent of the capital cost through the Habitation Water and Sanitation Committees (HWSCs). However, the higher income groups have contributed a major part of its share.
- The implementation of the project in 21 habitations has been completed. The villagers were availing safe drinking water facilities. However, the project is yet to be handed over to the HWSCs.
- The CWSS has given high priority to awareness building, even though it took a long time not only for collection of 10 per cent capital cost contribution from the villagers but also for taking the responsibility of O&M.

- With the implementation of SRP in 21 habitations, the quality and quantity of drinking water is assured at the doorstep. This has brought about a significant change in the livelihoods of people
- The NGOs/SOs were withdrawn from the project during 2002 and the entire project responsibility of implementation of the project was assigned to the Rural Water Supply Division (RWS) of Panchayat Raj Engineering Department (PRED) in the district.
- The RWS has by-passed the awareness creation in phase-II villages. However, the RWS has modified the implementation norms of sector reforms based on field conditions. In these circumstances, there is a fear that Household Water and Sanitation Committees (HWSCs) may not discharge their responsibility of O&M effectively.
- The selection procedure of villages/habitations has been changed after discontinuation of NGOs as Supporting Organizations (SOs) from the SRP. Currently, RWS is a SO in the entire district for the implementation of SRP.
- The RWS is giving priority to all the villages in the district and is also making use of the funds of MP/MLA funds.

Suggestions and Recommendations
Dakshina Kannada District

- We are not sure, if the system of releasing the entire amount of the first installment of Rs. 11 crore at a time is pragmatic and viable. It needs to be staggered within the first instalment also. Periodical progress reports should be the basis for frequent and adequate releases of the budgeted amount under SRP.
- Having accepted and adopted the principles and practices of democratic decentralisation mainly through the panchayats, there is need for greater role and participation of the panchayats in SRP. At times, the roles and objectives of the panchayat do not converge with those of the DWSCs and VWSCs. Therefore, some review of the institutional roles and interfaces need to be made between the panchayats and VWSCs.
- Greater thought needs to be given to aspects such as inter-sectoral coordination between the health, education and social welfare sectors in the context of convergence of development related services like drinking water and sanitation.

- Rainwater retention capacity of the soil is low in the sample district. Therefore, it is suggested that ground and roof tap rainwater harvesting structures should be promoted for augmenting the water resources. In addition, care should be taken to seal the bottoms of rainwater harvesting structures to control the excessive seepage due to the nature of the regional porous and laterite soils.

Chittoor District

- Priority should be given to the 21 pilot habitations for release of third instalment of budgeted amount and completion of the project in all respects including handing over of the project to HWSC.
- Instead of completely eliminating the role of NGOs in SRP, the RWS should identify select effective NGOs and take assistance wherever necessary instead of giving full responsibility to SOs, as stipulated in the earlier (SRP) procedures.
- In selection of habitations, priority should be given to the drinking water problem villages rather than mere upgradation/ improvement of water systems in FC villages.
- Training/awareness building regarding various components of the project should not be confined to HWSC members alone but should also include the Panchayati Raj functionaries. For this purpose, the RWS should build up their software training wing at the district level.
- Uniform ten per cent capital cost contribution from the stakeholders should be relaxed, especially for the BPL families. It should be five per cent cost sharing for the BPL families.
- Rain Water Harvesting and water conservation measures should be taken up by the RWS of PRED for sustainability of the project.

Bharat Nirman and Rural Water Supply

Bharat Nirman has been covered as a plan to build rural infrastructure within a four year period (2005-06 to 2008-09). Drinking water supply is one of the components of Bharat Nirman. It envisages coverage of all uncovered habitations and water quality problem habitations. In addition, coverage of habitations, which have slipped back from 'Fully Covered' to 'Partially'/'Not Covered' categories. The Department of Drinking Water Supply, Ministry of Rural Development, Government of India, has initiated steps to ensure that the targets of the rural drinking water component of Bharat Nirman are met within the specified time-frame. The Drinking Water component of Bharat Nirman is implemented through ARWSP. The requirement of funds under ARWSP has been reassessed keeping in view the objectives of Bharat Nirman. The State Governments and Union Territories have been asked to prepare their Action Plans. The progress (drinking water supply) of Bharat Nirman is being monitored periodically.

The targets and achievements set for Bharat Nirman are being monitored on-line on a web-based system. The software for the purpose has been prepared by the National Informatics Centre. This information is also linked to the portal in the office of the Prime Minister. The complete list of habitations, Gram Panchayat-wise, has been hosted on the website of the Department. Also, the monthly progress reports for the coverage and status of all habitations have been placed on the on-line monitoring systems, where all States can enter data regularly.

Coverage of Left-over Habitations of Comprehensive Action Plan (CAP) 1999

The Habitation Survey conducted in 1991 was updated in 1999 and a CAP 99 for coverage of these left-over habitations was formulated. There are still 55,067 uncovered habitations, 94,588 not covered and 50,479 partially covered of CAP 99 as on April 2005. Under Bharat Nirman, it is proposed to cover all uncovered habitations of CAP 99 by 2008-09.

Coverage of Water Quality Affected Habitations

The results of the quality survey (2000) revealed that there are 2,16,968 quality affected habitations. It is proposed to cover all (2,16,968) quality-affected habitations during the 4-year period of Bharat Nirman. While tackling the water quality problem, priority is given to arsenic, fluoride and salinity affected habitations. 90 per cent quality-affected habitations in these categories are covered through surface water alternative sources and 10 per cent through treatment by low cost technologies. In respect of iron, however, 30 per cent quality affected habitations will be covered by surface water sources and 70 per cent by treatment. In regard to nitrate-affected habitations, 100 per cent habitations are covered through surface water alternative sources.

Coverage of Slipped Back Habitations

As per the assessment of the 10th Plan Working Group 2.8 lakh slippage habitations are existing in the country. This figure is likely to increase as reflected from the raw data of the 2003 Habitation Survey Results.

Coverage of Habitations under Bharat Nirman

Table 3 shows the coverage of habitations under drinking water supply of Bharat Nirman. 5413 habitations are proposed to be covered under Bharat Nirman by the different states. Out of 5413 habitations, 1210 habitations are under remaining CAP-99; 3856 are under slipped back habitations and; 347 habitations are water quality affected habitations. Altogether, 5299 (actual covered) habitations are covered under Bharat Nirman programme during 2005-06.

Table 3: Coverage of Habitations under Bharat Nirman (2005-06)

Sl. No.	*State*	*Remaining CAP-99*	*Slipped Back*	*Water Quality Affected*	*Total*	*Total (Actual) Covered*
1.	Arunachal Pradesh*	54	8	54	116	62
2.	Bihar*	0	830	3	833	831
3.	Chattisgarh	0	734	6	740	735
4.	Gujarat*	11	709	62	782	727
5.	Himachal Pradesh*	1	0	0	1	1
6.	Jharkhand*	0	4	0	4	5
7.	Karnataka	278	14	118	410	491
8.	Kerala*	716	793	0	1509	1517
9.	Maharashtra*	2	0	0	2	2
10.	Meghalaya*	67	134	17	218	217
11.	Mizoram*	81	10	0	91	91
12.	Orissa*	0	2	0	2	2
13.	Rajasthan*	0	618	87	705	618
	Total	1210	3856	347	5413	5299

Source: Downloaded, Department of Drinking Water Supply, MoRD, GOI on 20 August, 2006.

Suggestions

- This is the high time to protect the groundwater for the future generations because we have been exploiting the groundwater through powerful submersible pumps; that water is being used for agriculture, industry, drinking water, etc. Due to this, the groundwater table in many parts of the country is depleting day-by-day. The groundwater recharge through rainwater harvesting programmes is on top priority of the Ministry of Rural Development and the results are positive. It is suggested that rainwater harvesting could also be included in Bharat Niman, especially, to the slippage villages.
- Ancient rainwater harvesting structures, for example, temple tanks, *Tuikurs, Khals* and *Chaals* are one of the oldest sources catering to the needs of drinking water and domestic use. These structures are replicas of the culture and heritage and management of traditional institutions. However, the review of literature indicates that a large number of the ancient rainwater harvesting systems are under severe threat or dormant. Therefore, these structures should be rejuvenated, which can be used for drinking water purposes. This component could be included in Bharat Niman.
- The farmers should be educated and trained in low water consumption modern methods like drip irrigation. In addition, they should be given incentives under Bharat Nirman by the Agricultural Department, if they grow low water consumption crops.
- Traditional water treatment methods like *Thetaam kottai* (seeds treatment for reducing turbidity, being used in some of the villages of Ramanathapuram district, Tamil Nadu) should be encouraged by the central and state Governments under Bharat Nirman.
- Usage of plastic vessels made with recycled plastic is a common phenomenon in rural areas. Studies of NIRD revealed that these vessels are being used for carrying and storing the drinking water. Obviously, consumption of this water (storing in plastic vessels) could create health problems to the people. Therefore, there is a need to create awareness through intensive IEC on

discouraging the usage of plastic vessels for storing drinking water.

REFERENCES

1. Annual Report—Ministry of Rural Development, 2005-06.
2. Downloaded, Department of Drinking Water Supply, MoRD, GOI on 20 August, 2006.
3. Ramaswamy Iyer (2003), Ground Water Legislation, Water Issues, Concerns, New Delhi, pp. 100-08.
4. P. Durgaprasad and P. Siva Ram, *et. al.* (2003), Sector Reforms in Water Supply and Sanitation in Karnataka, NIRD, Research Monograph, 2003, NIRD.
5. P. Siva Ram (2004), Community and Government Initiatives in Roof-Top Rainwater Harvesting for Drinking Water in Rural Areas of Aizwal District of Mizoram State—A Field Inquiry, *Journal of Man and Development*, Vol. XXVI, No. 2, June, pp. 105-14.
6. P. Siva Ram (2003), Planning and Management of Canal Based Rural Drinking Water Supply Schemes—A Study of Bathinda District, Punjab State, *Indian Journal of Social Development—An International Journal*, Vol. 3, No. 2, 2003, December, pp. 229-39.

18

WHRL Project and Drinking Water

V. Reddappa Reddy and C. Dheeraja

There is hardly any mandal or village in desert-prone Anantapur district in Andhra Pradesh that is not facing acute shortage of water for domestic consumption. A significant chunk of population of the district is also facing health hazards like weak and brittle bones, deformation of physique, teeth and gum-related diseases and discolouring of teeth due to heavy concentration of fluoride in the available drinking water. In fact, fluoride concentration beyond the acceptable level of 1.5 ppm is a norm rather than an exception in many villages in Anantapur district. The fluoride concentration level is getting aggravated in recent years due to the decline of the water-table owing to continuous droughts and extraction of water from progressively deeper bowels of the earth for irrigation and domestic purposes. The critical impact of drought on fluoride levels was identified in the routine monitoring of wells by the Water, Households and Rural Livelihoods (WHRL) project that indicated a widespread increase in fluoride concentrations of around 30 per cent during the 2002-03 drought in Kalyandurg mandal of Anantapur district. The enormity of the flouoride problem is such that UNICEF is supporting the cause of de-fluoride water filters by providing subsidy in the district. The supply of filters being not very penetrative, the need for an alternative became crucial. Hence, the major challenge to develop context specific, prioritized, sequenced, realistic and patient approaches to solve the domestic water problem.

Reprinted with permission, *Kurukshetra*, September 2005, pp. 11-15.

The Natural Resource Institute of University of Greenwich has undertaken an experiment aiming at the supply of fluoride-free drinking water in Kalyandurg mandal in Anantapur district under WHRL research project. The project was undertaken with financial support from the Department for International Development (DID), United Kingdom and field-level support from Accion Fraterna, one of the wings of Rural Development Trust (RDT), a local voluntary organisation working for the welfare of the poor of Anantapur and neighbouring districts.

The WHRL research project could be termed as a late adjunct to the Andhra Pradesh Rural Livelihoods Programme (APRLP). Under APRLP, the Watershed Development Programme (WSDP) is undertaken with the prime aim of enhancing the livelihood opportunities of poorer sections of Anantapur district by undertaking soil and water conservation and ecological balancing activities. As part of APRLP, *'water-audit'* was conducted in Kalyandurg mandal. The water audit of both irrigation and domestic sources covered the preparation of the inventory of wells in use and disuse, depth of wells, water-table in wells, water-use patterns and chemical analysis of water. The audit revealed disturbing trends with regard to drinking water, viz.

(1) progressive deepening of wells in all the villages;
(2) competition between different social groups for scarce water, weaker sections facing the disadvantage;
(3) water for irrigation often comprised the amount and/or quality of groundwater available for domestic supply;
(4) high concentration levels of fluoride in the currently used drinking water sources;
(5) though not in short supply, the quality of drinking water is absolutely dangerous for human consumption in a large number of villages; and
(6) WSDP largely focussed on promoting irrigation and neglected drinking water issues, and in some cases making the drinking water supplies worse.

The above scenario called for the integration of efforts towards solving the drinking water needs with the soil and water conservation and irrigation enhancing measures of WSDP. The WHRL project was undertaken to test the scope and compatibility of integrating the WSDP for solving drinking water problems supporting innovative approaches to promote better water management and establish mechanisms to use better quality water for drinking and contaminated water for agriculture. The project adopted a participatory approach in conjunction with specialist analysis of secondary data in the conduct of rapid surveys of fluoride levels in domestic water points and it envisaged identifying the specific water-related challenges faced by social groups within each village, and combining local knowledge, social and economic acceptability criteria, and information from the specialist analysis to match potential solutions to the challenges in each village.

It was envisaged replicating and upscaling the WHRL experiment throughout the district and even in the other areas similarly affected with fluoride concentration in drinking water. Hence, our analyses mainly aim at truthfully documenting the process of the experiment. The main objectives of the current documentation are:

(1) to identify and analyse the important field-level processes followed in executing the project;
(2) to document and analyse the process of peoples' mobilisation and participation while undertaking the project;
(3) to document the efforts made in making the project sustainable; and
(4) to identify the gaps in project implementation, if any, and suggest measures of helping replication and up-scaling.

Profile of the Project Villages

Since the study was undertaken in two villages in Kalyandurg, a critically driest mandal—mean annual rainfall being 524 mm—in Anantapur district, presenting a brief comment on the mandal may be relevant. Important characteristics as revealed by a team of experts of APRLP water audit showed the delicately poised ecological and environmental situation of the mandal appearing on the threshold of desertification. As a rule of thumb, out of every ten years, five are drought years, two of which are severe and one of which is catastrophic. The mandal was characterised with potential evaporation exceeding rainfall in all but a few months in any year. With regard to the groundwater-table it was noted that there has been a dramatic increase in groundwater extraction for irrigation and domestic purposes during the last 10-15 years. As a result, the shallow wells completely failed and extraction from deeper aquifers through bore wells has been the norm; between 100 and 150 metres being the depth of the bore-wells, on an average. Net groundwater extraction for irrigation, domestic and livestock use in the mandal was estimated at 11.0 per cent as compared to the estimated groundwater recharge being approximately 10.0 per cent, indicating that current levels of extraction in the mandal are not sustainable.

Apart from the natural problem of fluoride, 'social exclusion' of weaker sections, viz., Scheduled Castes and Scheduled Tribes, is also a deeply ingrained fact of life in many villages in Kalyandurg mandal as in the case of many villages in India. The discrimination identified in participatory assessment falls into two categories. Firstly, prohibition on Scheduled Castes and Scheduled Tribes directly accessing water from open wells and, secondly, forced preference of 'upper' castes at water points meant for 'lower' castes. Participatory assessment by the water audit team showed that, 'greater distances walked has a disproportionate impact on the lives of women and children as in households they take primary responsibility for fetching water'.

The strain faced by women and children of Battuvanipalli village in fetching water for domestic use until recently could be well understood from a statement made by an elderly person of the village, 'parents used to fear giving girls in marriage to Battuvanipalli as the women of the village were known to face year-long hardships in fetching water to meet the domestic needs, and the girls of the village used to feel relieved when they were given in marriage to other villages'.

For the last six years, the people of the village depended on the Rural Water Supply (RWS) scheme managed by the local Panchayat for domestic use of water. In addition, two hand pumps were in working condition in the village. These water sources contained about 4 ppm of fluoride, as compared to a safe level of 1.5 ppm. People learnt of the problems of high fluoride concentration levels from RDT staff before the initiation of the WHRL project. But they were unaware of the next step, as they noted that all the villages around theirs have a similar fluoride problem. So, they resigned to their fate, as they could not imagine migrating enmasse to another village having safe drinking water

Pathacheruvu village, a hamlet of Golla revenue village, is on the banks of Pathacheruvu vanka. The total population of the village is 216. During the pre-project days, the women of the old colony of Pathacheruvu used to collect water from nearby irrigation wells and Those of the new colony from two hand pumps; one located in the colony and another close to the nearby temple for domestic use.

Mobilisation of the Community

The process of project execution was not common in the two villages. In Battuvanipalli, lot of groundwork was done in mobilising the community for project execution. The mobilisation of the community involved two different stages, viz., awareness building about their problem and preparing the community for the experiment for solving the problem.

Awareness Building about their Problem

The field staff of APRLP undertook a detailed water audit of 70 wells within a radius of 2 km of Battuvanipalli village for ten days covering both shallow wells and bore-wells. As part of the audit, each of the wells was given a number, quantity of water measured, quality of water tested in the labs and a '√' or '×' mark was written at a prominent place close to the wells based on the lab results about the quality of water, indicating whether water from a particular well is useful for drinking purposes or not. While participating in the audit activity, the APRLP staff also interacted regularly with youth and women of the village on the fluoride content in the drinking water. The day-to-day visits by the staff to the water bodies, quantity and quality measurement of water, using hitherto unknown equipment for the measurement and regular discussions with the community, especially with youth, on fluoride content and its effect on humans, helped in creating awareness among the people.

Preparing the Community for the Experiment

With a view to positively use the evolved awareness and prepare them for the experiment, a 'gramsabha' was organised. The issues identified in the water audit, especially the scarcity of drinking water and level of fluoride concentration and possible repercussions when the same water is used for drinking purposes, were discussed. The discussions in these meetings also covered linking the cases of physical deformities, teeth and gum-related problems and discolouring of teeth found in the village to the water audit results. An exposure visit was arranged to another village not having a fluoride problem to help village youth and women understand the severity of the problem. By and large the people realised their folly in ignoring the linkage between fluoride concentrations and related health problems.

Using the RIDe Framework

Another gramsabha was organised for undertaking an assessment of resources, infrastructure, demands and entitlements with regard to drinking water in the village. With the participation of the community, the entire scenario of drinking water in the village was put into a Resources, Infrastructure, Demands/entitlements (RIDe), a three-dimensional framework. The first dimension of the framework helped identify 'resources', i.e., the water resource base in time and space (quantity, quality, etc.) and institutions that manage the resources. In the second dimension, people identified the available infrastructure, i.e., the systems (hardware and software) to extract, treat and convey water for different purposes, and institutions that manage the systems. The third dimension helped assess the demand and entitlements, i.e., the requirements of people/users and the institutions that represent them. The RIDe framework exercise helped the community in assessing the gaps and concerns and areas for intervention. Then the village youth decided to do something to overcome the problem and became enthusiastic to become part of the WHRL experiment.

Towards a Solution

The water audit helped understand the fluoride concentration levels in each of the 70 irrigation and drinking water wells in the radius of two kilometres of Battuvanipalli, and help single out an irrigation bore-well having fluoride concentration within the permissible level. By sitting with the youth, the WHRL staff has identified a number of possible solutions. Some of them were later discarded during community-level discussions. Ultimately, on the suggestion of the community and on their own assessment, the WHRL staff decided to dig a bore-well in the temple land close to the village tank and improve the water-table by enhancing the inflows into the tank by putting gates in upstream structures constructed under WSDP that impeded the runoff. They dug a bore-well accordingly. But the bore-well failed them, as it did not yield any water. Later one more bore-well was dug in the middle of the village tank. Though a sufficient quantum of water was found in this bore-well, the fluoride concentration level was of 3.68 ppm, beyond the permissible limit, bringing all their efforts to naught.

Then the scope for swapping of bore-wells between the irrigation bore-well of a farmer that recorded permissible levels of fluoride and the one dug for WHRL project was discussed in the community meeting. Water output from both the bore-wells being more or less the same and both bore-wells are located not far away to one another. The community hesitated to broach the idea as the concerned farmer had 12 acres of papaya crop under the bore-well at that time. After the harvest of the crop the community sent village elders and the WHRL staff to discuss the scope for exchange of wells with the farmer. The farmer agreed after explaining the purpose of exchange and legal rights that he is going to enjoy over the WHRL bore-well. The terms like, 'holiness, god's grace and community goodwill' earned by the farmer if he agrees to give the water to the entire community was liberally used to the best of their abilities by the elders and by the WHRL staff in their persuasion with the farmer. The persuasion did not fail and the farmer agreed to exchange his bore-well with the WHRL bore-well. The farmer also agreed not the dig any well within a radius of 200 metres from this well, and for the provision of passage to the well for starting the motor every day and for repair purposes. But after interactions with his family and well-wishers he refused the exchange offer. The community and the WHRL staff had no answer for a genuine problem raised by the farmer. The WHRL bore-well was dug in a tank-bed, a common property. The exchange of bore-well dug in his own land with a bore-well dug in common property made little sense to the community too. Then the farmer came forward with an alternative of selling the rights over his well instead of swapping his bore-well. The community and WHRL staff agreed to the proposal. The monetary consideration of Rs. 62713 included cost of digging a bore-well, electrification and pipeline cost for bringing water to his fields from the new bore-well to be dug.

In Pathacheruvu, the condition was that all the existing wells faced a fluoride problem, except one irrigation bore-well owned by a local temple priest. The WHRL staff identified the area around this well as a fluoride-free zone. Then it was decided to seek a small patch of land in this safe zone and dig a bore-well. The owner of the fluoride-free bore-well agreed to donate a small patch of his own land for digging a bore-well 25 metres away from his currently used bore-well. The donor (owner of the land) viewed that the population in the village is small, hence, there may not be much impact on the water-table affecting his well due to the extraction from the project bore-well to be dug. Another reason as told by the donor for the offer was that about 30 per cent of the population of the village belong to his caste, Boya, and many of them are his blood relatives. However, he laid a condition that the fluoride-free drinking water must be supplied to the temple to which he has the priesthood, and where regular marriages and other functions take place. WHRL staff agreed to this condition. The farmer also agreed to the condition that no other bore-well shall be dug within a radius of 200 metres from the project bore-well.

By adopting persuasion, facilitation and mobilisation techniques in Pathacheruvu, and monetary consideration along with the above three techniques in Battuvanipalli, the community good was prioritised over individual good.

The Outputs, Outcomes Impact

In Pathacheruvu village, one bore-well of 100 metres depth was dug, electricity connection secured from the concerned line department, an electric motor of 5 hp installed, pipelines measuring 1.5 km laid underground, one ground level tank with a capacity of 5000 litres and seven water taps installed, two pistons measuring 2500 litres each were constructed and six taps installed to the pistons, one cattle trough (an open structure meant to provide drinking water to the cattle) constructed and 28 underground rainwater harvesting structures constructed at a rate of one for each household. The rainwater harvesting structures were designed to collect water from the rooftops of households meant for improvement in the water table.

The community is getting the project water since October 2003 in the village and the impact seems two-fold. The women are spending much less time in fetching drinking water, are facing much less physical strain as they were only to carry the water from the water tap rather than physically excruciating themselves in hand-pumping the water from deep bore-wells and carry to the homes and are able to spend more time either in leisure or in other household activities. The community has said in one voice that, except the very old, none of them are facing joint pains and teeth-related problems since two months.

In Battuvanipalli, one bore-well, electric motor of 5 hp and electricity connection were acquired from a farmer, underground pipeline measuring 1.5 km laid, seven water taps installed and one cattle trough constructed.

Three checkdams in the catchment area of the local irrigation tank constructed under WSDP were arranged with sluices so as to allow the rainwater to flow unhindered to the nearby tank. The sluices have the provision to be closed once the tank gets filled; helping the storage of water after filling the tank, meant to improve the water table.

The community is getting the project water since November 2003. On an average, each household collects between 60 to 75 litres (four to five pots) of water from the project taps everyday. This water is used only for cooking and drinking purposes in Battuvanipalli village. It was limited to cooking and drinking due to the fear of possible extraction of more water from deeper aquifers and such extraction resulting in higher concentrations of fluoride levels, as people have come to be aware of the fact that the extraction beyond the current aquifers is likely to lead to higher levels of fluoride. The FGDs revealed that there was no report of joint pains and gum and teeth-related diseases, common earlier, from January 2004.

Peoples' Participation

The solutions do not serve the intended purpose, unless a sequence of interventions and activities have put as much, or even more emphasis on the long-term sustainability of interventions and putting the management capacity in place. To make the village Panchayats responsible for future maintenance of the systems (both physical and financial) the bore-wells and other infrastructure established by the WHRL project were handed over to the Panchayats in both the villages. The Panchayat of Pathacheruvu has agreed to meet 50 per cent of the maintenance cost of the project bore-well, pipeline, tanks and taps. The community agreed to contribute the remaining 50 per cent. To meet this 50 per cent, it was decided to collect five rupees per household per month. The Panchayat also agreed to meet 100 per cent of the electricity charges for pumping the water from the bore-well.

In Battuvanipalli, the community formed a Water Committee with 18 members, meant to look after the day-to-day maintenance of the project infrastructure and its management. The community collected Rs. 12,000 for the maintenance of the project from households following the 'ability to pay' principle: 25 households paid Rs. 100; 34 households paid Rs. 50; and 54 households paid Rs. 35. Three households were exempted from paying, as the community believed that they have no means to pay. The starter of the well was lost due to theft, and the community replaced the same on the same day, and the necessary amount of Rs. 2889 was met from the funds collected. One person was appointed as 'water man' since January 2004 by paying him Rs. 500 per month. His responsibilities include timely pumping of water every day from both project and Panchayat bore-wells and cleaning both project and Panchayat tanks once in a week. With a view to minimise the misuse of safe project water the community passed a few important resolutions: children should be discouraged from going to the taps for fetching the water (fearing wastage); the project water must not be used for washing of clothes and utensils and for bathing purposes and the project water must not be used for drinking by cattle.

The manpower contribution of people can be found in two areas in the execution of the project: mobilisation, facilitation and persuasion of their cohabitants, and the contribution of manpower for undertaking physical activities. The contribution differed slightly between the villages. In Pathacheruvu, the community contributed manpower in digging and laying the pipeline. In Battuvanipalli, the infrastructure included laying of the pipeline for a distance of 1.5 kilometres. The community itself laid the pipeline without assistance from any technical personnel.

Hydrological Monitoring

As already pointed out, the fluoride concentration levels and water-table are positively correlated, i.e., more the depth of the well, higher is the fluoride concentration level. Then the understanding principle is that the water from the project wells must not be exploited beyond a permissible depth. To keep abreast of the information whether water pumping is taking place within permissible depths or not, periodical hydrological monitoring is undertaken. The fluoride concentration levels are also studied periodically from the water samples collected from the project wells along with other wells in the two villages. The results show that the project wells continue to show permissible levels of fluoride concentration (1.48 ppm in Battuvanipalli and 1.44 ppm in Pathacheruvu), and the other wells showing beyond permissible levels (2.45 ppm in Battuvanipalli and 2.46 ppm in Pathacheruvu).

19

Drinking Water Quality Assurance in Villages

Dinesh Chand

Water is a physiological necessity for humans and animals. According to Wolf, "mean water intake by man per day is 2200 g or 3.1 per cent of the body weight." This daily quota of water must not carry contaminants antagonistic to his well-being. The Government of India has recognized access to safe and adequate drinking water for communities as one of the thrust areas. At present, India has scored significantly on adequacy, but is lagging far behind on water quality aspects.

The United Nations' population projections indicate that India will be among 34 countries of the world, which are likely to face severe water shortage by the year 2025. As per estimates, the country's annual fresh water requirements (i.e., about 1050 billion cum) by that year will be almost at par with its exploitable water resources. Thus, the preservation of safe water and protection of water quality of existing sources become priority areas.

Health Risks

In developing countries like India, most of the diseases such as gastroenteritis, diarrhoea, dysentery, cholera, enteric fever, etc. prevail due to unsafe drinking water clubbed with poor environmental sanitation. The country is also increasingly facing the problem of excess chemicals like fluoride, arsenic, nitrates, salinity and iron in groundwater sources due to either geo-climatic factors or man-made problems. Generally, the rural population suffers the most from such microbial or chemical contaminants in drinking water. As mentioned in "Agenda 21" of the UN Conference on Environment and Development (UNCED), "an estimated 80 per cent of all diseases and over one-third of deaths in developing countries are caused by the consumption of contaminated water, and on an average as much as one-tenth of each person's productive time is sacrificed to water-related diseases."

Inadequate sanitation adds to the microbial contamination of drinking water and food, leading to an increased number of carriers and cases. Person to person spread of diseases results because of poor hygienic practices or ignorance about them. The microbial contamination of drinking water from its abstraction till consumption is to be especially avoided because of its high degree of simultaneous infection in the community.

Status in Rural Areas

Since the launching of the National Drinking Water Mission in 1986, the pace of coverage increased manifold. Over 95 per cent of the rural habitations (i.e., 14.223 lakh) of the country (leaving only 9652 habitations uncovered as on 1.4.2004) now have access to drinking water with an investment of over Rs. 450,000 million through installation of over 37 lakh hand-pumps and 1.73 lakh piped water supply systems.

While the physical achievement has been impressive, the bacteriological and chemical contaminants in drinking water supplies/ sources have posed a serious threat to public health. The nation-wide survey of habitations completed in the year 1994 shows that over 43.5 million people living in 1.42 lakh habitations are at health risks due to presence of excess fluoride, arsenic, salinity, iron and other chemicals including nutrients, pesticides and insecticides contributed through agricultural run-off.

In India, over 85 per cent of RWS systems are based on groundwater aquifers. The depletion of groundwater has been identified as one of the major factors responsible for chemical deterioration of drinking water sources. In rural areas where access to a reticulated water supply is not available, groundwater is often utilized along with development of rainwater tanks, gravity feed schemes, wells and bores.

Generally, the surface water used for piped water supply systems has contaminants like high suspended solids, organic/inorganic loads, bacteria counts, etc. and is usually treated before being supplied to the community having Water Quality Monitoring (WQM) at the treatment plant site. There are fair chances of bacteriological contamination during transmission/handing over of water to consumer.

Organic substances and pathogens lead to increased health risks, especially in riverside populations that consume raw river water. The problems are compounded where industrial wastes containing heavy metals or other toxic chemicals are discharged into rivers/streams.

Presently, Water Quality aspects are being administered by water supply agencies, Public Health Departments/Central Water Commission, Groundwater and Pollution Control Boards of Centre/States/GSI (Geological Survey of India), Research Institutions/Universities and Non-Government Organisations (NGOs), according to their aims. These aims differ from agency to agency depending on their individual sub-sectoral role and responsibility within the water sector.

The States are having a different set-up for drinking Water Quality assurance activities without strong central supervisory/coordination mechanisms. Attempts have been made to formalize linkages at various levels and to facilitate routine testing/monitoring. However, a systematic drinking water quality assurance system has failed to develop. At present, the following systems are in place in some of the States:

(i) The Field Engineers of the water supply agency organize the collection of water samples and the Chemist in-charge of State/Zonal/District Laboratory conducts quality testing/analysis.

(ii) The reports are submitted to the Executive Engineer/Senior Chemist who supervises the work of the laboratory as well as field operations.

(iii) The Executive Engineer (PHE)/Senior Chemist submits a report to the Chief Engineer and other concerned officials on a monthly basis.

(iv) The Chief Engineer (PHE) casually passes on the results to DDWS.

(v) The data so generated are not systematically compiled and consolidated at any level for the purpose of planning and future monitoring of the water quality. However, initial data are used for selection of sources of a particular scheme and designing the treatment facilities.

Realising the importance of regular drinking Water Quality assurance and the need for creating an infrastructure, the Ministry of Rural Development had taken a policy decision to establish a District Level Water Quality (DLWQ) laboratory in each district of the country way back in 1989-90. 555 DLWQ laboratories, including over 100 laboratories by states from other resources have been sanctioned to various states and UTs so far. It was expected that such a network of the laboratories will help in developing effective Water Quality assurance system and thus prevent diseases after forging linkages with State Health Departments.

This may perhaps provide only a partial solution to the problem. An effective Water Quality assurance system depends on institutionalization with adequate infrastructural and financial support to ensure availability of quality water on a sustainable basis. In reality, the Government agencies could do the initial and occasional quality checks only. A typical institutional framework for National Water Quality Assurance is exhibited in Fig. 1.

Assurance Programme

Proper sanitary conditions, provision of microbiologically and chemically safe drinking water, and sufficiency in quantity are three main parameters of public health protection. These parameters are intertwined and no clear demarcation is possible. The water quality assurance programme may consist of two complementary components, viz., (a) monitoring, and (b) surveillance.

(a) Monitoring

Water quality monitoring involves sampling and testing of public supply sources at specific intervals to assure adherence to prescribed standards. The programme should focus on two major goals: (a) to maintain the quality of water supplied to the consumers, and (b) to

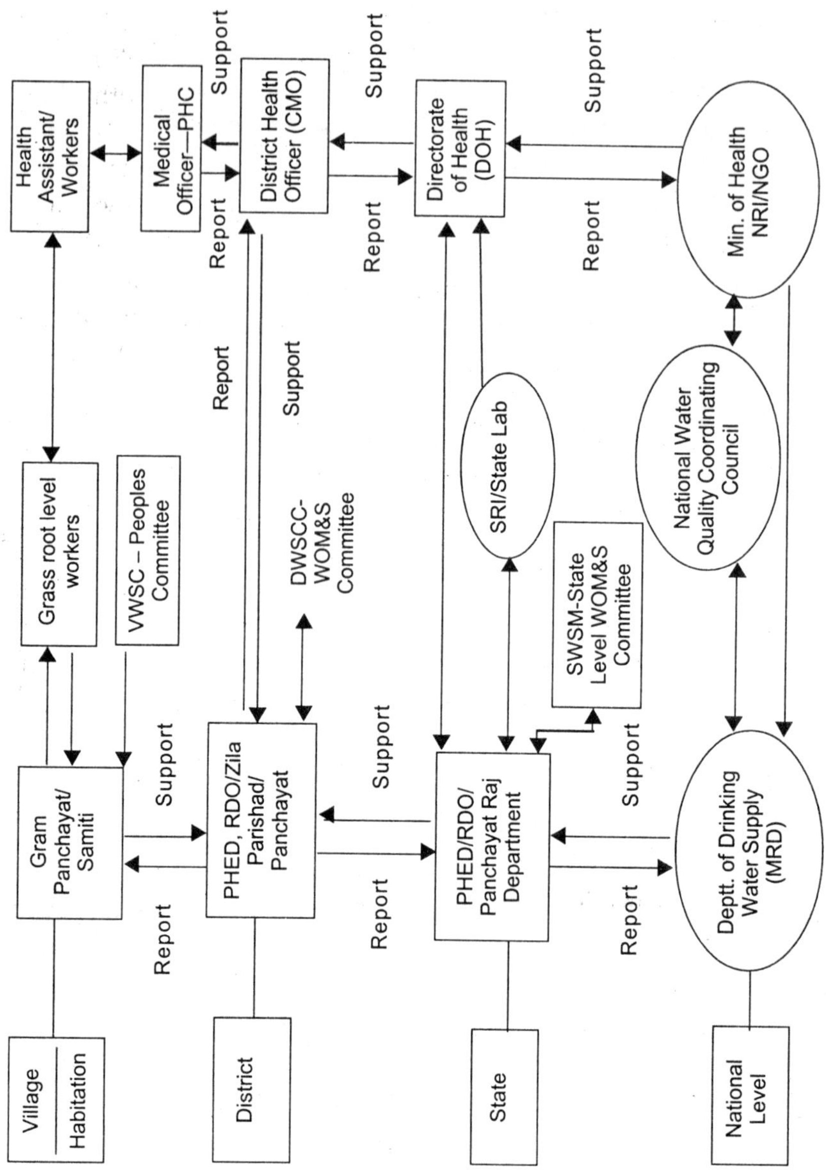

Fig. 1: Typical Institutional Framework for National Water Quality Assurance Programme

protect the water quality of sources for future generations by initiation of corrective measures.

In most of the developing countries, the actual sampling and laboratory analysis is generally carried out by government agencies. Keeping in view the magnitude of the problem, lack of finance and trained personnel, the government may involve communities and NGOs/other institutions to carry out water sampling and its analysis through local institutions or by using portable kits for initiating action to protect the sources wherever necessary. The properly devised monitoring programme should be cost-effective, and capable of detecting contaminants and defining the extent of contaminant plumes. Thus, the programme should also aim at these:

(i) To maintain acceptable levels of water quality of aquifers which have been developed extensively for drinking purposes on a sustainable basis.
(ii) To maintain acceptable water quality of surface water bodies including rainwater storages, which are being used for drinking purpose.
(iii) Status of water quality of an aquifer in landfill or other disposal facilities, which has been developed extensively for water use.
(iv) Control use of fertilizers/pesticides and excessive irrigation resulting in return flow to a shallow groundwater table.
(v) Check salt-water intrusion in coastal areas from entrapped connate water bodies in developed aquifers.

Goals

The water monitoring goals should be determined clearly. Typical goals might be one or more of the following:

(i) To meet regulatory requirements.
(ii) Determine site-specific baseline of groundwater quality and hydrological conditions.
(iii) Determine causes of groundwater quality deterioration in certain areas.
(iv) Determine the impact of a particular activity on the water environment.
(v) Determine regional groundwater quality trends and background groundwater quality.

The different goals mentioned above may be broadly categorized in two groups of monitoring, viz., (i) Management; and (ii) Contaminant Determination.

System

A detailed evaluation of a number of generic factors is needed for effective collection and analysis of water quality data. Some of the significant factors to be considered for a monitoring system are as follows:

(1) **Constituents:** A few specific constituents for monitoring are as follows:

(i) Microbiological contamination of water sources.

(ii) Chemical contamination due to the geo-chemical environment, water movement and source of groundwater contamination.

(iii) Contamination from fertilizers/pesticides, etc. used for agriculture.

(iv) Selected parameters related to sanitary landfill contamination.

(v) Measurement of conductivity at various depths for salt-water intrusion.

(2) **Analytical Facilities:** A well-equipped laboratory having trained personnel at each district level (and also at block level—if in a particular area the endemicity of drinking water-related diseases is predominant—optional), and suitable field kits at GP/Village level are a must.

(3) **Frequency:** Based on the preliminary information about the existing water supply system in a specified area and also the extent to which the sources are contaminated and type nature of contamination, extent and frequency of monitoring may be decided on the following basis:

(i) To divide a region based on administration, physiography and priority considerations;

(ii) To identify and make preliminary ranking priority sources in each area which needs immediate attention;

(iii) To examine the sources having greater potential hazards which contaminate drinking water sources and determine

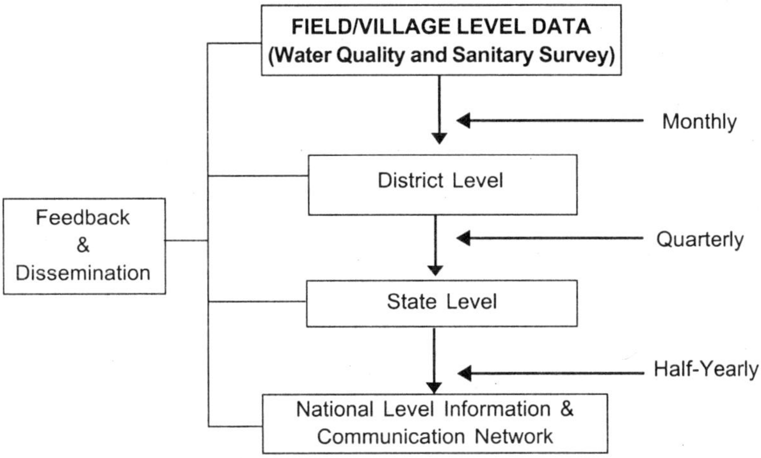

Fig. 2: Communication Network

what information already exists, what information is needed and at what cost.

A flow diagram for a reporting system is exhibited in Figure 2.

(4) **Network Design:** The successful design of water quality monitoring network and its operation may be based on the following considerations:

(1) The information-gathering and fulfilment of the monitoring process are integral parts of the management and decision-making process.

(2) Information-based management is more efficient and it tends to reduce risk (hence loss) when a choice has to be made between several alternatives. The information available on water quality, parameters of different aquifers, within or on the out skirts of the village and distant source may help plan a scheme based on alternate cost effective and viable safe water source to an endemic village with hand pump/local drinking water source.

(3) Because of the inter-relationship and interdependence, two sets of goals can be defined; one is for the overall water resources management plan, while the other deals with the monitoring of contamination status.

These are the overall management objectives for the particular monitoring system design and it depends on physical and financial conditions. Obviously, design objectives should be reasonable as compared to the financial allocation and interrelationships among the above factors.

(b) Surveillance

The surveillance of drinking water quality from the public health point of view involves mechanisation, management and a number of other activities including follow-up action to keep a constant vigil on the safety and acceptability of drinking water supply.

(1) Objectives

The objective of the drinking water quality surveillance is to identify potential health hazards and take preventive action to eliminate or minimise their impact on human health. In most developing countries, the principal risks to human health associated with small community water supplies are microbiological in nature.

(2) System

The surveillance is "a systematic approach to identify, assess, prevent and control health risks associated with water supplies." Surveillance will find out what is wrong, what is the magnitude of the problem and how to put the system right. It will also assist in developing more general activities, e.g., operators, training and hygiene education to the villagers to prevent waterborne diseases and to promote safety of water supplies.

Broadly, surveillance comprises the following five steps:

(i) Identification of health risks and assessment of their severity with the entire water supply system (source, treatment, distribution and use);

(ii) Determination of critical control points at which the identified risks can be eliminated, prevented or minimised;

(iii) Specification of criteria that indicate whether or not the risks have been controlled;

(iv) Identification and implementation of appropriate corrective action; and

(v) Establishment and implementation of protocols to monitor each critical control point to check that it is under control.

(3) Programme Elements

Surveillance of drinking water quality is an uninterrupted and vigilant public health assessment, and watchdog of drinking water supplied to the villagers. The key elements of a surveillance programme may include:

(a) Surveillance monitoring for health risk and remedial measures,
(b) Sanitary survey,
(c) Data processing,
(d) Evaluation,
(e) Remedial and preventive action, and
(f) Institutional analysis.

A surveillance plan may include the legislative and institutional support for surveillance, strategies for its implementation, community participation, dissemination and information sharing, and requirement of human and financial resources.

Since the objective of surveillance is to protect human health it is best carried out through state health departments or district health officers. The surveillance agency and the water supply agency should, therefore, make combined efforts to meet the common goal.

(c) Implementation Methodology

Once the assurance plan has been developed, strategies for its implementation must be formulated. A basic concept that should be used in any country is to determine the status of water quality assurance system and formulate a realistic programme keeping the local situation, human and economic resources of the country in mind, and meet the specified objective, then move on to the next stage of assurance programme in a phased manner. A summary of the broad steps is given below:

- Inventory of water supplies and status of quality assurance system.
- Design forms for data collection and analysis.

- Capacity development.
- Planning preliminary survey including sanitation survey.
- Undertake field work.
- Collate and interpret results.
- Evaluation and dissemination of information among water supply agencies/planners/consumers for improvement at critical points.

The steps to be followed during a surveillance study may include:

- Interaction with concerned agencies responsible for O&M of water supply schemes.
- Review of O&M aspects of raw water sources, water treatment plants, distribution systems, etc.
- Review of the existing surveillance programme.
- Assessment of prevalence of water-borne diseases.
- Water quality assessment through sampling and analysis of water samples collected at different points for various physical, chemical and bacteriological parameters.
- Analysis of the findings, identification of deficiencies in the existing system and suggestions on the remedial measures in the system.

(d) Information Management

Adequate, accurate record-keeping and documentation are essentials. Clearly, the information collected and analysed by the surveillance agency is to be provided to the water supply agency. The information may include at least the following:

- A summary of quality of the service and sanitary conditions of the supply system;
- Identification of health risk elements; and
- Suggestions for appropriate corrective measures by the water supply agency.

(e) Capacity Development

The development of human resources through appropriate education and training to make the water quality monitoring a success is an essential pre-requisite for a quality assurance programme. This may be achieved through a well-planned programme for all personnel associated with water quality testing, analysis and surveillance programmes. The educational and scientific institutions, NGOs and voluntary agencies including women's groups may be involved.

Community Participation

No programme can succeed without involvement of the beneficiary community. Thrust should be given to educate them to form a positive opinion on health aspects of drinking water and its handling at the household level. The main objective of such activities is to make people conscious about the importance of drinking water quality and its impact on health. Implementation of each of these activities requires planning, involvement of various institutions/organisations and coordination at different levels. The role of women in health education and community participation is very vital. Once they are convinced and empowered, they may prove helpful in spreading the message.

Health education and community involvement can be promoted through the following means:

- Introduction of water quality aspects in the curriculum of health workers, gram-sewaks, agricultural extension workers, other village level workers, hand pump/PWS mechanics, etc.;
- Electronic and traditional media like models, local newspapers/puppet shows, newsletters and posters in local languages, village camps, documentaries, video films, slides, pamphlets, etc. for promotion of awareness among villagers and target groups;
- Community involvement from inception of water supply and sanitation projects and during their maintenance;
- Inter-sectoral coordination among various stakeholders, namely, Health, Agriculture, Rural Development, Social Welfare, Education, PHED/Water Supply Agencies and Zilla Parishads should be established; and
- Introduction of health education related to water and sanitation in schools.

These should be used to convey the following messages:

(i) Importance of personal and domestic hygiene to ensure potable drinking water at the user's end.

(ii) Education about the drinking water standards and their impact on the human body.
(iii) Knowledge of necessary water treatment processes and monitoring.
(iv) Integration and linkages with other programmes, viz., health, education, water supply and water quality assurance, environmental sanitation, etc.
(v) Community participation aspects in water quality assurance programme.

Conclusion

Water quality assurance is an integral part of a safe drinking water supply programme. It determines the state of the system, in terms of both quality and quantity and provides the status of the water quality of the source at a particular location to gain a perspective on long-term water quality at selected sites.

Making the system functional, however, will require continual data generation to gain a better understanding of the statistical characteristics of water quality variables and the relationship between water quality and human health as well as the hydrological cycle. Without this understanding, technicians/engineers would continue to be good at collecting data, but not in using the data for extracting the valuable information it provides. Ultimately, the data collection and analysis should essentially result in suggestion of corrective measures to protect 'water quality'. Surveillance in turn shall serve as a tool to authenticate the process of monitoring and gauge the success of the system adopted.

REFERENCES

"Guidelines for Drinking Water Quality," Volumes 1-3, Published by World Health Organization, Geneva (1984).

United Nations Conference on Environment and Development (UNCED): Agenda 21: "Programme of Action for Sustainable Development." Chapter 18: "Protection of the Quality and Supply of Freshwater Resources," United Nations, NY (1992).

"National Workshop on Water Quality and Surveillance in Rural Areas," Technical Papers, RGNDWM, M/O RAE (1997).

Gorchev, H.G., "Global Perspectives on Surveillance and Control of Drinking Water Quality," Workshop on Water Quality and Surveillance in Rural Areas (1997).

"Sources and Nature of Water Quality Problems in Asia and the Pacific," Report No. ST/ESCAP/1875, United Nations, New York (1998).

Dinesh Chand, "Drinking Water Supply to Villages," *Kurukshetra*, Vol. 47, No. 10, July (1999).

——, "Drinking Water Quality Assurance to Rural India," Annual Conference (17-18 Dec. 1999), Indian Association For Environmental Management, Nagpur (1999).

——, "Management of River Water Quality: An Overview," National Workshop on Assessment and Management of Environmental Impacts in Hydro-Water and River Valley Project (9-12 May, 2000).

20

Sustainable Rural Water Supply

Dinesh Chand

In 1986, the Government of India created the National Drinking Water Mission and subsequently, renamed it as the Rajiv Gandhi National Drinking Water Mission in 1991, with the mandate to provide financial, policy and technological support and develop a multi-pronged approach relating to the rural water supply sector. The prime objective of the Mission was to provide at least one source of drinking water in villages during the decade period and subsequently focussed on the following major objectives:

- To ensure coverage of all rural habitations, especially to reach the un-reached with access to safe drinking water;
- To ensure sustainability of the systems and sources;
- To tackle the problem of water quality in affected habitations and to preserve the quality of water by institutionalizing water quality monitoring and surveillance through a Catchment Area Approach; and
- To adopt community participation in the rural water supply programme through sector reform projects in the country on a pilot basis.

With an investment of about Rs. 400 billion on rural drinking water supply in the last fifty years, it has been possible to fully cover over 86.9 per cent of about 1.4 million rural habitations with drinking water facilities, with about 11.7 per cent partially covered and about

1.4 per cent yet to be covered. The Mission could achieve coverage of the decade target by and large. In this process, certain important issues have emerged which need immediate attention to achieve sustainability of water supply assets.

The Government has accorded the highest priority for rural drinking water to ensure universal access as a part of policy framework—a global desire to surge ahead and achieve the goal of reaching the un-reached as evident from the massive financial and technical inputs to the sector from both Central and State governments. However, private sector investment or community support were absent. India has declared 2003 as the 'Year of Freshwater' in keeping with the United Nations Resolution declaring 2003 as the 'International Freshwater Year'.

Despite this impressive coverage with the installation of more than 3.5 million hand-pumps and over 116 thousand piped water supply schemes, in many parts of the country, the people face water scarcity almost every year especially during summer months. In the past few years, many parts of the country have faced severe drinking water scarcity thereby meaning that our water supply systems are failing to sustain, despite huge investments. The examination of sustainability issues of drinking water supply as well as systems has, therefore, become imperative.

Source Sustainability

Sources of water in the country include rainwater, snowfall, the river systems and groundwater. Rainfall in India is dependent largely on the southwest and northeast monsoons, on shallow cyclonic depressions and disturbances and on violent local storms. In India, the per capita average annual freshwater availability has reduced from 5177 cubic metres in 1951 to about 1869 cubic metres in 2001 and is estimated to further come down to 1341 cubic metres in 2025 and 1140 cubic metres in 2050. This is certainly going to be a cause of concern for all of us.

In our country, about 85 per cent of the drinking water systems are based on groundwater sources, which utilises only 5 per cent of the total groundwater extraction. The groundwater depletion has also aggravated deterioration of its quality due to excess fluoride, arsenic, iron and brackishness, in many parts of the country. This has compelled

PHE Departments, to either abandon low cost hand-pumps for adopting the costly and complicated piped water supply schemes or cumbersome treatment technologies or to exploit groundwater from different deeper depths.

The rapid and accelerated use of groundwater to meet competing demands from various sectors has led to an alarming decline in the groundwater level in many areas and consequent stress on groundwater resources. Tubewell and pump technology has been responsible for raising agricultural production and meeting the domestic and industrial water needs. Over-exploitation of groundwater and non-completion of surface water schemes have resulted in marked lowering of groundwater levels. The situation is grave in seven per cent of the country's area where the stage of groundwater depletion exceeds 85 per cent of the annual replenishable recharge. Besides, it has reached the critical stage in 11 per cent of the area where over 65 per cent of the groundwater is developed. The major impact may be seen in Rajasthan, Gujarat, Andhra Pradesh, Tamil Nadu, Karnataka, Madhya Pradesh, Orissa, Haryana, etc. In general, the demand for fresh water from different sectors has been growing against a finite available quantity, resulting in a scarcity situation spread over 1,203,863 sq. km in 1205 blocks of 223 desert and drought-prone districts. Further, a study shows that per capita availability of water, which was around 5000 cubic metres per year at the time of independence, has drastically fallen to 2000 cubic metres per year at present. Apart from the increasing mismatch in supply— demand scenario caused mainly due to rapidly growing population and ever increasing desire for higher levels of water supply, gross mismanagement of water resources, coupled with negligence of traditional systems and also the practice of collection and use of rainwater by individuals/ communities for their domestic use, further aggravated the situation in the form of falling water levels and its quality and prevalence of water-related diseases in these areas.

There is another problem inherent in such over-exploitation of underground aquifers. Chemicals such as fluoride, arsenic, salinity ingress along coastal areas and nitrate tend to rise beyond the permissible limit. This gets manifested in the form of various water-related diseases. All this notwithstanding, the rural drinking water supply agencies have concentrated their efforts on the exploitation of groundwater from different depths.

Since such rainwater harvesting systems are cost-effective, easy to build, operate and maintain by people/communities themselves, it offers a substitute as well as is complementary to existing water supply systems. Thus, rainwater harvesting including artificial recharge could be one of the solutions.

Attempts are also made by the Government of India to address the sustainability issue through initiating a Sub-Mission on sustainability for taking up projects of water conservation and rainwater harvesting under ARWSP/PMGY. Out of the 20 per cent fund earmarked under these programmes for Sub-Mission projects/ schemes, 25 per cent fund could be utilised for schemes on sustainability. In addition to this, the community may take up water harvesting/recharge activities to benefit drinking water sources under Swajaladhara programme.

There is a need to regulate the extraction of groundwater. A model bill to regulate and control the development of groundwater drafted by the Ministry of Water Resources was circulated to all the State Governments for enactment by their respective State Assemblies. But few states have adopted it.

System Sustainability

India being a vast country, the assets created are spread over a very wide area making it difficult or rather impossible for the government agencies to maintain them efficiently and effectively. The rural people consider these assets as government property and they refuse to own and maintain them thus rendering the assets unsustainable. The analysis reveals that the following major factors are responsible for system failure:

Lack of Users' Involvement

The rural water supply programme has so far been driven by a supply driven top down approach, entirely managed by government agencies like PHED/Water Boards in the form of purely engineering-based solutions and centralised decision-making bodies. There has been a lack of involvement of the community—the primary stakeholder—in the planning, choice of technologies, construction and management of the systems resulting in lack of ownership by the community towards the systems. In addition to this, the linkages with other potential partners, viz., local bodies, private sector, NGOs, local entrepreneurs, etc. have also been almost non-existent.

In fact, these systems were conceived and designed by a government department and were imposed on the end-users and generally executed with limited evaluation of the local requirements, preference of technology, its affordability and willingness to pay for the service. As such, selection, planning and design of the schemes do not take care of the financial affordability of users in terms of capital cost and recurring cost.

Poor Operation and Management (O&M)

Since the beginning of the programme, the government undertook responsibility of O&M neglecting community participation completely. This changed the perception of the rural people that water is a social good to be provided free of cost by the government, rather than a scarce resource that should be managed by local level institutions, as an economic asset. This 'dependency culture' has also been responsible for poor O&M. Business as usual, people were neither aware of the technological aspects nor its choice. Non-involvement of people in the design and implementation of projects often leads to use of sub-standard quality materials, poor workmanship and inadequate maintenance. The studies indicated that the people would be willing to maintain and operate the schemes when they:

- own the assets or share the cost as per their financial affordability;
- are involved in the process of selection and installation of schemes;
- are capable/trained to undertake simple repairs; and
- know the government will not maintain the asset and provide funds for it.

Slippage/Reverses of Coverage

It has been observed that once fully covered habitations are bouncing back to the partially covered or uncovered category and once partially covered ones becoming uncovered habitations. These habitations are reflected as covered but on the ground these may not last long as covered due to the following reasons other than sources going dry due to depletion of local groundwater level:

- Increase in population due to growth with passage of time.
- Systems outlived their life span or becoming defunct due to poor/non-maintenance.
- Disuse of sources due to quality deterioration, or over-drawal of water or other natural causes.

Inappropriate Selection of Technology

As on date, there is no mechanism in normal implementation of programmes that users/user groups make choice of technology/type of the scheme. This has resulted in adopting rarely user-friendly technology which is difficult to maintain. In most of the cases, these technologies were beyond the affordability and capacity of the community as far as capital cost or cost of O&M are concerned. Over the years, it developed a psyche disowning the whole system as "government system not to be touched." In case of any breakdown, the thinking was that the government agency is duty bound to correct it without any charge.

The only possible solution to make Rural Water Supply (RWS) schemes sustainable is to decentralise their planning implementation and O&M by making the beneficiaries and Panchayat stakeholders responsible for the assets. This would be possible only if the users are motivated enough to become owners of the facilities by sharing a part of the capital cost and also shoulder the full responsibility of creation of facilities and O&M. If active participation of stakeholders ensures system sustainability, scientific management of water resources contributes towards source sustainability by and large.

Financial Sustainability

Financial viability is essential for sustainable service delivery in the sector. An estimate shows that providing safe drinking water to all rural habitations in the country with a minimum satisfactory level of service would require an investment of about Rs. 450 billion. Further, at the present price, about Rs. 2000 crore per year would be required to keep the existing assets functional. The permissible O&M expenditure at this stage is only upto 15 per cent of the State and Centre funds put together. Hence, the resource gap between available funds and estimated total expenditure would work out to the tune of Rs. 1300 crore. In view of increasing constraints, it would be a difficult task for the government alone to mobilize such huge investment singlehandedly following a "supply driven" approach. Therefore, a productive and pro-active involvement of the user community and other stakeholders in resource mobilization and community participation in the implementation process as well as O&M of the systems has become imperative. To translate the above strategy into practice, it requires massive efforts to transform the prevailing mindset of the major partners—the users, community, PRIs, government agencies, NGOs, etc.

Field studies have shown that when users are involved in the process of planning and implementation, O&M of facilities, they are likely to be willing to pay for dependable water supply and they are confident that they will control the funds, which are collected for O&M.

A review of USAID and other donor literature relating to sustainability of development projects reveals that sustaining the long-term benefits of potable water supply projects requires successful action at all levels from the facility investment level to the regional water authority through the national government:

- At each water supply project or facility, steps must be taken to provide the capability for effective O&M. Efficient personnel with appropriate training must be obtained to manage and operate the facility. Systematic O&M procedures must be developed and followed. Necessary equipment and spare parts must be provided. Electric power must be reliably available.
- At the regional water authority and host country levels, action must be taken to ensure that the necessary institutional strength and financial resources to support O&M will be available over time. Some combination of user charge revenues and government subsidies must be developed to support the continued provision of potable water. This requirement is particularly difficult to meet in the Central Asian Republics because mechanisms for water pricing and cost recovery are limited and the economies are presently weak and depressed.

Institutional Sustainability and Policy Intervention

Institutional arrangements for implementation and delivery of services are critical from its sustainability point of view particularly with the community-based approach. The institutional arrangement may be adopted depending upon the local situation from Gram Panchayat System/VWSC, NGO with technical support needed from government at the local level. The institution's capability needs to be built-up properly for the success of the system. The local set-up of the institution should be up-linked with the district and State level department/institution responsible for monitoring the programme on behalf of the State Government. The district/state level departments should shoulder responsibility to disseminate the information of the latest developments and technologies elsewhere.

After the 73rd/74th Amendments to the Constitution of India, the subject of rural water supply was placed under the Panchayati Raj Institutions (PRIs—rural local bodies) making them responsible for it in their respective areas. The Government of India is supporting the process of empowerment and capacity building of the PRIs to enable them to discharge their responsibilities. In every village, Gram-Sabha, the general constitutional body of the village having all adult villagers as members, has to be fully involved in reviewing the implementation and management of drinking water systems and sources. However, there is need for adequate legislation to provide the basis for effective institutional arrangement for efficient and equitable water allocation and administration without overlaps/gaps to avoid confusion and jurisdictional uncertainties to facilitate consistent enforcement. It should also cover legislators to be well informed about water-related issues. Because water resource development and management is a highly specialised area, particular effort is required to present materials to decision-makers in a form that is easily used.

There is also need for an appropriate level of framework for inter-agency coordination particularly as competition for water increases and the fragmentation of responsibilities do exist supported with inadequate data collection, dissemination arrangement and weak coordination mechanisms on water-related issues. The World Bank, in its Review Report (1998), has made the following findings of much interest on India's Water Resources Management Sector:

(i) Water is becoming an increasingly scarce resource in India, its finite and fragile water resources are depleting, yet it continues to be used inefficiently on a daily basis in all sectors, while various sectoral demands are growing rapidly.

(ii) The current approach emphasises development of water resources and construction of new infrastructure under a top-down, supply-oriented and fragmentary framework.

(iii) The present institutional arrangement in India, including central, state and local institutions, and both formal and informal structures, do not enable comprehensive water allocation, planning and management.

(iv) Existing organisations, furthermore, lack the capacity in key management areas as well as effective mechanisms for implementation.

(v) Appropriate economic incentives for efficient water use and conservation are lacking on various levels, thereby impacting negatively on water provision and usage in these sub-sectors.

(vi) The absence of appropriate direct water pricing, and lack of adequate application of other economic and financial incentives at the sub-sector level has also served as an obstacle to the smooth transfer of water between sectors and states.

(vii) Supporting technological and informational systems to enable effective planning and management of water are also weak.

(viii) The current situation in water service delivery in India is, in general, characterised by a vicious circle of inadequate financial allocations to the sector (particularly for O&M) and inefficient and bloated service institutions, which have led to poor quality and unreliable services, user dissatisfaction with their services, and an unwillingness of users to pay for those services. The inadequate resources generated by the sector due to low prices and user unwillingness to pay for services further undermine sector financial resources contributing to a perpetuation of the circle. The end result is a sector that has become unsustainable.

(ix) The area types among water sectors (both rural and urban) areas due to the varied and desegregated institutional structures that make up the RWSS and UWSS sub-sectors within the states in India.

Further, the GWSS Assessment Report, 2000 identified similar sector constraints, viz., (i) financial difficulties, (ii) institutional problems, (iii) inadequate human resources, (iv) lack of sector coordination, (v) lack of political commitment, (vi) insufficient community involvement, (vii) inadequate O&M, (viii) poor water quality, (ix) insufficient information and communication and lack of hygiene education as equally applicable to India.

Acknowledging the necessity to involve local community or community-based organisation for sustainability of the systems, the following necessary elements are identified:

- Community mobilisation and capacity building,
- Community share in the capital investment,
- Community ownership and control,
- O&M and management by the community, and
- Dependable water source to meet community needs.

Government Initiatives—Sector Reform

Former President K.R. Narayanan (1998) said, "India today needs a people's movement to meet its water needs and to protect its water resources—encouraging a people's movement means a redefinition of everybody's role." Keeping this in view, the Government of India redefined the strategy in the drinking water supply sector and recognised it for reform to adopt community participation in RWS programme and launched the Sector Reform Project in districts in 1999 on a pilot basis and subsequently, Swajaladhara based on its principles was introduced in December 2002 in the country.

In order to achieve the desired goals, the Government of India had brought about policy changes by introducing reforms in the rural drinking water supply sector in 1999. A paradigm shift has been evolved in the sector, where the emphasis is on demand responsive approach, creation of awareness amongst the people, empowerment of local communities and ensuring their effective participation in the planning, choice of technological options, implementation, O&M and management of drinking water supply schemes.

Efforts are focused on the community's willingness to manage and operate the drinking water supply schemes for which they should have a feeling of ownership. A part of the capital cost (10 per cent) and full O&M cost is to be borne by the community. In this new approach, the Government's role is primarily that of a *facilitator* and *enabler* rather than a *financier* and *provider* of facilities. Presently, the pilot projects in 67 districts are in progress. With the issue of Swajaladhara Guidelines, the community may also take up water harvesting/water recharge activities benefiting drinking water supply sources after mobilising 10 per cent of the capital cost of the structure.

After experience gained and once the area specific models are developed through these pilot projects in the first phase, the models would be further perfected and replicated to the remaining districts of the country.

Recently, Prime Minister A.B. Vajpayee called for making water conservation a national mission and appealed for a collective address to the problem of water shortage, which is assuming critical proportions with every passing year, by conserving every drop of water and gave five valuable suggestions as under:

1. Let every household, colony, Panchayat and municipal body consider how to save and implement rainwater harvesting, water recycling and other measures.
2. Implement Central schemes like Swajaladhara and Hariyali and similar schemes of State governments.
3. All users of water should conduct a water audit to see how water can be saved. As a first step, he directed his office to implement a plan to achieve at least 10 per cent reduction in the usage of water.
4. Clean up polluted rivers, lakes and ponds. Measures to prevent pollution should be widely debated and acted upon.
5. Scientists should take up development of low-cost water-saving technologies as a major challenge.

Conclusion

Having achieved appreciable physical coverage of habitations with the water supply system through the normal "supply-driven" and "cent per cent Government funded" programme, it is now high time to reorient the programme-approach. The present water resources scenario is critical, especially the status of groundwater exploration and availability is causing a lot of concern. Apart from the severe threat to sustainability of the sources due to indiscriminate groundwater use, water quality problem has emerged as a major issue adding a new dimension. Taking into account all the constraints relating to proper management and conservation and protection of groundwater sources *vis-a-vis* the action needed to be taken at different levels, a multi-pronged integrated approach with a well conceived mix of professional, technical, administrative and legal aspects with a focus on "community-based-demand-responsive" approach would pave the way for making sustainable rural drinking water supply in the country.

REFERENCES

WHO-UNICEF-WSSCC (2000): *Global Water Supply and Sanitation Assessment, 2000*, Report.

World Development Indicators, 1998.

"India—Water Resources Management Sector Review—Initiating and Sustaining Water Sector Reforms," World Bank, 1998.

Barot, J.M., *"Sustainability of Rural Water Supply,"* 21st WEDC Conference Kampala, Uganda, (1995)

"Towards Conserving the Elixir of Life," India Toady, August 04, 2003.

"Guidelines for the Implementation of Rural Water Supply Programme," Ministry of Rural Development (GOI), New Delhi (2000).

"Guidelines for Implementation of Schemes and Projects on Sustainability Under ARWSP and PMGY—RWS," Ministry of Rural Development (GOI), New Delhi, (2002).

"Guidelines on Swajaladhara," Ministry of Rural Development (GOI), New Delhi (June 2003).

21

Drinking Water Supply to Villages

Dinesh Chand

Water is not only a physiological necessity for humans and animals but also essential for agricultural and industrial development and the growth of any country. From time immemorial, man has accepted water wherever he found it and used it advantageously. Many people in the world today still pursue this course. But with the advancement of science, all men were not forever satisfied with mere acceptance of available water and tried to make it more responsive to their needs. This was usually done to protect and enhance the quality and to improve accessibility and availability. At present, India has achieved significantly in respect of availability but accessibility still needs to be attended to.

In most of the Asian countries, the utilisation of water is 85 per cent for crop land for irrigation, eight per cent for industrial activities and seven per cent for domestic purposes. A significant portion of water is wasted with 70 to 80 per cent evaporating or seeping into the ground before reaching the crops.

The United Nation's populations projections indicate that India will be among the 34 countries of the world which are likely to face severe water shortage problems by the year 2025. As per estimates, the country's annual fresh water requirements (about 1050 billion cum) by that year will be almost at par with its exploitable water resources compared to the current demand of approximately 600 billion cum. Thus, additional supply of water will become necessary.

Rural Water Supply Status

Since the launching of the Rajiv Gandhi National Drinking Water Mission (RGNDWM) in 1986, the pace of coverage increased manifold. Over 95 per cent of the rural population in 13.96 habitations of the country (leaving only 44,000 habitations uncovered) now has access to drinking water with an investment of Rs. 180,000 million through installation of over three million hand pumps and 1.16 lakh piped water supply systems.

While the physical achievement has been impressive, the bacteriological and chemical contamination of drinking water sources posed a serious threat to public health. The nation-wide survey of habitations completed in 1994 showed that over 43.5 million people living in 1.42 habitations were at risk due to problems of drinking water quality like excess fluoride, arsenic, salinity, iron and chemical pollutants such as pesticides and insecticides.

In India, over 85 per cent of the drinking water sources in rural areas are based on groundwater aquifers. The surface water used for the Rural Water Supply (RWS) scheme was usually treated before being supplied to the community and water quality monitoring was carried out at the treatment plant site. Hence, regular water quality monitoring has been considered as an important priority by the RGNDWM.

Associated Health Hazards

The major hazards associated with water supplies are microbiological in nature, ". . . an estimated 80 per cent diseases and over one-third of the deaths in developing countries are caused by the consumption of water and, on an average, as much as one-tenth of each person's productive time is sacrificed to water-related diseases." (Chapter 18 of 'Agenda 21' of the U.N. Conference on Environment and Development).

Safe drinking water, together with sanitation, has a direct bearing on working conditions, health of the people and their optimum producing capacity.

In India, water-borne diseases such as gastro-enteritis, diarrhoea, dysentery, cholera, enteric fever, etc. are due to the presence of bacteria in drinking water. In addition to biological contamination, a variety of chemicals due to geo-climatic factors like fluoride, arsenic, nitrates and iron, when present in drinking water beyond permissible limits recommended by WHO and BIS led to serious health hazards.

Water from different sources in the villages, including bore wells, hand pumps and tubewells, are often found contaminated as the coliform and faecal conform counts are much above the prescribed values. Although tap water is chlorinated, few sources maintain hygienic standards despite the dependency of village communities on these sources. Diseases caused by microbial pathogens in drinking water are concentrated in the developing world and, within the developing world, among the poorer urban and rural households in the poor countries. Those at greatest risk are infants and young children, the sick and the elderly.

Infectious and parasitic diseases that are known to be transmitted through the presence of pathogens in drinking water include hepatitis A and E, cholera, typhoid, cryptosporidiosis, giardiasis, amoebic dysentery and dracuncrullasis (guineaworm).

The global burden of the main diseases and death (morbidity and mortality) from microbial contamination of our environment is given below:

Disease	*No. of Cases*	*Deaths*
Cholera	384,400	11,000
Typhoid	500,000	25,000
Giardiasis	500,000	Low
Ainoebiasis	48,000,000	110,000
Diarrhoeal diseases	4,002,000,000	3,115,000
Guineaworm	122,000	Low

Water Quality Monitoring

At present, water quality monitoring in rural areas is being handled by the PHED/Jal Nigam/Jal Sansthan boards. However, keeping in view the magnitude of the water problem in the country, there is ample scope for additional participation of the private sector, NGOs and other agencies.

In India, the States have different set-ups for water quality monitoring activities without Central supervisory mechanisms. In order to formulate linkages and to facilitate monitoring of the activities at various levels, significant work has to be done. However, a water quality surveillance system does not exist. At present, in most States, the following system of water quality monitoring is being followed:

- The chemist in-charge of the zonal/district laboratory organises the collection of samples and quality analysis.
- The chemist then submits reports to the Executive Engineer/ Senior Chemist of the district who is in-charge of the overall supervision of the work of the laboratories as well as the field operations.
- The Executive Engineer (PHE)/Senior Chemist submits monthly reports to the Chief Engineer and other concerned officials.
- The Chief Engineer (PHE) passes on the progress report to the RGNDWM.
- The data so generated is not systematically compiled and analysed by the States for the purpose of planning and future monitoring programmes of water quality.

Realising the importance of water quality monitoring and the need for creating an infrastructure for assuring it, the Mission had taken a policy decision in 1989-90 to establish district-level water quality testing laboratories in the country; 418 district-level water testing laboratories and 110 portable testing kits have been sanctioned to various States and Union Territories so far. In addition, over 100 such laboratories have also been established by the States from their own resources. It is expected that such a network of laboratories will help in effective water quality monitoring and prevent the use of contaminated water and diseases caused by contaminated water and hygienic conditions.

Establishing laboratories and prescribing water quality standards may perhaps provide only a partial solution to the problem. An effective WQM and S system depends on the infrastructure and institutions to ensure provision of safe drinking water conforming to quality standards on a sustainable basis.

The government agencies can only conduct the initial and occasional quality checks thereafter. However, to ensure that the water remains safe from the source to final consumption, it is essential that all the people involved in its handling are aware and careful in ensuring quality.

Water Quality Assurance

Adequate sanitary conditions, provision of microbiologically and chemically safe drinking water and sufficient quantity are the three main parameters of public health protection. These parameters are intertwined and no clear demarcation is possible. The water quality assurance programme should generally consist of two complementary components, namely, monitoring and surveillance.

Monitoring

Quality monitoring of drinking water supply involves sampling and testing of public supply sources at specific intervals to ensure that drinking water standards are maintained. In areas known for suspected groundwater quality problems, domestic wells/local sources may be included in the regular monitoring programmes.

In most developing countries, the actual sampling and laboratory analysis is generally carried out by the State water supply agencies. However, keeping in view the magnitude of the problem, lack of finance and trained personnel, the Government must create awareness in the community and NGOs must carry out sampling and water analyses through local institutions or using portable kits and communicate to the Government agencies for building up the necessary database/initiating action for protection of the sources from contamination, wherever required.

Unobserved contamination, which persists for a considerable period of time, may lead to extensive damage to the aquifer. When properly devised, the monitoring programmes should not only be cost effective, capable of detecting contaminants and defining the extent of contaminant plumes but should also be tailored to the site under study. The great diversity of conditions requires a separate evaluation of these factors for each site. Thus, the monitoring should include:

- Maintaining sustainability of an acceptable level of water quality of the aquifer which has been extensively developed for water use;
- Level of water quality of an aquifer in sand fill or other disposal facilities which has been extensively developed for water-use;
- Use of fertiliser and excessive irrigation resulting in return flow to a shallow groundwater table; and

- Salt water intrusion in coastal areas or ingress of salt water from entrapped connate water bodies in a developed aquifer.

Monitoring Goals

Before a bore/dug well is drilled and water sample taken and analysed, the groundwater monitoring specialist should clearly determine the goals to be accomplished. Typical goals might be one or more of the following:

- Meeting regulatory requirements;
- Determining site baseline groundwater quality and hydrologic conditions;
- Determining causes of groundwater quality problems occurring in certain areas;
- Determining the effect of a particular activity on the environment; and
- Determining regional groundwater quality trends and background groundwater quality.

The different goals mentioned above could be broadly categorised into two groups:

1. Monitoring for Management, and
2. Monitoring for Contaminant Determination.

Monitoring System Considerations

A detailed evaluation of a number of generic factors is needed for effective collection and analysis of water quality data. Some of the significant factors to be considered while deciding on the general scope of the monitoring systems are:

Constituents

1. Monitoring for natural chemical contamination due to the geo-chemical environment, movement and source of groundwater such as fluoride, sulphate, carbonate, nitrates, bicarbonates, calcium, magnesium, sodium, potassium and pH.
2. Monitoring contamination from fertilisers would require analysis of phosphate, nitrate and potassium and chloride.
3. Selected parameters related to sanitary-land fill contamination

may be pH, heavy metals, organic carbon, phenols, other ions, conductivity, etc. at different levels in the aquifer.

4. In the case of salt water intrusion, the measurement of conductivity at various depths would be the guiding factor.

Analytical Facilities

It is very important to have a well-equipped laboratory having trained personnel at district and block levels if, in a particular area, the endemicity of drinking water-related diseases are predominant.

Extent of Monitoring

Based on the preliminary information about the existing water supply system in a specified area and also the extent to which the sources are contaminated, the extent and frequency of monitoring required should be based on the following considerations:

1. To divide a region based on administration, physiography and priority considerations;
2. To identify and make preliminary ranking priority sources in each area which needs immediate attention; and
3. To examine the sources having greater potential to contaminate drinking water sources and determine what data and information already exist and what data and information are additionally needed and at what cost.

Surveillance

The surveillance of drinking water quality from the public health point of view involves mechanisation, management and a number of other activities including follow-up action to keep a constant vigil on the safety and acceptability of the drinking water supply. It is also an indispensable activity to ensure that the investment made and assets created through drinking water supply schemes promote and protect the health of the consumers.

The objective of drinking water quality surveillance is to identify the potential hazards and take preventive and control action to eliminate or minimise their impact on human health to acceptable levels. The surveillance is "a systematic approach to the identification, assessment, prevention and control of hazards associated with water supplies." In most countries, the principal risks to human health associated with small community water supplies are microbiological in nature.

Broadly, the surveillance concept comprises the following five principal steps:

- Identification of hazards and assessment of the severity of risks associated with the entire water supply system (source, treatment, distribution and use).
- Determination of critical control points at which the identified hazards can be eliminated, prevented or minimised.
- Specification of criteria that indicate whether or not the hazard has been controlled.
- Identification and implementation of appropriate corrective action.
- Establishment and implementation of procedures to monitor each critical control point to check that it is under control.

Surveillance will find out what is wrong and put matters right. It will also assist in developing more general activities, for example, operator's training and hygiene education for the public in the prevention of water-borne diseases, to promote the safety of water supplies.

Surveillance of drinking water quality is an uninterrupted and vigilant public health assessment and monitoring of drinking water supplied to the public. The key elements of a surveillance programme may include:

1. Monitoring,
2. Sanitary survey,
3. Data processing,
4. Evaluation,
5. Remedial and preventive action, and
6. Institutional analysis.

The surveillance programme may include the legislative and institutional basis for surveillance, strategies for its implementation, community participation, flow and use of information and the required human and financial resources.

Since the objective of surveillance is to protect human health, it should best be carried out through State health departments or district health officers. Surveillance agencies and water suppliers should, therefore, not be in competition with one another; rather they should make an effort to meet the common goal of improved water quality.

Strategy for Implementation

Once the surveillance plan has been developed, strategies for its implementation must be formulated. A basic concept that should be used in any country, rich or poor, is to determine the level of surveillance now existing, formulate a realistic surveillance programme suitable to the local situation, human and economic resources of the country and meet the specified objective, then moving on to the next higher surveillance stage.

A summary of these common activities is given below:

- Inventory of water supplies
- Involvement of communities
- Design forms for data collection
- Training
- Planning preliminary survey
- Undertake field work
- Collate and interpret results
- Promote improvement at critical points
- Report to suppliers/planners/consumers

Information Management

Adequate accurate record-keeping and documentation are essential to the application of surveillance. Clearly, the information collected by the surveillance agency is to be provided to the water supplier and should include, at the minimum:

- A summary of the quality of the service being provided and condition of the supply, and
- Identification of hazards and required corrective action.

Human Resource Development

The development of human resources by appropriate education and training to make water quality monitoring a success is an essential pre-requisite for all efforts of quality assurance and treatment technology. For this, a well planned programme for all personnel connected with the Water Quality Testing and Surveillance Programme, as well as involvement of the educational and scientific institutions, NGOs and voluntary agencies including women's groups, are essential components.

Community Participation

No programme is a success without the participation of the community which is the beneficiary. The role of women in health education and community participation is very vital. Thrust should be given to educate them on the health aspects. The main objective of such activities should be targeting to making people conscious about the importance of safe drinking water and its relation with health. Implementation of each of these activities requires planning, involvement of a number of institutions/organisations and co-ordination at different levels. The important role of rural women in this regard should also be considered because if they are convinced and empowered, they would be of great help in spreading the message.

Health education and community participation could be undertaken through the following means:

- Introduction in the curriculum of health workers, gram sewaks, agricultural extension workers, teachers, hand pump mechanics and other workers.
- Electronic and traditional media like models, newspapers, newsletters and posters in local languages, village camps, documentaries, video films, slides, pamphlets, etc. be developed for use of the general public and target groups.
- Community involvement in the form of labour and land donation and helping in maintenance of facilities should begin from the start of the programme.
- Inter-sectoral co-ordination between different departments, namely, Health, Agriculture, Rural Development Social Welfare, Education, Public Health Engineering and Zila Parishads should be established by involving their staff to carry out health education programmes.
- Introduction of special health education to school-going children and teachers.

These means should be used to convey the following messages:

1. Importance of personal and domestic hygiene to ensure potability at the users' end.
2. Education of drinking water standards.
3. Effect of different water quality parameters on the human body.
4. Knowledge of the necessary water treatment processes and monitoring.
5. Importance of integrating other programmes, namely, health education, water supply and water quality monitoring, environment, sanitation, etc.
6. Community participation in water quality programmes.

Inadequate sanitation will result in microbial contamination of the drinking water and food, leading to an increased number of carriers and cases. Person-to-person spread of diseases will result because of poor hygienic practices or ignorance about them. Microbial contamination of drinking water from its extraction till consumption is to be specially avoided because of its high degree of simultaneous infection in the community.

Conclusion

Water quality monitoring is an integral part of the programme to provide safe drinking water to the community. It determines the state of the system, both in terms of quality and quantity and provides the status of the water quality of the source at a particular location and enables us to gain a perspective on the long-term quality at selected sites.

Making the system function properly, however, will require continual development of the data to gain a better understanding of the statistical characteristics of water quality variables and the relationship between water quality and the hydrological cycle. Without this understanding, technicians/engineers would continue to be good at collecting data but not in using the data for understanding the valuable data it provides.

REFERENCES

"Guidelines for Drinking Water Quality," Vols. 1-3, Geneva: World Health Organisation, 1984.

"National Workshop on Water Quality and Surveillance in Rural Areas," Technical Papers, RGNDWM, M/O RAE, 1997.

"Programme of Action for Sustainable Development," United Nations Conference on Environment and Development (UNCED), Agenda 21, Chapter 18: *Protection of Quality and Supply of Freshwater Resources*, 1992.

"Sources and Nature of Water Quality Problems in Asia and the Pacific," New York: United Nations Report No. ST/ESCAP/1875, 1998.

Gorchev, H.G., "Global Perspectives on Surveillance and Control of Drinking Water Quality," Workshop on Water Quality and Surveillance in Rural Areas, 1997.

Kurukshetra, July 1999, Reprinted with permission.

22

Drinking Water Supply: Availability in Rural Areas

Dinesh Chand

Rural drinking water supply scheme is one of the important basic service schemes and is essential to sustain life. Presently, the States are solely responsible for its implementation and their efforts are supplemented by the Centre through financial and technical assistance under the Accelerated Rural Water Supply Programme (ARWSP).

The Government of India introduced a national water supply and sanitation programme in the social sector way back in the year 1954. The financial assistance was also provided in the Fourth Five Year Plan to carry out identification of the problem villages (PVs). Later on, to accelerate the pace of coverage of PVs, the Centre introduced ARWSP in 1972-73 to assist the States and Union Territories with 100 per cent grants-in-aid and continued it till 1973-74. With the introduction of the Minimum Needs Programme (MNP) under the State Sector during the Fifth Five Year Plan (from 1974-75), ARWSP was withdrawn. However, it was reproduced in 1977-78 to focus coverage of identified PVs.

Surveys have been conducted to identify PVs in the country in 1972, 1980 and 1985. To expedite the coverage by providing at least one source within these villages during the International Water Supply Decade (1980-90), a Mission was launched called "Technology Mission on Drinking Water Management," by setting up "National Drinking Water Mission (NDWM)" which was one of the five Societal Missions in 1986. It was renamed as Rajiv Gandhi National Drinking Water Mission (RGNDWM), in 1991.

The National Policy, guiding the rural water supply (RWS) sector today, is contained in the Eighth Five Year Plan (VIIIth Plan, 1992-97), which states, "Safe drinking water supply and basic sanitation are vital human needs for health and efficiency (given that) death and disease, particularly of children, . . . and the drudgery of women are directly attributable to the lack of these essentials.' High priority was given to the coverage of villages without safe water supply or in which supply is less than 10 litres per capita per day (Ipcd) and to improve the level of service for villages which fall between 10 and 40 Ipcd. The VIIIth Plan also stressed on the following points:

(i) Water should be managed as a commodity in the same manner as any other resource;
(ii) The delivery of water services should be based on the principle of effective demand and should correspond to the standard of service that users are willing to maintain, operate and finance;
(iii) Local bodies (i.e., Panchayati Raj Institutions) should be responsible for operating and maintaining the system installed;
(iv) Local bodies should be free to levy and raise appropriate user charges for drinking water and sanitation services, undertaking operations and maintenance, if not further investment, and be self-sustaining;
(v) The private sector should be encouraged to construct and maintain schemes to the maximum extent feasible, and
(vi) Appropriate links should be forged between water supply and environmental sanitation.

These points address the challenges that have emerged in the sector. Moreover, the VIIIth Plan specifically emphasized the desirability of adopting an integrated approach in planning and implementation, which entailed the provision of primary health care, potable water, women's welfare, immunisation and sanitation facilities, all in collaboration with local administrations and user communities. Technical support to local administrations and user communities were to be provided by district departments.

The programme approach envisaged for the VIIIth Plan period was also continued in the IXth Five Year Plan (1998-2003). During this

Plan, strategies revolved around the following three distinct but interrelated issues:

(i) Accelerating coverage of the remaining uncovered habitations,
(ii) To promote sustainability of water supply systems and sources and to institutionalise water quality monitoring and surveillance, and
(iii) To institutionalise community participation in terms of capital and recurring cost sharing, planning, implementation, maintenance, etc.

Accordingly, the existing normative criteria has been modified in terms of allocation of Central assistance to States. Private sources within villages, which have access to the general public, were considered for the purpose of coverage in addition to public sources. A dual water supply concept is adopted for providing safe water for drinking and cooking, and chemically contaminated water can be used for other purposes in quality-affected areas. From the financial year 1999-2000, 67 districts have been identified for institutionalizing community participation in RWS programme (i.e., Sector Reform Concept) on a pilot scale with the assumption that replication would proceed after successful development of models in the country. A sum of 20 per cent of the total central funds (ARWSP) has been earmarked for this.

Table 1: Progressive Coverage of Problem Villages (PVs)

Year	*Problem Villages*	
	Identified	*Covered*
1972-80	1,53,476	94,000
1980-85	2,31,000* (Start of VIth Plan)	1,92,024
1985-90	1,62,000*	1,59,000
1990-92	3000 (Start of VIIth Plan)	—

*Including spillover from the preceding Plan.

To enhance the service level, the norms for implementation of ARWSP have been relaxed recently to allow a provision of 55 ipcd of drinking water with a source within 1/2 km in the plains and 50 metres elevation in the hills for the States which have achieved full coverage as per existing norms. These relaxations are subject to adherence of the principles of community participation through partial capital cost sharing (minimum 10%) and shoulder full responsibilities for subsequent operation and maintenance.

"An estimated 80 per cent of all diseases and over one-third of deaths in developing countries are caused by the consumption of contaminated water, and on an average as much as one-tenth of each person's productive time is sacrificed to water-related diseases," as indicated in Chapter 18 of "Agenda 21" of the UN Conference on Environment and Development (UNCED).

The status of coverage of rural habitations as on 1 April, 2002 is: (i) fully covered: 1,273,133, (ii) partially covered: 133,513, and (iii) not covered: 16,018. Thus, over 99 per cent of rural habitations have access to drinking water facilities having about 38 lakh hand pumps and 12 lakh piped water supply schemes installed. Obviously, the massive investments made during various Plans by the State and Central Governments resulted in quite impressive physical coverage. Table 1 shows that a large number of villages were identified as "Problem villages" during surveys conducted in 1972, 1980 and 1985. The identified PVs, all except 3000, were covered with at least one source of water supply till the beginning of the Eighth Plan (1992-97).

A massive survey of all rural habitations in the country to identify the status of drinking water supply and quality problems was carried out by the States/UTs during 1991-93 and validated by the Centre in 1994. The salient changes are as follows:

- For the first time, the unit of coverage was taken as a habitation/ mohalla/basti instead of a Census village to get a micro-level picture.
- The concept of partial coverage was introduced to assess the total availability of drinking water. The norm fixed for full coverage as provision of 40 Ipcd of safe drinking water from a public source within a distance of 1.6 km or on differential elevation of 100 m.
- The survey data revealed that 1,40,975 habitations (10.69%) remained NC and 4,30,377 as PC as on 1.4.1994. It was further indicated that 5.26 per cent of rural population did not have any public water source as per the norms.
- As many as 2.17 lakh habitations had water quality problems,

taking into account the subsequent coverage during succeeding years and updated further in June 2001.

Table 2: Coverage of Rural Habitations

Type of coverage	*No. of habitations*	*%age of total habitations covered*
Total	1,422,664	—
Fully covered (FC)	1,275,695	89.67
Partially Covered (PC)	131,052	9.21
Not Covered (NC)	15,917	1.12

An estimated amount of Rs. 38,000 crore has been invested by the Centre together with State governments for the rural drinking water facilities so far. Table 2 shows the status of coverage of rural habitations with drinking water facilities as on 31-07-2002.

This coverage may be true only at a given point and may vary on other times due to:

1. Unprecedented growth of population in certain habitations, particularly those nearer to urban areas,
2. Excess drawal of groundwater resulting in rapid depletion of water table,
3. Because of reason (2) above certain bores drilled in the past years may yield less or become dry, as they were drilled to shallower depths or outlived their life span, particularly more than 12 years old, and
4. Inconsistent rain and successive drought years are aggravating the situation due to lack of sufficient recharge of groundwater or lack of recharged water measures.

Thus, many habitations are bound to change from FC to PC habitations or PC to NC habitations. The settlements (mostly STs) and new colonies in and around urban and semi-urban areas are also adding up to the number of new habitations year by year.

Further, variations in groundwater levels are also causing changes in water quality resulting in increase of "No Safe Source (NSS)" habitations. The status with regard to slippage/reversal of coverage from FC to PC, PC to NC habitations and PC to NSS (quality affected) is not accounted for in the coverage. Table 3 shows the status of water quality habitations as reported by the States.

The Central outlay for the Rural Water Supply Sector for 2002-03 is Rs. 2235 crore.

Sustainable development can only take place when we use the resources for our needs and not for our greed as Mahatma Gandhi once said. The United Nations' population projections indicate that India will be among the 34 countries of the world, which are likely to face severe water shortage problems by the year 2025.

Being a tropical country, India is fortunately getting an average precipitation of about 4000 billion m^3 (BCM). Nearly three-fourth of it is, however, lost as run-off to the sea and remaining about 1000 billion m^3 is available as ground and surface water for use. It is estimated that by 2025 the total water requirement will exceed the available water resources. There are, however, vast spatial and temporal variations in the precipitation. About one-third of the county's area is thus drought prone. Some areas of the country are affected by excess salinity, fluoride, nitrate and arsenic in the groundwater and microbial contamination making it unfit for human consumption. The quality of water is also facing problem due to large fertilizer use, and poor solid waste management.

Table 3: Status of Quality Problem Habitations

Nature of Quality Problem	*No. of Affected Habitations*
Excess Fluoride	36,988
Excess Arsenic	3,553
Excess Salinity	32,597
Excess Iron	138,670
Excess Nitrate	4,003
Other reasons	1,400
Total	217,211

Almost 85 per cent of rural drinking water needs are met from groundwater, although only 5 per cent of total groundwater extraction is needed for domestic water supply while irrigation accounts for 90 per cent and industry takes the remaining 5 per cent. The rapid development in groundwater-based irrigation in many States has caused groundwater depletion, because of which the life of the drinking water supply source becomes short. Highly subsidised irrigation electricity tariffs have led to an indiscriminate and disproportionate level of groundwater extraction.

State-wise evaluation of groundwater development indicates that Punjab, Haryana, Tamil Nadu, Rajasthan, Gujarat and parts of Uttar Pradesh register a high to very high level to development ranging between 45 to 94 per cent of the annual recharge. The report on "Ground Water Resources of India" categorised 249 units out of 5683 units (blocks, taluks, mandals and watersheds) in the country as "over-exploited" (level of development being more than 100 per cent of recharge), 179 under "dark" category (level of development between 85 to 100 per cent of the recharge) and 595 under "gray" category (level of development between 65 to 85 per cent of the recharge).

The present requirement for rural water supply is at the rate of 40 LPCD for human population and with an additional 30 LPCD for livestock in desert areas. This level of water supply works out approximately to 30 BCM. Taking into account the population growth, demand of water supply connection to houses, the projected demand by 2025 at 70 LPCD for drinking water supply, including provision of 30 LPCD for livestock population in the DDP areas, works out to 52 BCM.

Recently, it has been noticed that groundwater depletion has aggravated water quality problems due to excess fluoride, arsenic and brackishness in certain areas, forcing the Public Health Engineering departments to abandon low cost hand pump-based systems and to undertake costly and complicated piped water supply schemes. The need for regulating the extraction of groundwater arises from the following considerations:

- Protection of resource against over-exploitation;
- Protection of resource against quality degradation; and
- To ensure social equity and to guarantee minimum provision to all sections of society.

In order to assess the actual scenario with regard to the quality problem, the State governments have started to carry out a 5-10 per cent stratified sampling survey, taking the block as a unit. On identification of the quality affected blocks, 100 per cent survey of the sources in those blocks would be carried out.

New Initiatives

A detailed review analyzing the reasons for recurring slippage in the status of coverage revealed that among various factors responsible for the slippage, a Government-oriented supply-driven approach without community involvement is the most critical one. Further, the free supply of water, though a fundamental social right, has also made the community ignore the scarcity value of potable water. It was also found that the per-capita monthly charges for operation and maintenance of hand-pumps and piped water supply is well within the affordable limit of even poorer sections of society. In view of the above and in the context of the 73rd and 74th amendments of the Constitution empowering the Panchayati Raj Institutions, the Government of India, ushered in sectoral reforms in the rural drinking water supply on a pilot basis. The salient features of the reforms are:

- Demand responsive approach;
- Peoples' participation right from planning unto monitoring;
- Cost recovery;
- Transparency in the entire process; and
- Promotion of a sense of ownership amongst the users.

In order to ensure long-term sustainability of the sources and systems, the Government of India has introduced reforms in the RWS sector which, *inter-alia,* envisages institutionalization of community-based rural water supply systems by incorporating the following basic principles for ensuring peoples' participation: (i) adoption of a demand-driven responsive and adaptable approach of villagers to ensure their full participation and ownership in the project in the choice of scheme design, implementation, control of finances and management arrangements through software activities like IEC and HRD, (ii) shifting the role of the Government from direct service provider to that of facilitator; and (iii) partial capital cost (10%) sharing either in cash or kind or both and 100 per cent responsibility of operation and maintenance by the end-user. Sixty-seven districts in 26 States all over the country have been identified for implementing this concept on a pilot basis. These projects, based on an integrated approach, aims at tackling the major issues of sustainability of the sources and systems and degradation of water quality.

The National Agenda for Governance of the Government of India stipulates that safe drinking water should be provided to all habitations on a sustainable basis by 2004. In order to achieve this objective, it is necessary to adopt prioritization on the following pattern: (i) Highest priority to be given to ensure coverage of remaining NC habitations with sustainable supply of safe drinking water; (ii) coverage of PC and quality affected habitations with safe drinking water on a sustainable basis and to institutionalize water quality monitoring and surveillance systems; and (iii) the SC/ST population and other weaker sections to be given priority while ensuring coverage of NC/PC habitations.

In view of the above and to regulate and develop groundwater resources in a scientific manner, it is high time to press State governments for enactment of legislation.

Conclusion

It is obvious that the physical coverage has been impressive under normal "supply driven" with 100 per cent funded and free supply programme by the Government. However, the ground situation has not been so good as expected from this achievement. Thus, it is now envisaged by the Central Government that these programmes should be reoriented towards "community-based demand responsive approach" as soon as possible. Basically, this approach aims that the community would get ownership and empowerment to shoulder the responsibilities of taking up their choice of schemes not only for water supply but also revolutionise the total developmental activities on a long-term sustainable basis in rural areas. However, the water resources scenario presents a rather critical picture, especially the status of groundwater development and availability is causing a bit of concern. Apart from the severe threat to sustainability of the sources due to indiscriminate groundwater development, quality problem in drinking water emerging as major issues has added a new dimension to the problems in the sector. Taking into account all the constraints relating to proper management and protection of groundwater source *vis-a-vis* the action needed to be taken at different levels, a multi-pronged integrated approach with a well conceived mix of professional, technical, administrative and legal steps and with emphasis on community sensitization and empowerment would pave the way for achieving the cherished goal of a demand responsive, community-based, rural drinking water supply in the country on a sustainable basis.

REFERENCES

"Groundwater Resources of India," Central Groundwater Board, Ministry of Water Resources (1995).

"List of 'dark' and 'gray' Blocks," National Bank for Agriculture and Rural Development, Mumbai (1997).

Report of the National Commission for Integrated Water Resources Development, Volume-I (1999), Ministry of Water Resources, Government of India.

Dublin International Conference Statement on Water and Sustainable Development, World Metereological Organisation, Geneva (1992).

Guidelines for Implementation of Schemes and Projects on Sustainability under Accelerated Rural Water Supply Programme (ARWSP) *and Prime Minister's Gramodaya Yojana* (PMGY-2001).

WHO-UNICEF-WSSCC (2000): *Global Water Supply and Sanitation Assessment,* 2000 Report.

"Guidelines for the Implementation of Rural Water Supply Programme," Ministry of Rural Development (GOI), New Delhi (2000).

Tripathi, S.K. and Kumar, Anil (2000), *Rural Water Supply Programme in India: People's Participation in Drinking Water Supply; Sector Reforms; the Emerging Scenario,* Government of India, New Delhi.

"Annual Report, 1994-95," Ministry of Rural Development, Government of India, New Delhi.

23

Solar Photovoltaic Water Pumping System for Drinking Water Supply

P.R. Singh and R. Prasad

Water is a critical need for most human activities like household use, agriculture and industrial operations. In developing countries such as India, the bulk of the population lives in rural and remote areas with no access to clean and safe drinking water. Generally, natural surface water sources have provided the bulk of the water for rural area requirements. However, over the years, due to overuse, these sources have become scarce and contaminated. It is difficult to depend on groundwater sources in areas where there is no grid connectivity and groundwater aquifers are deep. Solar Photovoltaic (SPV) water pumping system, that use power generated by photovoltaic conversion process using solar energy, is an alternative solution for providing water in such areas. The pumping systems have an application in far-flung villages and arid areas. Adoption of the SPV system applications is in its infancy and social acceptance is crucial for further developing the programme as well as defining implementation strategies.

The present case study analyses parameters that highlight the sustainability of the services of a SPV pump and its suitability to a region devoid of piped water supply as well as proper electricity. The results make a positive case for the pumping systems through a case study of a 900 Wp capacity pump installed in village Harpalpur of District Sultanpur in Uttar Pradesh. The pump provides water for domestic use to a population of 410 human and 202 cattle heads. The beneficiaries' views on its performance and impact have also been detailed.

Hand pumps, open wells and ponds are still the major sources of drinking water for domestic use in rural areas and are often unhygienic and unsafe. Recently the SPV pumping systems have been introduced which has proved to be an effective choice in the rural context. Due to higher cost, lack of knowledge about the utility of this option and maintenance facilities, the technology has yet to take off. Hence, the significance of the technical and socio-economic feedback in popularizing the SPV system has been realised. The Energy and Resources Institute (TERI) attempted to gather the techno-social perspective of the beneficiaries on the performance of a 900 Wp SPV pump installed in the village.

The entire study area gets optimum sunlight almost throughout the year. That provides an opportunity to introduce a SPV pump as a viable alternative for providing water in the village, which is also a non-polluting and thus environment friendly choice.

Project Area

Jagdishpur block is situated in Sultanpur district of Uttar Pradesh. Sultanpur district is located at the south-east of Lucknow. The district is surrounded by Bara Banki and Faizabad districts in the north, Jaunpur and Azamgarh in the east and Rai Bareli in the west. Jagdishpur town is 85 km away from the state capital, Lucknow. The block is densely populated and mainly rural in character and the main occupation is agriculture. These 56 per cent families are below the poverty line, economically backward and the literacy level is low. The size of land holdings is small and most of the farmers are marginal or small farmers. The land under forests is almost negligible with only 0.4 per cent area under forests.

The population of 570 (79 households) covers an area of 199 hectares. The major community in the village is Hindu and very few households are of Muslims. The major occupation is primarily agriculture-based. Almost half of the houses are electrified but the supply is highly erratic and voltage is often low. The village draws water from open wells and handpumps (Table 1). A scheme for supplying pipe water was commissioned but has been running dry for years.

Table 1: Water Sources in Village Harpalpur

Village	*Open Wells (No.)*	*Hand pumps (No.)*
Harpalpur	6	42

In both the systems in the village (handpumps and wells) water is lifted manually. At the time of study, there was no clean and safe source of drinking water for the village cattle. The existing sources were not sufficient to meet the needs of both humans and animals. During the rainy season, water in the wells was muddy or turbid and infested with human and household waste. The contamination makes the water a carrier of water-borne diseases like typhoid, dysentery and cholera. In a situation of scarcity of water, the cattle were being taken to the nearby stream for drinking and washing. In recent years, the discharge of toxic material from the Jagdishpur industrial units into the stream is also posing a threat to the cattle. Consequently, some animals have perished. Hence, it was felt necessary to provide safe water to the villagers for domestic use. In such a situation solar water pumping emerges as a viable option to get safe drinking water to them.

Village Selection

The first step of implementation is the planning process. The district has almost 2500 villages located in 22 blocks. Due to a very large number of villages, Jagishpur block was selected for this study. From within the block again few villages were short-listed that are in the proximity of village Lakhnipur where TERI has worked in the past. As a result of this past association, and good rapport with the villagers, the response was forthcoming. Detailed information was collected through group discussions and interviews with key persons, such as the Panchayat Sarpanch.

The study was conducted with an objective to evaluate the performance of the SPV pump and observe its social impact on the users. For achieving this, a household level primary survey was carried out after one year of the installation of the pump. The sample households were selected on the basis of distance from the location of the pump.

Solar Pump Project

The solar pump activity in Jagdishpur is part of a project "village level implementation of energy efficient interventions in Jagdishpur block," UP. The project, sponsored by the Bharat Petroleum Corporation Ltd. (BPCL), is being implemented by TERI. The pump was installed in April 2000.

During the implementation stage, programmes were organized to educate school students, panchayat members and block level government officials of Jagdishpur block regarding local energy and environment issues and technologies promoted in the project. It is hoped that successful demonstration of the technologies and creation of local knowhow in technical and managerial aspects of these technologies, will help in propagation of technologies in future in Jagdishpur block with minimum external assistance.

Water Demand

Assuming that the minimum daily requirement per head for human and livestock is 60 and 45 litres respectively, the total demand in the village for potable water was computed to be about 30,000 to 35,000 litres. The demand may rise during summer, festivals, marriages or social functions. Therefore, it was decided to install a pump, which could pump at least 10 per cent more than the present demand. So the water demand in the village was estimated to be approximately 38,500 litres per day.

Harpalpur requires potable water to feed 410 human and 202 cattle heads. Since there was no potable water storage facility inside the village, the livestock was forced to consume industrial wastewater flowing almost within one kilometre from the village. This often caused diseases to animals and sometimes proved fatal. In response to this, a submersible pump of 900 Wp was installed which could pump 50,000 litres of water per day. This system would work upto a total height of 100 ft. The discharge from the pump would vary with the intensity of the sunrays from morning till evening. It would be maximum around noontime.

Site Selection

Selection of a suitable site for installing the solar pump was considered on the basis of parameters that are important for long time functioning. The parameters included easy approach to maximum households in the village. Safety from theft, breakage, animals and felling of any tree and path of the village cattle were also considered. Identifying the common land was an important criterion for installing the solar pump in Harpalpur. Accordingly, a site was selected which lies in the main village way and is easily approachable from all households. The water table of an open well varies from 20 ft during winter and more than 25 ft in summer. This site was located in Harpalpur at a distance of 5 km from the block headquarter, Jagdishpur.

The shadow free 10 m × 10 m site was finalised after several rounds of meetings and discussions with villagers. It was also decided that the land ownership for the site should stay with the village panchayat to avoid any conflict in the future.

Installation

During installation of the solar pump, meetings were called in the primary stage to know the willingness of the residents of the village. The potential benefits were discussed. Some villagers were already aware of the solar pump because they had seen the solar pump in the nearby village of Lakhnipur. A positive response was received from all the villagers.

The solar pumps were installed in the village after the completion of boundary wall and the preparation of borewell. A 900 Wp SPV pumping system installed in the village was supplied by the Central Electronic Limited (CEL), Sahibabad, Uttar Pradesh. The technical specifications are given in Table 2.

A storage tank of 5000 litres capacity and a trough for animals to drink water were also constructed, attached to the pump. The discharge from the pump is first released to the storage tank and then taps have been raised out from it so that water can be used for drinking, bathing and for delivery to the animal trough. The animal trough is also connected through an overflow pipe of the tank. This tank provides water after sunset. A bathing area was also constructed and for the safety of the system, a boundary wall was constructed.

Peoples' Participation

The villagers wanted to develop a water source as there was an acute shortage of potable water. Moreover, they now had access to the new technology. They not only donated labour during the installation but also provided financial support for the construction of the site. Though an engineer from the system supplier guided the installation, the villagers prepared the site, dug the borewell, installed the pump and constructed the storage tank, water trough, bathing area as well as the boundary wall. An experienced electrician did the series-parallel connection of the solar modules.

Table 2: Technical Specifications of the Installed System

Components	*Technical Specifications*
Solar Module	900 Wp (24 modules, each of 37.5 Wp)
Capacity of Motor	0.75 HP
Make of Pump	Submersible, Grundfos make
Suction Head	Upto 30 M water level
Water Discharge	50,000 litres per day

The villagers played an active role throughout the project. The pump and the facilities are treated as a common property of the village and are managed by the village panchayat. It is worth mentioning here that the involvement of the people is crucial in the achieving desired results in such human endeavour.

Operation and Maintenance

The proper management of the SPV pumping system is necessary for effective delivery of services. A study carried out by the Administrative Staff College of India (ASCI), Hyderabad showed that about 24 per cent of the solar pumps surveyed were found to be non-functional at the time of study. The survey also indicated that about 19 per cent of the users were not satisfied with the performance of installed solar pumps, due to lack of maintenance, non-availability of spare parts, lack of awareness of technology among the users, etc. (MNES, 2001-02).

To avoid failure on all accounts, the village panchayat has been made responsible for the following activities of the SPV system and associated facilities:

- Management of fund in case of repairs;
- Proper operation of the system;
- Security of the system; and
- Guarding against misuse.

For routine operations and maintenance, a local person was deputed by the village panchayat. The person was trained to operate, repair and clean the modules and adjust their orientation, etc. The person has been provided with some spare parts to undertake minor repairs.

Users' Perspective

The people have opined that the solar photovoltaic pump requires minimal maintenance and is easy to operate. The SPV pump operates on freely available solar energy. This saves diesel and electricity expenditure and there is no fear of power cuts or scarcity of diesel. Unlike a diesel pumpset, it does not produce noise and pollution. The pump is easy to operate and handle. The cost of operation and maintenance is negligible.

The system performed satisfactorily throughout the first year. In summer, the output did not decrease because of the submersible pump. Initially in the power switch, MCV used to get burnt, and had to be replaced.

Social Impact

During festivals or family gatherings, the pumping system proves extremely beneficial and essential. For social functions, water collection as well as storage was one of the major time-consuming activities. It was often considered one of the major concerns. People felt that the SPV pump has relieved them of the pressure, besides providing them the required water. Moreover, they could utilize their time for more productive activities. Also they could enjoy social gatherings and participate meaningfully.

In summer, the demand as well as scarcity of water rises, adding to the drudgery of women in fetching water. The most important tangible benefit that people identified was the easy availability of water throughout the year. About 55-60 households of Harpalpur village are regularly fetching water from the SPV pump. Especially, the women appreciated that it was easier for them to fetch water for domestic use and the pump had reduced their drudgery drastically. In fact, some women have started washing utensils and clothes close to the pump site. Men and children enjoy taking bath at the facility created for the purpose.

As the water storage tank provides water during non-sunshine hours also, people are increasingly becoming dependent on the facility. It was observed that due to the continuous availability of water, the users living close to the installation site have developed a preference of fetching water from the pump as compared to traditional water sources.

According to villagers, the water trough has become a boon for livestock. The impact of the solar pump was judged from the fact that cattle are now habituated to drinking water from the trough whenever they are on way to and while returning from the grazing fields. Villagers have reported that cattle prefer the trough and now sometimes refuse to take water during stall-feeding. Having realized the potential benefits, the villagers are planning to clean/maintain a pond, which is near the pump for bathing cattle in summer.

The solar pump is a cheaper option in the long-term, compared to other sources like diesel pump, or the conventional rural water supply scheme. Perhaps the most significant gain from the success of the project is the high technological awareness generated amongst villagers. The installed pumping system in Harpalpur is serving as a demonstration of the technology for the Jagdishpur area. Impressed by the performance of the pump and its benefits, the inhabitants of the nearby villagers have started demanding similar systems in their villages.

Conclusion

A SPV pump was installed for drawing potable water in village Harpalpur, which was devoid of adequate and safe drinking water. The study revealed that the villagers accepted the installation and the site is serving as a positive demonstration of technology in the Jagdishpur block area. The SPV pumping system has been established as a viable alternative for providing potable water for domestic use. The study further highlighted that the sustainability of a SPV system may be ensured by developing proper understanding of the technology among users, providing repair as well as maintenance facility and establishing a successful demonstration.

The villagers learnt about the technology, contributed physically as well as financially for the installation and owned the responsibility of managing the system. This is an example of a ground reality that reflects a sense of community ownership. Though certain technical support by a repair unit was sought, the villagers were satisfied with the performance of the pump, which yielded water almost throughout the year. The beneficiaries appreciated the features like easy availability of water, especially during festivals and functions, reduction in drudgery of women and provision of water beyond the sunshine hours, etc. An enhanced inclination of preferring the SPV pump for fetching water, over the traditional sources was observed in the study area. Finally, it may be noted that such locally suited and need-based technological choices can make a difference in peoples' lives.

REFERENCES

Ministry of Non-Conventional Energy Sources (MNES), Annual Report, 2001-02.

Implementing Water Supply and Distribution System in Village Lakhnipur, Report submitted to Round Table 16 of Den Helder, the Netherlands, 1997.

Solar Photovoltaic Borewell Water Pumping in Lakhnipur, *Sun Power,* Vol. 5, No. 1, pp. 25-28, March 1999.

Solar Photovoltaic Pump: Alternative Option for Rural Water Demand, *Kurukshetra,* January 2000.

Implementation of Energy Efficient Technologies in Selected Villages of Jagdishpur, District Sultanpur, U.P. (Report No. 98RE62)

Part III

PARTICIPATORY WATERSHED MANAGEMENT

24

Participatory Watershed Management

S.S. Khanka and Anjan Bhuyan

Watershed management is an evolving concept in India basically associated with the proper storage and re-harvesting of rain run-off by appropriate management of natural and man-made watersheds. The approach to watershed management is participatory in nature; people friendly, location specific, process-based and geared to cater to the problems and needs of the local/rural communities. It requires that all stakeholders in watershed management—including users, policy-makers, researchers and others— recognize that participation is not simply another way to deliver the same technological solutions. Participation, in fact, implies that the stakeholders will willingly and enthusiastically work together to set criteria for sustainable management, identify priority constraints, evaluate possible solutions, recommend technologies and policies, and monitor and evaluate the impacts on the watershed.

I. Watershed and Watershed Management

A watershed is a geographic unit that collects, stores and releases water. Collected water comes in the form of rain, snow and in coastal fog. It is stored in lakes, ponds and sub-surface soils and geologic formations. Rivers and streams, as well as groundwater flow, then release this water. Watersheds are based on the geography of the area. A watershed is the land area where water flows across on its

Reprinted with permission, *Kurukshetra*, July 2006, pp. 12-16.

way to a creek, stream, wetland, pond, lake or river. Watersheds are also referred to as drainage basins or catchments because they "drain" and "catch" rain and snowmelt water that falls onto the land. Watersheds are defined as a location. For example, a watershed can be defined as the area contributing to a farm pond, or to lake contributing to the Platte River at its mouth. The boundaries of a watershed are determined by the elevation of the surrounding land, with the highest elevation points marking the boundary. (Fig. 1)

Based on the size, shape and land-use pattern of locations, watersheds are categorized into different groups. The categorization could also be based on the size of the stream or river, the point of interception of the stream or the river and the drainage density and its distribution. The All India Soil and Land Use Surveys (AIS&LUS) of the Ministry of Agriculture, Government of India, have developed a system for watershed delineation like water resource region, basin, catchments, sub-catchments, and watershed. The usually accepted five levels of watershed delineation based on the geographical area of the watershed are:

(1) Macro-watershed (> 50,000 hect)
(2) Sub-watershed (10,000 to 50,000 hect)
(3) Milli-watershed (1000 to 10,000 hect)
(4) Micro-watershed (100 to 1000 hect)
(5) Mini-watershed (1-100 hect)

A watershed could be described as fan-shaped (near circular) or fan-shaped (elongated). Hydrologically the shape of the watershed is important because it controls the time taken for the runoff to concentrate at the outlet. Watersheds may also be categorized as hill or flat watersheds, humid or arid watersheds, red soil watershed or black soil watershed based on criteria like soil, slope, climate, etc. Depending on the land-use pattern, a watershed could again be classified as highland watersheds, tribal settlements and watersheds in areas of settled cultivation.

Watershed management is an alternative process of integrated decision-making regarding uses and modifications of lands and water within a watershed. It is a typical form of ecosystem management, which includes the entire watershed system, from uplands to headwaters, to wetlands and river channels. It focuses on the

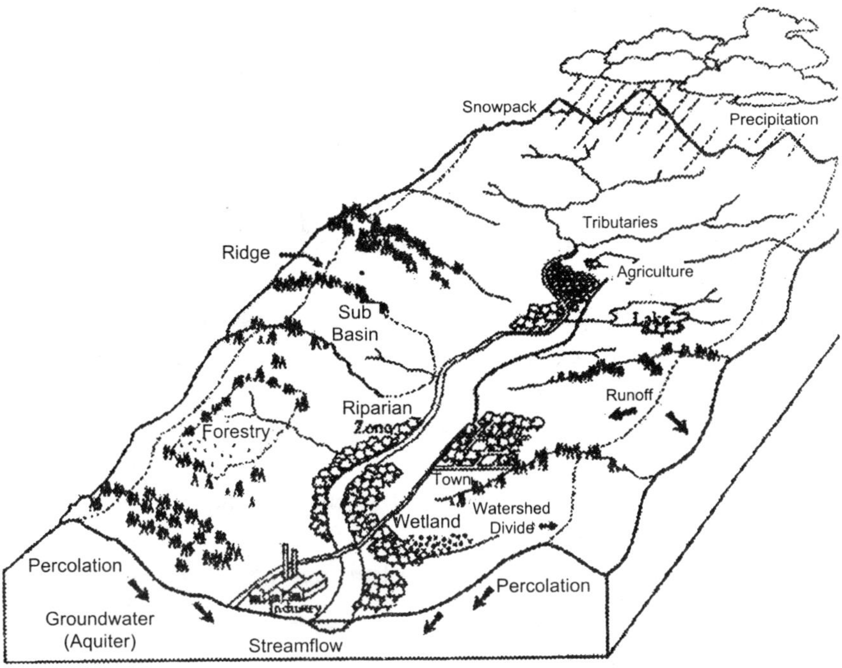

Fig. 1: A large-scale watershed with diverse components and geography
(Adapted from the web page of University of Nebraska on behalf of the University of Nebraska-Lincoln Extension)

processing of energy and materials (water, sediments, nutrients and toxics) down slope through this system.

One of the major objectives of watershed management is the routing of precipitation through the pathways of evaporation, infiltration, and overland flow. This routing of groundwater and overland flow defines the delivery patterns to particular streams, lakes and wetlands; and largely shapes the nature of these aquatic systems.

II. Participatory Watershed Management (PWM)

A. *What is PWM?*

People's participation is gradually being recognized by government agencies as an essential component of all developmental efforts including watershed management. The implementation of participatory watershed management practices has enabled communities to overcome problems and gain more control over their natural resources and livelihoods. Increased expectation due to involvement of the local people may not always be accomplished. But the advantages of people's participation are not only many but sound also. Participation can ensure effective utilization of available resources. In real terms community participation means voluntary sharing by the users' group of their time, energy and money on the programme and adopt the recommended measures and practices on a sustained basis.

Watershed initiates a participatory process for the optimum utilization of water resources in a given area. It promotes skill management, regulation, control and conservation of water to facilitate maximum agriculture and allied operations in watershed areas. The unique feature of a watershed is that it involves all the stakeholders in the process of planning, decision-making and management of the watershed. It enables willing and active participation of the farming community along with the implementing agency.

B. Why PWM ?

In practice, people have varying goals and values relative to uses of local land and water resources. Human modification of lands and waters directly alter the delivery of water; sediments and nutrients alter aquatic systems. The need for and significance of watershed management is imbued with multiple advantages it offers to:

(1) Assess the nature and prevailing status of the watershed ecosystem;
(2) Define short-term and long-term goals for the system;
(3) Set objectives and determine actions needed to achieve the objectives;
(4) Assess both benefits and costs of each action;
(5) Implement desired actions;
(6) Evaluate the effects of actions and progress toward goals; and
(7) Re-evaluate goals and objectives as part of an iterative process.

The process of watershed management provides a chance for stakeholders to balance diverse goals and uses for environmental resources, and to consider how their cumulative actions may affect long-term sustainability of these resources. The guiding principles of the participatory process are partnerships, geographic focus and sound management.

It is because of its holistic approach that watershed management has become an important interdisciplinary science involving social, ecological and economic considerations. Common goals for land and water resources must be developed among people of diverse social backgrounds and values representing to the stakeholders of watershed management. We feel that an understanding of the structure and function—both historical and current— of the watershed system is required, so that the ecological effects of various alternative actions can be anticipated and duly considered. The decision process also must weigh the economic benefits and costs of alternative actions, and blend current market dynamics with considerations of long-term sustainability of the ecosystem.

C. How PWM—The Indian Experience

People's participation is the core element for the success of the PWM process. Under PWM, the local dwellers and neighbouring villagers (coined as stakeholders) participate voluntarily in the entire process. However, the system of PWM may be centrally authorized or led by NGOs of the locality itself.

Although India is far behind in the modern technology of PWM in global perspectives, the very idea was rooted in the country in the late 1970's. In 1978, the Government of India (GOI) appointed a Working Group to formulate an action plan for flood control in the Indo-Gangetic Basin. Emphasising on the need of the Working Group, Dr. M.S. Swaminathan, Secretary, Agriculture and Rural Development, Govt. of India, emphasized: (i) the need for protecting the Himalayan Eco-system and drawing-up a detailed and effective programme of Eco-development; and (ii) to have a 'people-oriented' integrated plan with people's participation so as to evolve a strategy for appropriate land-use and maximum protection to the Himalayan environment. Accordingly, a team of officials from the Uttar Pradesh Forest Department prepared an overall development plan in Nov. 1981 for treatment for the catchment area of these rivers. In view of the overall Development Plan prepared by the Forest Department, the Govt. of Uttar Pradesh established a state level Watershed Management Directorate (WMD) in March 1982. It was proposed to take-up various activities required to control the serious problem of erosion and eco-degradation in the hills in an integrated manner through a multi-disciplinary force working under a single administrative authority (WMD). It was then envisaged that gradually the entire hill area of the State would be taken-up for treatment by the WMD over a period of about 20 years. A beginning in this direction was made when watershed management projects were undertaken in 1983 in the Himalayan region of Uttar Pradesh with financial assistance from the World Bank and the European Economic Community covering about 3000 sq. km. in 8 sub-watersheds of Nayar, Panar and South Bhagirathi watersheds. After the formation of the new state Uttaranchal, the Watershed Management Directorate working in the hilly region had started working as a separate department under the aegis of the Uttaranchal Government.

D. Pre-requisites of PWM

The possible pre-requisites of a successful PWM rest upon a carefully evolved process for execution of the PWM policy. Such a process (tentative) is delineated hereunder:

1. Identification of Area for Watershed Management

It is the primary task in framing a PWM programme. It is executed by studying rainfall pattern; hydrology, topography and soil characteristics of the area. In this connection, socio-economic developments and organizational changes in the area are also considered.

2. Workout Development Plan with Farming Community

This is itself a participatory process at the village level concerning the farming community. Initially, group meetings are conducted at individual villages for preparing an indigenous plan of execution on the basis of identified characteristics.

3. Village-level Meetings

In this stage, discussions are executed concerning the farming and non-farming communities in general relating to the data concerning population, land-use, water resources, status of water tanks and flow of precipitation. This would help in the generation of the idea of the type of watershed to be developed, prospective management plan, investments and subsequent stages of watershed development.

4. Multi-village Level Meetings

This is a common platform of the representatives from all the surrounding villages, which are going to be directly or indirectly effected by the project.

E. Components of PWM

The basic components of Watershed Management may be classified as land management, water management (precipitation, surface water inflow, groundwater inflow), water-use (evaporation, irrigation, drinking water), outflows (surface water outflow, groundwater outflow), and storage (surface storage, groundwater storage, root zone storage). These components are considered strategic in a successful PWM designated under a three-fold stratification of:

(A) Water Management Policy.
(B) Biomass Management Policy.
(C) Determining Long-term Sustainability Considerations.

The water management policy basically includes the following:

1. Rain Water Harvesting
2. Ground Water Recharge
3. Maintenance of Water Balance
4. Preventing Water Pollution
5. Economic Use of Water

Rainwater harvesting forms the major component of water management. The rainwater collected can be recharged into the ground. Roof top water harvesting, diversion of perennial springs and streams into storage structures, farm ponds, etc. are the methods widely used for rainwater harvesting. Percolation pits/tanks, recharge trenches/rain pits, recharge wells, ferro cement tanks, farm ponds, V ditch, bench terracing, etc. are some simple and cost effective rainwater harvesting structures.

Biomass management is another important component of PWM, which includes eco-preservation biomass regeneration, forest management and conservation, plant protection and social forestry, increased productivity of animals, income and employment generation activities along with coordination of health and sanitation.

Determination of sustainable considerations in PWM is qualitative in nature. So, there is every chance of de-motivation on the part of the stakeholders. However, quantitative generalizations regarding the sustainability considerations are tried to be formulated on the basis of the following premises:

1. Socio-cultural indicators
2. Economic indicators
3. Environmental/ecological indicators.

The socio-cultural indicators deal with the social and cultural well-being of the watershed dwellers. This includes factors like decision-making power of the community, empowerment of women, formation of farmer groups/Self-help groups, change in ownership of land, improvement in quality of life, harmonious social life, etc.

The economic indicators of sustainability consist of factors required for livelihood and economic well-being of the people; which consist of increase in income levels, availability of food and food security, improvement in standard of living, off-farm income to families, improvement in rural economy improvements in credit and market supports.

Environmental factors include tangible and non-tangible factors influencing the ecology of the community such as increase in the productive potential of resource-base, management of common property resources and improvement in bio-diversity of the region.

The number of components in different watershed management programmes may vary according to the objectives set and strategies made for the accomplishment of the goal. In the Indian context, the common components of the on-going PWM are:

Forestry is to halt deforestation, provide vegetative cover on degraded land and supplement fodder and fuel-wood resources available to the rural communities.

Agriculture, Support Irrigation and Soil Conservation aims to increase agricultural productivity in a sustained manner and to diversify crop production. This is being achieved through organizing farmers' training camps and exposure visits.

Horticulture is specifically designed to raise fruit production, diversify production and to conserve soil and moisture through establishing perennial tree crops with suitable ground cover on steep land, which is unsuitable for arable production.

Animal Husbandry with an objective to improve the productivity of livestock through breed improvement programme, reduction in the number of scrub/unproductive cattle and to ensure maximum utilization of fodder resources.

Energy Conservation by introducing energy efficient cooking equipment (such as pressure cooker, wood stoves) and use of alternative energy sources (such as biogas, solar cooker). The main objective is to reduce pressure on forests for fuel-wood.

Community Participation is viewed as the key of ensuring success of convergent planning and joint project implementation with the village communities.

Training and Awareness Programme is an essential ingredient for achieving the project's objectives which includes local villagers' training, motivators' training, training on organization building techniques, training of users' groups in the field of management of natural resource, exposure visits, etc. Regional academic and research institutions are involved for the benefit of the projects, so that full advantage may be taken of existing information and expertise from the institutions.

III. Concluding Remarks

WPM which seems useful in principle is not so simple in practice. There is research and evidence to believe that improving the social and economic conditions of the resources of the poor through redistribution of land and water resources by policies like PWM is beset with two serious problems:

One, it is a physically difficult task.

Two, the elite groups in the community tries to block such noble moves when it feels that it would be a loser in the PWM process either directly (diversion of water) or indirectly (benefit flows from a project go to others).

Considering such a non-conducive environment, the following steps are suggested to make the PWM more effective:

1. As much of the physical work and capacity building for

watershed management is done by the village people, the final decisions on the PWM should also be of these people.

2. The rate of women participation in all the levels of PWM should be increased considerably.
3. Expansion of general literacy is another precondition which would help in motivating stakeholders to preserve precious water-resources for their own benefit.
4. Last but by no means the least, the stakeholders should also be made well aware of multi-dimensional benefits the PWM offers.

We feel the sooner these steps are taken, the better it will be for the PWM and, in turn, community/village development.

25

Watershed Management and Grassroot Institutions

Dr. Sanjeev Kumar

People's participation and the role of grassroots institutions, e.g., Panchayati Raj Institutions (PRIs), Non-Governmental Organisations (NGOs), Self Help Groups (SHGs) and other social institutions, have become the hallmark of rural development in the present globalised world. PRIs and other social organizations are instruments of socio-economic and political change as well as agents of development. People's participation, empowerment and good governance are powerful tools that can give poor people a voice in the affairs of the state and government. At the same time, building community assets can have a positive impact on poverty and help reduce migration to cities. Small savings can serve as an effective entry point to other developmental activities. These institutions can better serve the interests of the poor if they are reoriented. Society and governments should retain the focus on poverty to improve rural livelihoods and to reduce growing social conflicts. This process demands effective participation of the people at large.

Participation has acquired a wider dimension with the assertion of democracy. Participation is also associated with political liberties and civic consciousness. To be able to exercise the right by the people, the prerogative to shape their own government and to steer it for their interests is also regarded as the participatory process. Shaping the

Reprinted with permission, *Kurukshetra*, December 2005, pp. 4-13.

local institutions for the beneficiary's goals is the element of self-expression amounting to participation. Here participation is generated through a dialogue among the stakeholders seeking the shape of local facilities. Similarly, these institutions are major agents of social change and can play an important role in the management of natural resources at the local level.

The participatory role of all people from top to bottom is crucial to successful initiation/design/financing/implementation of development programmes. There are many examples where a key person at the policy level gives a firm direction to generate programmes and a lowest functionary makes a programme succeed. At the lowest level, the failures come to our notice but the successes achieved by individuals under great odds go unsung, yet the people, who benefit do remember their contributions. The need of the hour is to prepare and make these local rural inhabitants capable of handling environmental problems as well as the problem of over-utilisation of natural resources.

While the importance of leadership to activate people and form them into an organization is acknowledged, it cannot be left as a one-time effort. It requires constant contact with the members and the people to acquaint them with the problem, enthuse them constantly and bring the project or development activity to culmination for their benefit. The responsibility largely lies with the field staff of the government or the project. It is the grit and dedication of the personnel at the cutting-edge level that results in the efficiency and achievement of participation. Some malleability and adjustment may also be required in the participatory process during the implementation stage. Participation would not be a set frame for all time to come but a phenomenon running with the programme. The local level facilitators and capacities have to be live to this course. The new post 73rd Amendment Act leadership at the Panchayat level is more literate and aware than the old traditional leadership. Therefore, they can handle the situation in a better way and government has to play the role of a facilitator.

The Problem

The application of participation is rooted in the logic that *people should have an opportunity for controlling their own fate, as much as possible.*

Participation has now become virtually synonymous with development projects. Participatory approaches are being tried in almost all sectors. However, the worldwide acceptance of participation has also bred some scepticism. Critics of bottom-up development have argued that the *participatory rhetoric, like, communism, was a noble dream but not very practical due to a naiveté about human nature* that it has become a political slogan among some governments which control the process by *prominent displays of participatory intentions* and that it is a good fund-raising device for NGOs which, by showing they are more participatory and less bureaucratic, are able to obtain substantial funding from various donors. Some of the scepticism and criticism of participation is both healthy and valid.

Hundreds of development initiatives involve some form of participation, but often there are no clear answers on who is participative, why participation takes place, and whether participation works as a process in itself, or as a vehicle for better delivery of services.

A popular vehicle for people's participation and for delivering services in natural resources management is users' groups. Thus, water-users' associations, forest-users' groups, and watershed committees, among others, have been formed all over Asia either as a complement to, or a substitute for, centralized government-controlled management, democratic in management style with the potential to meet the equity and efficiency objectives of development. Nepal's forest-user groups, for example, have established clear rules for the use and management of local forests and have specified the contribution to be made and the benefits to be derived by each member, and laid down penalties for breaking the rules. The natural resources can be managed better by managing the watershed area as a whole. The development and judicious utilisation of land, water and forest should be the main objective of the local people. Watershed, a natural entity in itself, combines forest management, land-use management and water management. It happens to be such a hydrologic or physiographic unit that it offers a very good unit for planning and implementing soil conservation, water harvesting, aforestation and environmental protection programmes. It also satisfies the area concept which is considered a rational basis for optimum development of available resources. Watershed programmes can be effectively implemented with the active involvement and cooperation of the beneficiaries.

Why People's Participation?

There is a close relationship between the environment and the people living within that area as the community derives sustenance from it. Increase in biotic pressure leads to over-exploitation and degradation of natural resources. Paucity of resources also leads to internal conflict giving opportunity to others to exploit the situation. It is thus necessary for people to realize the intrinsic relationship between population, poverty and the degraded environment they live in. The poor, in a developing country like India are left with no option but to degrade their own environment for their very own survival. Still, it is only they who can restore health to the environment thus ruined; outside actors can only facilitate but never substitute for stake-holders. Low cost and locally available technology with suitable intervention by latest advancements yields the best solution. It is clear that watershed development cannot be done in isolation. It is a natural entity and may contain different types of lands, namely, forest lands, community lands, government lands or private lands. Therefore, the entire watershed community is to be involved for the integrated development of watersheds and the assets created in such an effort are also to be maintained through the people of the watershed community in order to ensure sustainability.

Development of Local Institutions

The civil society organizations encompass various types of organizations such as cooperatives, trade unions, Non-Governmental Organizations (NGOs), community groups, self-help groups and others. In the Indian context, Panchayati Raj institutions, Swayam Sahayata Samooh (SHG) and NGOs are still in their infant stages and there is vital need for their involvement in the development of local rural areas.

In India, the 73rd and 74th Constitutional Amendments have given a new approach to development and social change. The Amendments aim at democratic decentralization and self-governance. Panchayati Raj Institutions (PRIs) were set up four decades ago to make real the basic conviction that the village Panchayat could play a major role in social transformation. Thus PRIs have been the prime instruments of decentralization at the grass roots in India.

The Panchayati Raj System envisages political and administrative decentralization as embodied in the 73rd Constitutional Amendment. It aims at greater participation and more autonomy to the people in the management of their own affairs. Another major instrument for people's participation is their organizing into community groups such as the NGOs. The emergence of NGOs can be a powerful force and process for greater participation by the people in a civil society. Tarun Bharat Sangh in Rajasthan and Disha NGOs have set the example for others on how to manage natural resources at the local level while involving local people in developmental activities. The problem of unemployment, hunger and poverty can be mitigated with the involvement of these institutions and people in the rural development and natural resource management process.

As per the guidelines for watershed development (revised-2001), the Zila Parishads and other Panchayati Raj Institutions (PRIs) shall have very important roles to play in Watershed Development Programmes. Wherever the DRDA has been made responsible for implementation of the watershed programmes, the Chief Executive Officer of the Zila Parishad shall be a member of the DWDC. The PRIs shall have the right to monitor and review the implementation of the programme and provide guidelines for improvements in the administrative arrangements and procedures with a view to ensure convergence of other programmes of the Ministry of Rural Development such as JGSY, SGSY, IAY, CRSP, Rural Drinking Water Supply, etc. At the village level, the Gram Panchayat shall be fully involved in the implementation of the programme, especially community organization and training programmes. It may use its administrative authority and financial resources to support and encourage the formation of SHG/UGS, the operation and maintenance of the assets created during the project period and the common property resources such as pasture lands, fisheries, tanks, plantations on village common lands, etc. The creation of local institutional capacity to manage natural and other resources through collective action, not dependent entirely on the structures and authority of the state, offers an important alternative to the bureaucratic approach, if such capacity can become viable. One of the reasons for ambiguity and confusion in much of the thinking about local institutions is that it has both a social and geographic meaning and neither may match the administrative definition given to the term.

It is useful to recognize that there are at least ten levels of decision-making bodies that range from the international level down to the level of individual decision-makers. Of these, levels six to eight come within the ambit of what is usually meant as local level.

1. International level
2. National level
3. Regional level
4. District level
5. Sub-district level
6. Panchayat level
7. Community level
8. Group level
9. Household level
10. Individual level.

The first two levels are far removed from local conditions and activities. The next three are closer to but still not local in any sociological sense, being essentially administrative entities. There is no basis or capacity at these levels for organizing activity to promote development except through formal political channels or through diffused market relationships. Steps needed by development promoters for large-scale people's participation, e.g., Go to the people, Live with them, Learn from them, Serve them, Love them, Plan with them, Start with what they know and Build on what they have are universal in nature and not restricted or applicable to the ground realities in China alone. These are thus the basic principles for ensuring people's participation. At the same time, in watershed projects essentially based on community participation, the following constitute part of capacity building:

Ways of approaching local community; Methods for facilitating group formation/institution building; skills for fostering group participation, especially women groups; conducting participatory planning session; going on sustaining participation, especially women groups. In this direction, an explicit training strategy for community participation can move around the theme of building critical capacity in the following areas:

- Participatory project managerial skills through building learning organization and team work;
- Skill building for facilitating group formation of women and men/pro-poor institution building;
- Skill building for fostering groups/institutions into planned actions for betterment of their livelihood, living conditions and quality of life; and
- Building skills for sustenance.

Self-Help Groups

Self-help groups are necessary to overcome exploitation, create confidence for the economic self-reliance of the rural poor, particularly among women who are mostly invisible in the social structure. These groups enable them to come together for common objectives and gain strength from each other to deal with exploitation which they are facing in several forms. A group becomes the basis for action and change. It also helps building of relationship for mutual trust between the promoting organization and the rural poor through constant contact and genuine efforts. Self-Help Groups play an important role in *differentiating between consumers' credit and production credit; analyzing the credit system for its implication and changes in the economy, culture and social position of the target groups; providing easy access to credit and facilitating group/organization for effective control; ensuring repayment and continuity through group dynamic; setting viable norms for interest rates, repayment schedules, gestation period, extension, writing off bad debts; and assisting group members in getting access to the formal credit institutions.* Thus, Self-Help Groups (SHG) disburse micro-credit to rural women for the purpose of making them enterprising women and encouraging them to enter into entrepreneurial activities. Credit needs of rural women are fulfilled totally through SHGs. SHGs enhance equality of status of women as participants, decision-makers and beneficiaries in the democratic, economic, social and cultural spheres of life.

The participation of SHG in the watershed development is one of the crucial and important roles. The guidelines envisage that each

Project Implementation Agency (PIA) shall carry out its duties through a multi-disciplinary team designated as the Watershed Development Team (WDT). Each WDT may handle 10-12 watershed development projects and may have at least four members, one each from the discipline of forestry/plant science, animal sciences, civil/agricultural engineering and social sciences. At least one member of the WDT should be a woman. Preferable qualification for a WDT member would be a professional degree. However, qualifications can be relaxed by the ZP/DRDA in deserving cases keeping in view the practical field experience in respective disciplines.

At the same time, the PIA shall also constitute User Groups (UGs) in the watershed area with the help of WDT. These groups shall be homogenous groups, who may be most affected by each work/activity and shall include persons having land holding within the watershed areas. Each UG shall consist of persons who are likely to derive direct benefits from a particular watershed work or activity. The UGs should actually take over the operation and maintenance of the completed community works or activities on common property resources.

The SHG is considered as a viable organization of the rural poor particularly women for delivering micro-credit in order to undertake entrepreneurial activities. Some of the studies on SHGs of the rural poor, particularly those managed by women, successfully demonstrated how to mobilize and manage thrift activities, appraise credit needs, enforce financial discipline, maintain credit linkages with banks, effectively undertake income generating activities, etc. Women play a central part in the provision, management, and safeguarding of water. The pivotal role of women as providers and users of water and guardians of the environment has seldom been reflected in institutional arrangement for the development and management of water resources. Acceptance and implementation of this principle requires positive policies to address women's specific needs and to equip and empower women to participate at all levels in water resources programmes, including decision-making and implementation in ways defined by them. In a nutshell, women are the agents of natural resource management as they are in regular interaction with land, water, fuel, fodder, food, livestock, medicinal plants, etc.

People's Participation in Watershed Management

People's participation may be of varied kinds and we must focus on the appropriate and experimented kind of participation so as to avoid adverse effect of the approach. At the root of some of the problems in natural resources management in South Asia and other countries is the form of participatory practice followed in development interventions. Some of the forms of participation, ranging from coercion to total local control, are as follows:

- *Manipulative*

Participation is pretence. People's representatives are on boards or committees, but lack power.

- *Passive*

People participate by being told what has already been decided. Announcement on projects are made unilaterally by the government agencies without listening to people's responses. The information collected belongs to an external professional; it is not shared with the people.

- *By Consultation*

People participate by being consulted, or by answering questions. External professionals define the problems, the information gathering processes, and thus the analysis. The professionals are under no obligation to accept the people's view.

- *For Material Gain*

People participate by contributing resources, e.g., in return for material gains from a project. The people have no stake in the participation process or in the project after it has ended.

- *Functional*

Participation is seen as a means necessary to achieve the project's goals. People may participate by organizing themselves into groups to help meet the pre-determined objectives of the project. The involvement may be interactive and involve shared decision-making, but the project authorities may have already made up their minds.

• *Interactive*

People participate in analysis, development of action plans and formation or strengthening of local institutions. The process of participation is as important as the end-result. Participation is seen as a right, not just the means for achieving a project goal. The use of participatory tool and inter-disciplinary methodologies help to increase awareness and learning among community groups. As groups take control over local decisions, they increase their stake in maintaining or changing existing structures or practices.

• *Self-Mobilisation*

People participate by taking initiatives to preserve a resource or change an existing social system, independently of external institutions. The people may develop contacts with external agencies for financial assistance or technical advice, but retain control over how the resources are allocated or used. A good example is the indigenous forest management systems initiated by the tribal people in Gujarat, which have functioned outside the scope of the forest departments. Self-mobilization can spread if governments and NGOs provide an enabling framework of support, even if they challenge existing distribution of power and wealth.

We may integrate functional, interactive and self-mobilisation for suitable results.

Problems in Planning and Implementation

Watershed programmes are implemented by the Zila Panchayat through watershed associations. A Project Implementing Agency (PIA), which may be a government department or an NGO, is assigned about 10 micro watersheds, each micro watershed covering about 500 hectares. The PIA forms a watershed development team that interacts with the watershed associations and provides technical assistance to the watershed association in the planning and implementation of the watershed programme. The residents of the area covered by the watersheds are also organized into self-help groups and user groups. In fact, these user groups are the beginning point as well as the end point for Watershed Development programmes. Their initiative is crucial to the success of the programme and they are the ultimate beneficiaries.

Evaluation reports have shown that watershed projects cannot succeed without full participation of project beneficiaries and careful attention to issues of social organisation. This is because their success depends on consensus among a large number of users. Moreover, collective capability and action is required for management of existing as well as new structures created during the project. Otherwise, the costs and benefits of watershed interventions are location-specific and unevenly distributed among the people affected.

The unfortunate truth today is that most projects have failed to generate sustainability because of the failure of government agencies to involve the people. Up to the end of the Eighth Plan period, 16.5 million hectares of rain fed/degraded land have been developed under different schemes. However, this does not get reflected in the data for Net Sown Area, which has remained almost stagnant at around 142 million hectares for the last 30 years. This indicates that there was no sustainability of efforts made.

This lack of sustainability can be attributed to a number of practices followed by the Government in the implementation of watershed development programmes. Strict orientation to achieve physical and financial targets discourages the project authorities to promote people's participation. There is considerable pressure to spend substantial resources by a fixed deadline leaving no room for pursuing participatory approaches. It is imperative for the successful implementation of the watershed projects that people participate in the planning and execution of the project right from the beginning. This would inculcate a sense of ownership among the people. Some other bottlenecks are:

- There is no arrangement for handing over of structures and maintenance of plantation after a project is completed.
- In the present form, schemes are planned and executed by district level officers who have very limited capacity to do so. There is need to train both government officials and functionaries of agencies.
- Little evaluation of the programme is done after it has run for a couple of years as it is taken for granted that once money has been spent, physical progress automatically results. But, this is far from the truth.

- Programmes are run departmentally with little vertical compartmentalisation. Horizontal linkages between various agencies are very weak. Thus, although watershed development may require integration of soil conservation techniques with plantation, there is little likelihood of effective coordination between the District Soil Conservation Officer and the District Forest Officer.
- Forest lands, non-forest pastures, wastelands and crop lands must be looked at in an integrated manner. As this is usually not done, treatment upstream to reduce soil movement does not benefit large farmers who are downstream. They see no advantage and are indifferent or opposed to this strategy. They would prefer to conserve and harvest water in the drainage line to be used for irrigation or to replenish groundwater. However, lands in the upper catchment areas must always be rehabilitated first.

Despite problems, there are many success stories. Successful and sustainable projects include Ralegaon Siddhi, revival of *johad* in Alwar, Sadguru Foundation's activities in Gujarat, Watershed Development in Jhabua and Sagar districts of Madhya Pradesh and externally aided projects like KAWAD, SDC, DANIDA in Karnataka, World Bank Project in Andhra Pradesh, DANIDA project in Tamil Nadu, World Bank aided Kandi project in Himachal Pradesh and Sukhomajri project in Haryana. All of these successful projects have some characteristics in common—emphasis on social issues, social mobilization, clear direction to the Government to accept principles of participatory management, transparent project monitoring and a strong sense of ownership by the local community. The Sukhomajri and Kandi projects resemble one of the best examples of people's participation in watershed management.

In fact, Ralegaon Siddhi has become a role model for people across the country to learn how people's involvement is instrumental to the success of watershed activities. It stands testimony to the fact that the key to rural economy is the development of watersheds and the key to development of watersheds is participation of local farming communities.

Building Local Partnerships

Participation, Partnership and People (three Ps) are the major concerns for the management of watershed. Through a partnership, different people and organizations work together to address common interests and concerns. Other terms such as *teams, alliances* and *groups* can be used instead of partnership. What you call your organization and how it is structured is up to the group. In fact, effective organizations are as unique as the watershed itself. In addition, partnerships often result in: More efficient use of financial resources; A spirit of sharing and cooperation; Fairness which minimizes the potential for negative social and economic impacts; More creative and acceptable ways to protect natural resources.

Typical Projects

Field trips and tours, meetings and workshops, canoe trips, volunteer monitoring, cleanup and restoration days, educational programmes for schools, civic groups, and other local organizations, media relations, opinion surveys, focus groups and partnerships can also be challenging. It takes time and skill to create successful partnerships. Maintaining motivation and enthusiasm is another challenge, especially if positive results do not happen quickly. All the relevant stakeholders must believe their efforts are needed. Remember, the benefits of partnerships usually far outweigh the challenges.

Who Should be Included?

The stakeholders are the right partners for the success for management of natural resources. In short, anyone with a stake in the watershed management plan should be involved. Success depends on involving a good mix of people and organizations in the partnership to put together and implement the plan. We will need to find people to play a number of roles. These roles include: Technical leadership, Communication education, Political liaison and Public policy. Some people who live outside the watershed may even have an important role to play because they benefit from or impact water or other natural resources within the watershed.

How to Build a Successful Partnership?

Building a successful partnership takes skill, time and patience.

Here are some specific strategies to help:

- *Mass Media:* Coverage of watershed events, Human interest stories, Understanding of local information needs, Ability to get information out quickly.
- *Landowners and Managers*: Trustworthy information sources, role models and peer pressure.
- *Financial Institutions*: Influence over management decisions, linkage with landowners, prestige for partnership, funding for programmes.
- *Agri-businesses and Industries:* Distribute information and influence decisions, Sponsor field days and demonstrations, Donate equipment and services, Funding for programmes.
- *Farm Organizations*: Credibility and visibility for programmes, Existing communication channels.
- *Environmental and Conservation Groups:* Knowledge of environmental constituencies, Awareness of problems and issues, Committed and knowledgeable memberships.
- *Local Elected Officials:* Political leadership and credibility, Land-use and resource management decisions, Financial support for projects.
- *Local Government Agencies:* Financial and technical support, Policies and decisions that affect the watershed, Logistics, equipment, and related support, Data collection and analysis expertise.
- *Chambers of Commerce:* Compatible, broader goals for local economy, Concerns and interests of businesses.
- *Students:* Influence over efforts in the future, Time and energy for *repetitive* tasks.
- *Teachers:* Influence over values and beliefs, Ability to shape future generations, Source of information.
- *Women's Groups:* Influence over family decisions. Interest and concern for health issues, Ability to mobilize and motivate members.
- *Religious Leaders:* Commitment to stewardship, Ability to appeal to higher values, Credibility and legitimacy.
- *Retired Persons:* Time and talent for teamwork, Understanding of local conditions, Credibility in community.

- *Civic Organizations:* Ongoing programme activities, Interest in and concern for community, Fund-raising skills.

Keys to Successful Partnerships

Establish a sense of need and direction—All partners need to know they are working towards a worthwhile purpose. They also need to know what is expected of them. Select partners based on existing and potential skills, not personalities—Partnerships will need technical, communications, problem-solving and interpersonal skills. Pay particular attention to early meetings and activities—first impressions mean a lot. People are often sceptical at the first meeting and may be suspicious of other partners. The group will probably need to set some specific ground rules related to meeting, participation, discussion, confidentiality, constructive feedback, and expected contributions. Start with a few short-term tasks that have a good chance for success—Be sure that early projects are realistic and will be seen as *winners* in the eyes of the partners. Challenge the group regularly with fresh facts and information—New information (that you will be gathering as a partnership) will help to better understand your situation and improve your effectiveness. Spend time together—It will take time to get the partnership working effectively. Spend time (outside of meetings if possible) to get to know each other. Use the power of positive feedback, recognition, and reward—People respond to positive incentives in the partnership setting just as they do as individuals.

All people with a stake in the watershed should be receptive to becoming a partner. Use the list to start with. In addition, consider the following three distinct groups: Those who are both affected by and interested in watershed protection. Those who are affected, but not interested. Those who are not affected, but are interested. While each partner should understand and agree to their own roles and responsibilities, all partners should be able to take part in any decision or activity where they have interest and expertise.

Leadership should emerge from among the members of the partnership. Someone will have to take the initial responsibility for getting members together. Once members are together, however, consensus will be necessary regarding leadership. Leadership or coordination involves the ability to get people to voluntarily commit to goals and accept responsibilities. A top-down approach will not generally work. The initial meeting(s) are critical to success.

An important way to build a partnership is to develop a clear sense of your purpose through a statement. Partners should develop a concise purpose statement that defines general goals and responsibilities.

A carefully worded statement will serve as a yardstick for decision-making, for measuring progress and will provide motivation for high quality. Make sure all partners are comfortable with the statement. Steps include: Ask for ideas from all partners; Discuss the ideas and draft a statement; Revise draft based on discussion; Write a final statement based on consensus; Solicit statements of commitment from all partners. This process may not be easy and will take time. Potential conflicts need to be discussed and resolved. Remember, it is important to keep the statement general enough to encourage widespread support, but specific enough to identify goals and measure progress.

To accomplish the purpose, the group will need to set short and long-term goals. These goals should include general strategies, e.g., increased support for watershed protection, goals for more specific activities, e.g., series of newspaper articles, tree planting, etc., focus on the future in setting clear and attainable goals. Do not let the past dictate the future.

Build the partnership around members' interests and strengths. Each member needs to contribute his unique talent. For example, some may be responsible for public contact while others will gather resource information. Individuals can provide new ideas and approaches. Yet, the group shares responsibility for decisions and actions, as well as for successes. All members should be able to express their opinions and offer constructive criticism.

Successful partnerships are built on clear and open communication. Discussion both during and outside meetings should be honest and open. Partners need to listen to each other and provide constructive feedback. Balanced participation will also promote a spirit of trust and cooperation. Because each partner has an interest in the success of the partnership, each should participate in discussions and decisions. It is also important to agree on decision-making procedures that encourage participation. Most effective decisions are made by consensus. This does not mean that everyone will be completely happy, but that everyone can live with the decision and feel decisions are fair.

There is no single partnership structure that will work in every watershed. Instead, your group should determine how formal the partnership needs to be. Partners could meet on a regular basis or only be contacted as needed. Some division of labour and delegation of responsibility should be there to take advantage of resources and expertise. Build on existing community organizations, such as informal groups of land managers, formal organizations and other community organizations. Your local soil and water conservation district, natural resource agencies, extension, conservation clubs, Chamber of Commerce, service organizations or a local business can provide valuable advice on organization and facilitation. Sub-committees could be formed for activities such as media relations, fund-raising or demonstrations. It may also be necessary to include representation from more than one country depending on watershed boundaries. If the watershed is too large, the group may want to sub-divide it into smaller watersheds with their own partnerships.

Partnerships are successful for a number of reasons. Your challenge is to determine what motivates people and make sure these motivations are met. Some individuals may contribute because their jobs involve such cooperation. Many people also enjoy working with others and meeting new challenges. They also may see the potential for professional and personal growth, as well as a sense of accomplishment. External factors can also motivate partnerships, including public expectations and organizational mandates for cooperation. Informal, social interaction can provide the glue that holds a partnership together.

Most people agree with the notion of partnership, at least in principle. However, partnerships may be unsuccessful for a variety of reasons. Past failures; Lack of commitment; Worry about lost independence; Lack of credit for own contributions; Personality conflicts; Power struggles or turf battles; Partners who do not agree on realistic roles and responsibilities; Differences in cultural and personal values.

How Partnerships Develop

Successful partnerships take time to develop. Expect some highs and lows. There are four main stages. These stages can be compared to how we learn to swim. Each involves specific feelings and actions.

If you understand and prepare for these different stages, you will find it easier to move through the difficult stages to reach success at the end.

- *The Forming Stage*

When a partnership is forming, people cautiously explore each other. Members are like hesitant swimmers. They stand by the side of the pool and stick their toes in the water. Feelings at this stage include excitement and optimism mixed with scepticism and anxiety. Activities include: Defining the job at hand and discussing how to accomplish it; Deciding what information needs to be gathered; Discussing concepts and issues identifying all the barriers to getting the job done.

- *The Storming Stage*

This is often the most difficult stage. Partners become impatient and begin arguing. They are like new swimmers. After they jump in the water, they are afraid they might drown and begin thrashing around. Feelings include resistance to change and negative attitudes about the success of the partnership. Signs include: Arguing about less important issues; Becoming defensive or competitive (choosing sides); Developing unrealistic goals; Increasing tension and jealousy.

- *The Normalizing Stage*

People accept their role in the team, as well as ground rules (or norms). Conflicts are reduced and competitors become more cooperative. Like experienced swimmers, people realize they are not going to drown and they help keep each other afloat. Feelings include acceptance of team membership and relief that things seem to be working out. Some activities are: Achieving harmony by avoiding conflict; More friendliness and sharing of problems; A sense of team cohesion and common goals.

- *The Performing Stage*

By this stage, the partnership has become an effective and close-knit unit. People begin to really work together. Like a winning relay team, the partnership works together well. Feelings include new insights about the partnership and each member's roles as well as satisfaction with the partnership's progress. Some activities are:

constructive change; ability to work through problems; closer attachment to the partnership.

Conclusion

Watersheds have become recognized as a key and discreet development unit in rural development. To achieve sustainable increase of productivity and management integrated approaches have been recommended. The intensification and diversification of production is viewed from a livelihood perspective. For sustainable livelihoods, the trade-off between agriculture productivity, equity and sustainability is critical. Therefore, there is need for people's participation for sustainable development of rural India. A bottom-up approach is needed so as to involve local people in planning, managing and division-making process. The bureaucracy should pay the role of a facilitator. The maximum involvement of people, PRIs, NGOs, SHGs and other peer social groups may be encouraged by the central and state governments. Awareness, education and motivation of the local inhabitants is the right way for the management of natural resources as well as wastershed development.

26

Water Conservation through Watershed Development

Prof. V.S. Gupta

As a life support means, water is the source and substance of life. It is also essential for realizing the full potential of the agricultural sector and the country's development.

During recent years, water has become one of the important subjects for national level planning and plan formulation, which led to the establishment of the National Water Resources Council as a national apex body with the Prime Minister as its chairman. The National Commission for Integrated Water Resources Development Plan (NCIWRDP) was established in 1996 to prepare an integrated water plan for development of water resources and other issues.

Several international level conferences have taken up issues related to water—its management, conservation and proper utilization.

At several forums held world-wide several principles were adopted on water conservation and management. These principles underline the fact that effective management of water resources demands a holistic approach, linking social and economic development with protection of natural eco-systems. Effective management links land and water uses across the whole of a catchment area or groundwater aquifer.

The participatory approach involves raising the awareness of the importance of water among policy-makers and the general public. Water development and management should be based on a participatory approach, involving users, planners and policy-makers at all levels. It means that the decisions are taken at the lowest appropriate level, with full public consultation and involvement of users in the planning and implementation of water projects.

Women play a central part in the provision, management, and safeguarding of water. The pivotal role of women as providers and users of water and guardians of environment has seldom been reflected in institutional arrangements for the development and management of water resources. Acceptance and implementation of this principle requires positive policies to address women's specific needs and to equip and empower women to participate at all levels in water resources programmes, including decision-making and implementation in ways defined by them.

Within this principle, it is vital to recognize the basic right of all human beings to have access to clean water and sanitation at an affordable price. . . . Water has an economic value in all its competing uses and should be recognized as an economic good. Managing water as an economic good is an important way of achieving efficient and equitable use, and of encouraging conservation and protection of water resources.

National Water Policy

The National Water Policy, 2002 in its preamble says: Water is a prime natural resource, a basic human need and a natural asset. Planning, development and management of water resources need to be governed by national perspectives.

The policy, adopted at the meeting of the National Water Resources Council (NWRC), held on April 1, 2001, states: Water is a scarce and precious national resource to be planned, developed, conserved and managed as such, and on an integrated and environmentally sound basis, keeping in view the socio-economic aspects and needs of the states. It is one of the most crucial elements in developmental planning. As the country entered the 21st century, efforts to develop, conserve, utilise and manage this important resource in a sustainable manner, have to be guided by the national perspective.

The Policy underlines the need to put into practice traditional conservation methods like water harvesting, including rooftop rainwater harvesting, so as to increase further the utilizable water resources. Paragraph 3.4 of the Policy lays particular emphasis on watershed management through extensive soil conservation, catchment area treatment, preservation of forests, increasing the forest cover and construction of check dams.

Harnessing Every Drop of Water— A National Priority

Addressing the NWRC meeting, the Prime Minister Sh. Atal Bihari Vajpayee said: "Let this meeting of the Council send out a powerful message that harnessing every drop of water is a national priority. We should lay special emphasis on specialized, localized and decentralized harnessing of water resources. . . . The Policy should recognize that the community is the rightful custodian of water. Exclusive control by the government water machinery cannot help us to make a paradigm shift to participative, essentially local management of water resources." The Prime Minister's address thus gave a resounding call for the recognition of the community as the custodian of water resources as also for a national movement for rainwater harvesting.

Fortunately, in several parts of India, a number of initiatives have been taken by local communities regarding water harvesting and watershed development. These community-driven initiatives were taken by panchayats and villagers themselves, sometime guided by village elders, scientists and social workers. Eminent broadcaster and journalist, Mark Tully devoted one complete chapter to water harvesting in his latest book, *India in Slow Motion,* on how panchayats in the Saurashtra region of Gujarat took up massive work of reviving traditional methods of harvesting water and building check dams in villages involving even religious leaders.

Likewise, community-based natural resource management work in the villages of Alwar district of Rajasthan has brought about a change in the lives of the people by empowering them through ridding the area of water shortages, starting women's banks and reviving traditional methods of water harvesting. The success story of this initiative has been highlighted by the United Nations Development Programme (UNDP) in a compilation of articles brought out to commemorate the International Year for Fresh Water.

In this context, Magsaysay award winner Rajinder Singh says, "Though most of our work has been in the area of water harvesting, we have also tried to empower people so that they can sustain themselves and fight for their rights without our intervention."

Explaining the concept of community-driven water harvesting, Singh says, "Our organisation—an NGO, Tarun Bharat Sangh (TBS) — provides aid in the form of financial assistance to the extent of 67 per cent. The rest, 33 per cent, is provided by the people in the form *of shram daan* (voluntary labour). Earlier, we used to provide help to the extent of 75 per cent, which we have reduced so that people's initiative can be strengthened further.

TBS has helped people construct nearly 7500 water harvesting structures in 11 districts of Rajasthan. Of these, nearly 1500 are in the villages of Alwar in the form of mud dams, concrete dams and ponds. Communities have made most of these with help from TBS over a period of 17 years and women have played a major role in these.

Singh says water management should not be looked at in isolation. Wherever harvesting has been done and forests have been regenerated, women have been the first beneficiaries.

Watershed Development

Watershed, a natural entity in itself, combines forest management, land-use management and water management. It happens to be such a hydrologic or physiographic unit that it offers a very good unit for planning and implementing soil conservation, water harvesting, afforestation and environmental protection programmes. It also satisfies the area concept which is considered a rational basis for optimum development of available resources. Watershed programmes can be effectively implemented with the active involvement and cooperation of the beneficiaries.

Successful Watershed Experiments at Sukhomajri and Bunga Villages

In Sukhomajri, a village nestling in the sub-Himalayan Shivalik hills, over-grazing and deforestation had left the environment badly degraded, with extremely high rates of erosion.

When the late Dr. P.R. Mishra, formerly director of the Central Soil and Water Conservation Research and Training Institute at Chandigarh, in 1977 tried to dissuade villagers from uncontrolled grazing in their watershed, his pleas fell on deaf ears. The village stream was carrying thousands of tonnes of silt to a large reservoir which supplied water to Chandigarh. So, Mishra decided to build a small dam to hold back the monsoon rain. Enthused by the results, the villagers promised to protect the watershed, so that, the silt could accumulate in their own reservoir. The forest department also took a daring step to let the villagers manage the watershed. The villagers, in turn, banned all grazing on it and levied a charge on every family collecting fodder from it. In five years, irrigation helped the villagers double their grain production, turning the village from a food importing to a food exporting one. As the grass and trees regenerated in the watershed, the villagers began to get more fodder. Hunger and destitution disappeared.

Likewise in village Bunga, in the foothills of the Shivaliks, 22 kilometres from Panchkula, the village farming community, mostly Gujars, resorted to cattle-rearing during the rainy season and agriculture during the *rabi* season. They led a nomadic existence, leaving their village along with cattle during summer and returning during September-October. Till recently, there were no bunds, no irrigation canals and no water storage structures, the run-off rain water denuded the vegetation cover and resulted in heavy soil erosion.

An Integrated Watershed Development Plan for covering about 1000 hectares of agricultural as well as forest land was finalised for the village in August, 1982. The major objectives of the project were afforestation in 200 hectares of hilly catchment area, soil conservation and irrigation through construction of three mini earth-filled water harvesting embankments to store rain water for providing irrigation in command areas. With visible benefits accruing from the project, the villagers themselves started protecting the catchment area against grazing and illegal cutting of vegetation. Anyone found grazing cattle in the catchment areas was imposed a fine by the Hill Resources Management Society (HRMS). The standing grass of the catchment was sold by the society to the highest bidder for a year.

The HRMS is patterned and based on the Sukhomajri village model. The participation of the villagers in the society, which works on the pattern of a cooperative society is more democratic than a village panchayat. Whereas elections to the society are held every year, elections to the panchayats are held every five years. The panchayat works more in accordance with the rules and procedures established by the state department, the HRMS frames its own rules, passes its resolutions and works in a more autonomous manner. It has also constituted a sub-committee known as pani-panchayat which regulates the distribution of water for irrigation purposes and lays down rates.

The Bunga Watershed Project is not an isolated project of its kind. The entire foothills range in Haryana are dotted with such projects. Many more watershed projects have been identified in the state.

Water Harvesting—A Movement

The Ministry of Water Resources and the Global Rainwater Harvesting Collective recently organised a National Workshop for Voluntary Organisations on drinking water and sanitation. The eminent development activist and doyen of NGOs in India, Bunker Roy, could get together about hundred grass-roots groups and voluntary organisations from across the country to discuss low cost rural solutions and share community-based success stories in an effort to change the water policy.

The workshop sent out a strong message that the government should get out of supply of water for irrigation and domestic needs. It should restore traditional step wells, tanks and water ponds, which have survived hundreds of years and hand over their maintenance to local communities.

Discussing the recommendations of the workshop, Senior Development journalist Usha Rai says, "The Global Rainwater Harvesting Collective is focussing in two areas—collecting rainwater from roof tops of schools and hospitals and in revitalising wells and hand pumps that have gone dry. This is done by directing surface water into open wells within the village. The use of stored water is controlled by the community. There are several such excellent projects being managed by voluntary organisations that need support. They do not require large sums of money that government projects do."

REFERENCES

'Community-based Natural Resource Management in Alwar'—an article by Rahul Gupta in *UNDP News*, July 2003, New Delhi.

National Water Policy, 2002, Ministry of Water Resources, Government of India, New Delhi, April 2002.

'Water-Asia's Environmental Imperative' (1997), Asian Media Information and Communication Centre, Singapore.

'Water before Roti, Kapada aur Makan' by Usha Rai, *Grassroots*, August 2003, Press Institute India, New Delhi.

27

Integrated Watershed Development Project

Meenu Arora

Integrated watershed development projects are being implemented in the country in the plains and hills to improve the productivity potential of the project area in the states evolving watershed treatment technologies through community participatory approaches. The associated objective of the project is to assist the states with institutional development and to consolidate progress already made in harmonising approaches to watershed development and management among various programmes operating particularly in the Shivalik hills.

Integrated Watershed Development Project (IWDP) Hills-II has been taken as a follow-up project of Integrated Watershed Development Project (IWDP) hills that was closed on 31 March, 1999 to fill the gap and designed to recognise the need for policy and institutional arrangements to ensure long-term sustainability. Integrated Watershed Development (Hills-ID) project has been operational in Haryana, H.P., J&K, Punjab and Uttranchal states of the country since 15 September, 1999. The Integrated Watershed Development project Hill-II is being implemented in Akhnoor and Ram Nagar sub-watershed of the Shivaliks of Jammu and Rambiara and Rajwara sub-watersheds of Karewas of the Kashmir Valley. The major objectives of the watershed project are to conserve and protect the natural resources base from degradation through active participation of people. The ultimate aim of the project is to improve the quality of life of rural people in these poor regions through various demands-driven intervention.

The project places special emphasis on the building capacity of communities to take responsibility for maintaining assets created under the project. The project consists of two main components:

(i) Institutional strengthening.
(ii) Watershed development and protection.

Under the project, strengthening the institution will be by improving the community capacity building, strengthening policy reform, human resource development, providing income generating activities for women, improving information management, monitoring and evaluation and to support project coordination and management. Secondly, the project will protect water for development use through sub-watershed treatment, fodder and live stock development and rural infrastructure development.

The project will contribute significantly to decrease soil erosion, increasing water availability and alleviating poverty in the project area in the state.

Institutional Development

The watershed Development Council (WDC) at the central level is acting as coordinator and convener of the project for overall watershed development policy matters and would be responsible for facilitating and monitoring of the project. The project is being implemented by the States headed by the Watershed Project Implementation Office (WPIO) by the DDO at district level and at grass-root level by the Village Development Committees (VDC)/Village Forests Committee (VFC) and by people participation. The development work is done with the beneficence contribution in the shape of cash, material and labour.

Watershed Structure

Overall excellent work has been done on various aspects of watershed management in remote and difficult areas in a short period. However, there is still scope for further improvement. Watershed management includes protection, conservation and improvement of land for more efficient production by accelerating measures to conserve soil and moisture on farm grazing lands and forests. Even though it is an integrated participatory and sustainable area development programme, it is not a rural development programme for construction of road, bridge, school and other community development works.

Land treatment measures are expected to reduce run-off soil erosion, increase recharge rise of water level and improving agricultural and silvi pasture productivity. When watershed management activity becomes a long-term activity, its effective, excellent, noticeable results will be seen in project areas. Erosion control and water conservation will be useful to specify catchment area tackled, for construction of check dam, brush dam, loose rock dam, dry store dam and drop spill way under the guidance of technical experts of line departments. Development activities of pasture and silvi pasture through providing planting material (trees-root slips), fertiliser, etc. is one of the main activity under the project and fencing of the area are equally useful to prevent uncontrolled grazing by cattle.

Livestock Development

The main objective of the component is to increase the milk yield and wool production by improving the breeds through artificial insemination, improved veterinary care, reducing disease stress and also ensuring fodder availability. Awareness for keeping/providing high milk yielding milch animals and better quality of livestock cultivation of fodder crops and grasses on degraded land and to create willingness in farmers to pay for the services are of importance for the sustainability of the project.

So far, 125 units of cows, 76 units of sheep/goats and 832 units of poultry have been provided under the project and this has helped in increasing the income of the beneficiaries. Crossbreed cows are not being encouraged/provided to the beneficiaries below the poverty line as they are not in a position to maintain them and they are being equipped with either poultry or sheep/goat units as an ideal alternative. Fencing for closure of area for silvi pasture is a good activity with a little high cost and would help in introduction of improved area for cattle and uncontrolled grazing would also be reduced. Stream bank erosion control practice is mixed with field bunding and for such condition crates are being used and are quite popular.

The women participatory Self-Help Groups (SHGs) are being provided skill training in tailoring and mushroom cultivation and for its marketing, etc. to supplement their income for the family.

Crop Improvement

To make long-term arrangement to provide improved seeds of high yielding variety which farmers can store and use for 2-3 seasons. Farmers can produce their own seed and share with other farmers.

VDG/VFC members share different roles and responsibilities and chairmen of committee require to be trained with well designed comprehensive courses, training material, etc. to manage effectively the implementation of the project.

To augment income and involve women in activities, which provide supplementary incomes the formation of self-help groups is done for mushroom cultivation, tailoring and small cottage industries activities.

Geographic Information System (GIS) and Information Management, Monitoring Evaluation (IMME)

The overall progress of this component is not very encouraging though efforts are on to set up hardware and software for the unit and IT consultants are being hired for setting up IT units and execution of the IT system in project management. The Geographic Information System (GIS) and remote sensing have a lot of potential in natural resource management activities and this needs to be fully integrated into the Information Management, Monitoring Evaluation (IMME).

IT consultants with project staff need to work for developing methodology and utilisation of the database and that can help in planning, prioritisation and selection of project activities and sites which help in execution of project activities by continuous monitoring mechanism and help in assessing the impact of the project.

It needs development of effective linkages with the Directorate of Environment and Remote Sensing, Directorate of Land Records for acquisition of remote sensing data and village maps to sort out priorities of the activities on the lines of NWDPRA.

Financial Management

The Financial Management Technical Support Consultant should provide training to all accounting staff and to the VDCs for smooth functioning of the computerised financial management system and maintenance of proper record of implementation of the project.

Social Issues

Active participation of disadvantaged groups like SC/ST/OBC and women in the executive committees shows an improvement in the participatory process. Due to insurgencies prevailing in certain states the majority of people of these groups are deprived of the direct benefits of the project.

Training

Periodic training to all the line departments officials and field functioning, i.e., VDC/VFC members is required for proper maintenance of accounts, etc.

Forestry

Pressure on grazing lands have adversely affected the vegetative cover and led to accelerated soil erosion. Various measures to check and reverse this degradation process and increase the biomass production through afforestation and augmentation of natural regeneration besides soil conservation measures and drainage line treatment have been initiated and is doing well. There is need to improve and bring uniformity in the approved five models of forest and VCL sector under the project. There seems to be enough scope of improvement in the nursery management and procurement of seedlings and other material.

Achievements

In all the four SWS of Jammu and Kashmir State 34 Self-Help Groups were formed covering 719 members. 94 VDCs/VFCs were prepared during the year 2000-01. 66 VDCs were prepared during 2001-02 upto August covering total 791 beneficiaries (including 616 male members, 175 female members and 187 SC/ST members). Similarly, progress and physical achievements will be monitored in all the project states and are expected to achieve the target of the project.

Specific Suggestions

The main focus should be on land and water conservation

management and minimum priority on rural/community-base activities:

- Use of pond water for micro-irrigation for growing vegetable crops near the pond rather than using for human bathing and livestock drinking only.
- Hand pumps/shallow wells can be supported for drinking water near the pond.
- Plastic mulches can also be attempted for conservation of water.
- Size of pits for planting fruits can be minimised for reducing the water coverage.
- Soil testing facility should be developed for appropriate suggestion of use of fertiliser and manure.
- To avoid duplication in efforts for the same activity, use of special studies for developing plan and new micro-enterprises.
- Training plan should be rescheduled and need-based.
- Use of GIS for pre- and post-development—information for maintaining/increasing the water table and conservation of soil moisture.
- GIS and MIC should be strengthened.
- Effective linkages and coordination with the local institutions will help effective implementation of the project.
- Information gap should be minimised.
- Regular quarterly review meetings by the implementation staff and steering committee.

Courtesy: *Employment News*, 12-18 April, 2003.

28

Integrated Watershed Development: Technology-Based Model

Sunil K. Agarwal

India being an agrarian country depends a great deal on natural resources for production of food and economic development of the rural areas. About 72 per cent of its population live in villages and about two-thirds of its workforce is engaged in agriculture and allied sectors. Hence, natural resource management and rural development are the mainstay of India's growth strategy. But excessive biotic and abiotic interferences reported in recent years particularly due to population pressure and natural hazards have caused considerable degradation of natural resources of land, water, vegetation and groundwater aquifers. Serious concerns are being expressed regarding deteriorating resource-base, loss of biodiversity, pollution and environmental degradation. Recent Human Development Reports reveal that more than 350 million Indians fall below the poverty line. A vast majority of people have no access to primary education, basic health care or even clean drinking water. They are vulnerable to natural disasters and have very little margin of survival. According to another estimate, the burgeoning population of India is expected to exceed 1225 million human beings and 600 million livestock by 2015, requiring nearly 275 mt of food grains, 1083 mt of green fodder and 235 mm^3 of fuel wood against current production of 209 mt of foodgrains, 513 mt of green fodder and 40 mm^3 of fuel wood. The per capita cultivated land area which was 0.53 ha in 1950, 0.195 ha in 1990 is projected to be 0.121 ha by 2025 and 0.087 ha by the year-2050—is a major challenge to meet all basic necessities from per capita arable land area. A vast extent of cultivable rainfed land can be made more productive with year round employment opportunities. Thus, natural resources are the most critical part of the livelihood strategies and farming systems, including livestock management and horticultural development and provide food, fuel wood, fodder, timber, compost, etc. for local communities. Therefore, natural resource management is at the core of the decentralized planning processes requiring a proactive movement of the people in view of the fact that most of the natural resources are in the common access management domain. Such emerging challenges and a widening gap between demand and supply in the country calls for conservation, judicious and sustainable use of natural resources with an urgent need to make all out efforts to ensure that appropriate Scientific and Technical (S&T) inputs and Research and Development (R&D) outputs are put to use at the grass-roots level for the benefit of society.

Watershed Development: Current Scenario and Future Needs

In terms of approaches, the watershed-based development has now emerged as a major area to take care of such problems related to resource management in different agro-eco-regions on the principles of watershed-based resource identification, planning and implementation. There are several well-cited success stories on watershed development and management focussing more on biophysical aspects. But the need is now being felt for an appropriate approach requiring greater focus on socio-economic concern, community participation, institutional building, people's empowerment, conflict resolution, gender issues, equity and alternative activities for landless and productive employment generation through location specific needs and considerations. Here it is worthwhile to mention that the watershed is not just about soil and water conservation, but it is associated with individuals, villages, community and economic status of the area. It is a holistic development programme for the given area.

Different developmental agencies and S&T institutions are involved in watershed development programmes in the country like National

Watershed Development Projects to improve and maintain natural resources through improved agronomic and management practices based on watershed basis to help people in remote rural areas with degraded natural resource base. In this endeavour, it is strongly felt that watershed development and management with appropriate strategies and systems approach can play an important role in re-greening and re-nurturing depleting natural resources in a given watershed area. Such an effort will help by inbuilt mechanism for promoting conservation of resources, improving socio-economic life of the local people, promoting and conserving the environment thus contributing effectively to livelihood and environmental security. Technology intervention has also become a necessity and as an important tool in this approach for developing/modulating and transferring sustainable technologies that are cost effective, acceptable and affordable by the people either for construction of water harvesting structure or setting up of fodder bank or seed bank or improve agricultural and agro-processing techniques for value addition at the village itself. In this direction the following are the essential components for watershed development to enhance sustainable livelihoods.

Integrated Development with Systems Approach

The above needs may be fulfilled through integrated watershed development and management at micro-level focussing on need-based technological interventions and applications for sustainable production systems and quality improvement of rural livelihoods with participatory "systems approach" for capacity building and technological empowerment of local community to make them self-reliant in managing and using natural resources in a sustainable way. Participatory implementation and monitoring with strong networking amongst all the stakeholders and developmental agencies can generate adequate on-farm and off-farm employment opportunities, food and nutritional security and improve the quality of living.

Systems approach involves designing of programmes to infuse technical skills in local people and enhance capabilities of artisans/ small and marginal farmers/landless labourers through application of S&T inputs for creation of sustainable livelihoods. This bottom-up approach emphasizes development of a complete process of identifying needs, appropriate technology design and development, systems engineering resulting in creation of systems based on sustainable technology packages and maintenance of assets created. The process takes into account the local resources/skills available, the problems of the existing economic structures, gender and environment friendliness of the technology package and long-term sustainability of the entire programme.

People's Participation and Empowerment Based on Local Felt Needs

It is being realized that to succeed in watershed development approach for sustainable natural resource management, land and water conservation measures and other interventions should be initiated based on the socio-economic-environmental concerns. The programme should be formulated in response to the felt needs of the local community and based on local resources potentially available in rural areas such as labour, artisanal skills, land, water, forest and livestock. Participatory development implies intensive use of locally available information based on experience and knowledge of the rural people and, in the process, attempts to realize their latent capabilities. These efforts are supplemented with information and resources available from the Government and other sources with a view to enhancing local productivity.

The local community should be involved from conceptualization to the decentralized implementation stage, which will be more effective and fruitful than piecemeal approach. Since traditionally they are directly or indirectly dependent on these natural resources, their active participation becomes crucial to the success of such watershed development and management initiatives. Emphasis should be given to enhance the capacity of people by "learning by doing" and innovating in a changing environment and taking collective decisions and actions by involving all the stakeholders.

Involvement of Voluntary Organizations: Linkage Support and Networking

In order to facilitate effective participation, it is now being felt strongly that voluntary organizations with scientific and technical expertise can play a crucial role in development and dissemination of technology along with social engineering and motivation work; providing a strong communication link between the users and S&T

agencies; maintaining forward and backward linkages; standing as a guarantor/facilitator for loan and support services for the end users and providing marketing linkages, thereby playing a vital role in improving profitability and aptitude to use the technologies. Such organizations often are local in nature or associated with external groups (S&T institutions, developmental agencies) having strong linkages and networks working for their collective and mutual benefits.

Technology Needs and Back-up Support: Appropriate Package for Sustainable Livelihoods

Appropriate technology package transfer should consider socio-economic concerns and size of the population, composition and structure of household, basic and secondary needs of the people to address the problems of unemployment, underemployment, inequalities in income and assets and over-exploitation of natural resources. It is imperative to match people's needs with development and application of an alternative set of technologies for optimum utilization of resources and for alternative employment opportunities in the farm as well as the non-farm sector to solve the problem of the vicious circle of poverty and shrinking natural resource base. The immense diversity of our country's natural resources and prevalent local situations suggest introduction of location specific and need-based technological interventions, which could pave the way for desirable shift in the lifestyles and consequent improvement in quality of life. The main role of science and technology could be to make such necessary intervention, which may blend with the lifestyles of the people. These interventions must aim at providing simple affordable scientific solutions, which help the individual save on time and energy for the same life routine, thus creating opportunities for work in the non-traditional areas and augmenting income. Thus, science and technology can play a critical role as a provider of options and knowledge to the people specially with reference to the weaker sections and women which are either dependent on some natural resource which they own or those having no access or rights to such natural resources. For this S&T is a necessity in watershed development by addressing long-term problems of drought, fodder crisis, epidemics, drinking water shortage, health and sanitation, improved dietary habits, nutrition, housing, etc., and day-to-day problems like improved technology for routine work, value addition to products, shift towards non-conventional energy sources, etc. In this process, the need is to find ways of making the people cultivate the habit of using the natural resources specially wood, bamboo, medicinal plants and other forest products more judiciously through the application of sustainable technologies, which must be environmentally sound and compatible with socio-economic concerns to gain acceptance among the rural people.

Case Study: Technology-based Integrated Watershed Development Model

The Society for Rural Industrialization (SRI), a science and technology-based field group in Ranchi, took up the challenge for developmental and execution plan in 1996 for Tati watershed area, Angara block, Ranchi, based on sound social and technical considerations. This watershed area consists of 8 hamlets (Tolas) with 485 ha of arable and 120 ha of non-arable land having a population of 2880 with more than 80 per cent belonging to the tribal community. This area is characterized by undulating topography, poor soil fertility and large-scale migration of people. The main activities of the inhabitants are rainfed agriculture and collection of minor forest produce which are sold in the local market. Since rainfed agriculture is undependable, in the event of crop failure, the villagers either go for collection and sale of wood or migrate in search of sustenance.

Keeping the above in mind, the technology packages with a systems approach were appropriated and adopted for engineering and vegetative measures and socio-economic intervention under the guidance of locally constituted watershed development groups with representatives of each tola committee and women's representatives. Box 1 shows the treatment work on watershed basis for developing and managing resources, institutional and cultural development, economic and ecological benefit. The results provide clear pictures of the changes and evaluate the effect of appropriate technological application in this integrated and holistic watershed development and management work done over time for enhancing sustainable livelihoods. In this model, problems were addressed to generate the following assets essential for enhancing sustainable livelihoods:

1. Natural Assets

For this, efforts were made for above and below groundwater rain water harvesting, storage and its judicious usage; vegetative check dams; farm ponds (dohar well); channels; production plantations of various types like fodder, forages and grasses to fetch quick returns initially and timber for long-term benefits ensuring immediate community participation.

2. Physical Assets

Mechanical check dams; drainage work; gully plugging; agro-processing centre; production-*cum*-demonstration training centres for poultry; community centres; *pucca* roads, etc.

3. Human Assets

New employment opportunities with specialized skill and knowledge about processes, quality production, value addition and marketing in the area of biodynamic gardening, organized compost making, nursery raising, bamboo crafts, energy plantation *(Casuarina equistifolia, Prosopis juliflora)* as biomass fuel, mud tile making, rope making from *Sabai* grass and *sunhemp* fibres, and trading activities, etc. have generated immense confidence amongst local tribal people and self-help groups due to enhanced income level, reduced drudgery and additional-off farm employment leading to sustainable growth.

4. Financial Assets

Above interventions were found to be economically viable with direct employment and enhanced income in new trades; agro-processing; livestock rearing; etc.

5. Social Assets

Formation of watershed committee, Women's SHGs, tola committees; monetised (thrift, informal and infrastructure bank) and non-monetised (biomass, service and labour bank) banking structure has helped in increased participation and collective decision ensuring social security.

Box 1: Impact Assessment: Technology-based Participatory and Integrated Watershed Development in Tati Watershed Area of Angara Block, Ranchi, Jharkhand

Parameter	*Index of assessment*	*Status and Impact*	
		Pre-intervention 1996	*Post-intervention*
1	2	3	4
Land and water management	Arable land status	Agriculture: 90% by traditional method & 10% by improved method	50% by traditional, 50% by improved method yielding 15-20% increase in productivity.
	Non-arable status	Utilization once in three years	Mixed cropping in every year, 20-25% increase in average annual yield.
	Moisture level	Very poor	10-20% improvement in treated land.
	Soil fertility in treated land	25 to 30%	48 to 60% improvement
	Run-off	60%-75%	20%
	Soil loss/ton/ha/year	3 ton/ha/year	2 ton/ha/year
	Animal grazing	Open method	Controlled, now stall feeding
	Groundwater recharge	10%	25%
	Rise in water table	0.3 metre during summer	.5 metre increased in summer
	Water harvesting structure	Nil	Construction of 11 nos. WHT
	Plantation for fuel/fodder	Only in natural forest	40 ha.
Afforestation and value addition	Practices	New plantation by 10% people.	New plantation by 30% people. Tree cutting (40-60%), bamboo-based article making
	Utilisation	Tree cutting for timber and own family 90% Nil for fodder and lac	40% people started plantation for fodder/lac.

(Contd.)

Box 1: (*Contd.*)

1	*2*	*3*	*4*
Capacity building technological empowerment, self-sustainability	Practising trades	• 2 types, mason & carpentry	• 23 types
	No. of trained manpower	• (25 nos.)	• 352 nos.
People's participation in planning, implementation and maintenance stage	• Small farmer • Medium farmer • Larger farmer • Women	Low	• 40-50% • 40-50% • 20-25% • 60%
Economic level/income generation opportunities	Income from farm activity	By seasonal vegetable and local variety of paddy only.	30% increased in total yield by improved variety of seed and other techniques.
	From non-farm activity	60% family used to be engaged in wood/leaf selling and daily wage work	• 20% family engaged in skilled job/ shops • 40% engaged in daily wage work.
Women's emancipation	Activity of women	90% women were engaged in wood selling, agriculture and vegetable selling, etc.	60% are now engaged in compost-making and food-processing, etc.
	Women's organization	Nil	50% are organized in groups having informal bank.
	Interaction with outside society	Nil	20% can interact with Bank/block officers.
	Nutritional garden	Nil	20 trained women have initiated.
Men's emancipation	Organisation building	Tola level committee for social and cultural activities.	Tola level for agriculture and economic activities.
	Initiative in new activities	Nil	Fishery, Nursery raising, Piggery, Animal health care.

Impact Assessment

The details of the impact of the intervention with growth indicators for social and technical benefits is available in Boxes 1 and 2. Besides groundwater recharge, rise in water table was spectacular with tremendous environmental benefits through erosion control. Due to this and techno-managerial training, youths are now able to operate and maintain pump sets, nursery and other off-farm activities; women are taking interest in construction of improved *chulhas,* biomass gardening, production of cash crops like chilli and oil seeds with more and more participation of small and marginal farmers in diversified agricultural activities and making value added products. Mobile lift irrigation has helped in timely transplantation of paddy and increase in yield. Health and orientation camps on cleanliness, prevention and cure of diseases; education on mother and child care, family planning through *nukkad natak;* night coaching centres for children; biomass-based power generating system for night illumination, irrigation and small industry have contributed immensely from the social security point of view. A group of people has also been trained to make use of *Lantanna,* an invasive biomass available in the area for making value added low cost articles like furniture and using this unwanted weed as a fuel in gasifier. For ensuring the involvement of people, structures were created for internal resource generation by formation of new groups, Village Level Organizations (tola), Apex Committee at the watershed level, strengthening and stabilizing the structure through various inputs in the form of training, creating work opportunity alongwith social and environmental security, and introduction of informal system of non-monetized and monetized banking structure managed and controlled by villagers linked to the Panchayati Raj Institutions for further continuance and sustainability. Such diversified livelihood options have resulted in negligible migration of the people, stability and social cohesiveness.

In the success of the above, the guiding principle has been to provide enough flexibility and space to help the people and groups to come out with their own plan in technological and societal areas like eco-regeneration, etc. This factor has contributed in a significant way enabling people to shed the inhibition and doubts and share the responsibilities together. The people are able to access the technical, social and economical consequences of their management decisions.

Now, with the convergence of various programmes and technical backup support by nearby institutions over the last seven years, the micro-planning system is well strengthened and entirely owned by the community organizations.

In this Tati watershed model, SRI has shown that joint management of land, water, vegetation, livestock and human resources can be made through sound strategy and multi-sectoral approaches for integrated watershed development with diversified livelihood options in a participatory manner. Women's involvement, socio-economic upliftment of landless and disadvantaged sections of the community, equitable sharing of benefits and responsibilities were found important elements for long-term sustainability of such interventions. Diversification for new micro-enterprise and off-farm activities, health and nutritional programmes, location specific production activities linked with value addition at source and dovetailing market linkages—provided better sustainable livelihood opportunities thus, in turn ensuring immediate community participation in land, cover and water management measures. Bottom up approach, access to non-formal education, intensive and transparent interaction with stakeholders for blending traditional knowledge with new technology inputs have facilitated technology adoption. As a result, the community is now able to mobilize and manage regular development programmes for infrastructural development and welfare activities in the area. This model further suggests that watershed programme is a holistic approach of development in which various programmes have to be converged like drinking water, health management, income generating activities, etc. It has become imperative now to strengthen such pro-active movement so that wealth is generated in our rural areas and the state-of-art technologies are available at the grass-roots level in our effort to create sustainable livelihoods through S&T interventions.

Conclusion

Such initiatives have contributed to the ecological stabilization of the Tati watershed area with increased groundwater level that, in turn, has breathed a new life in natural resources of the project area. This model also highlights the role of NGOs and networking needs for interfacing with S&T institutions and support agencies and, above all, the systems approach for technology-based integrated watershed

Box 2: Participatory Integrated Watershed Management: Technological Interventions and People's Empowerment

Activities	*S&T Interventions and Technical Support*	*Problems: Benefits and People's Empowerment*	
		Pre-intervention	*Post-intervention*
1	2	3	4
Agronomic measures: • Cropping pattern	• Demonstration of double crop, triple crop and cash crop suitable for the area	Mono-cropping	• Double cropping pattern followed—60% people • Triple cropping—20%
• Integrated pest and nutrient management	• Training on herbal pesticides & storage technology • Training on use of biomass for making different types of composts	Chemical pesticides were used by the people	• Herbal pesticide for pest control along with scientific storage technologies at family and community level • 60% farmers using organic fertilizer • Organized women's group in vermi-compost technology and marketing support
• Horticulture	Training on plantation including nursery raising	No horticulture plantation by local family	• Each family planted 6-8 fruit plants per year
Vegetative measures	• Arhar plantation • Contour and graded bund with pits • Check dam • 5% model • Strip vegetative terracing • Vegetative hedge	• Nil. • Severe land erosions and degradation, 60-75% run-off	• People trained in production of grass & energy plantations • All families are sustainably using the output for above production • 10 families are getting regular income from selling of grass/rope-making or broom-making

(Contd.)

Box 2: (*Contd.*)

1	2	3	4
	• Plantation. • Savai grass cultivation on high slopes • Broom grass cultivation on high slopes		• Increase in production of the treated land
Increased productivity of arable and non-arable land	• Land and water management and treatment (techniques introduced)	90% traditional farming Utilization of land once in a year in non-arable land	• 50% traditional farming • 50% modern technology • 20% more yield • People got trained in modern agriculture • People utilizing once in a year • 20 to 25% improvement in treated land
Improve post-harvest technologies and agro-processing	• Training on post-harvest management • Agro-processing training on pickles, chips, tomato, imli, etc. • Value addition to agro-forest produce	• Traditional method followed for post-harvest • No agro-processing technique followed	• People aware of storage of post-harvest material and quality processing • Common facility centre for processing and production • SHG formed on agro-processing for income generating activity
Animal husbandry	• Training of 30 people on animal health management	No trained manpower	• Trained people available at tola level
Aquaculture	• Renovation of ponds, preparation of spawn and culture techniques	No trained manpower	• Quality fish production and income generation

Employment opportunity	• Mandays granted during implementation of work component of the project • Vermi compost technology • Processing technology (Jackfruit, etc.) • Energy farming • Bamboo structure building • Gasifier operation & maintenance, etc.	Traditional farming/absence of non-farm activities	• 30% of the present employment is through new skill-related jobs/opportunities.
Health	• Health camps; training on [illegible] planning and immunization	Poor health	• 25% water borne diseases compared to 60% earlier
Drinking water & irrigation	• Water harvesting tanks, farm ponds, and channels, irrigation well built	Scarcity of water for irrigation and drinking	• Availability for irrigation facility for 50 ha of land • Drinking water facility for 24 hrs. • Controlled run-off and water conservation
Habitat, electricity, etc.	• Low cost construction technology • Installation of biomass-based power generating unit and gasifier • Night coaching centres and functional literacy	Poor habitat, no electricity, *kuchha* lanes, poor housing	• 25% families own *pucca* house against 5% as recorded earlier • 68 families getting power for night illumination, irrigation and small industry • 900 families to get power by another 100 KW BMG system • 8 coaching centres and 8 biomass banks • *Pucca* road

(*Contd.*)

Box 2: (*Contd.*)

1	*2*	*3*	*4*
Benefit cost ratio from technological intervention	• Different technologies introduced • Training provided • Linkages established	Nil	• Direct benefit accrued per year is around 2.5 times the investment cost • Indirect benefits are environment protection, social security and improved quality of life
Conservation and equitable sharing of benefits	• Introduction of technologies suitable for marginal farmers or families owning primarily non-arable land	Selling wood from forest	• Compost production • Tamarind processing, bulk processing of fruits and vegetables • Oil expelling • Masala grinding • Energy farming and selling the biomass in power generating units, etc.
Strengthening of people's institutions for credit and marketing	• Committee formation on Tola level and apex level on cultural and village development • Group training • Linkages with marketing group federation, etc.	Community organization, poor	• Tola level committee—8 nos. • Watershed committee—1 • Marketing channel developed • Women SHG—16 nos. • Cultural/sports—1 no. • Community Centres—3
Ecological soundness & biodiversity conservation	• Introduction of environmentally sound technology packages like vermi-composting • Conservation and sustainable use of resources	Poor awareness	• 100 acres area with plantation (200 families involved) • 16 SHG group for composting, etc. • Awareness through Eco-regeneration camps/training

development. Hence, concerted efforts are urgently required to develop and adopt an integrated approach through appropriate technological interventions in participatory mode to offset the looming crisis of natural resource degradation and increased demand of food for sustainable livelihoods. The need is to convert weaknesses into strengths and threats into opportunities by involving people in all management aspects related to conservation measures and repair of structures, diversified agriculture/farming activities and benefit accrued should be shared or utilized to strengthen watershed development work, thus, building a sense of self-reliance rather than dependency in the rural areas. It ensures social development, natural resource and infrastructural needs of the community by enabling them to work with all actors and developmental agencies to access multi-sectoral technical and financial inputs for solutions to their day-to-day activities/problems. For strengthening these efforts, it is essential that S&T institutions as technology providers and voluntary groups as facilitators should forge an alliance for nurturing rural livelihoods in different parts of the country through well designed integrated watershed development programmes focussing on area specific needs.

REFERENCES

Baumann, P. and Sinha, S. (2001), *Linking Development with Democratic Processes in India: Political Capital and Sustainable Livelihoods Analysis*, Natural Resource Perspectives, 68, ODI.

Farrington, J., Turton, C. and James, A.J. (eds.) (1999b), *Participatory Watershed Development: Challenges for the 21st Century*, Delhi: Oxford University Press.

Gaur, O.R. (1999), *Role of Self-help Groups in Natural Resource Management—Cooperative Experience*. Workshop on People and Participation in Sustainable Development of Natural Resources, (Environment Improvement in Rainfed Areas—EIRA), held during October 26-28, 1999 at Nagpur, Maharashtra, pp. 18-23.

Samra, J.S. (1998), *'People's Participation and Community Organizations in the Management of Watersheds,' Journal on Rural Development*, 18(3): 421-37.

Samra, J.S. (2000), *Assessment of Participatory Process of Watershed Management in India:* in ICIWRM-2000, Proceeding of International Conference on Integrated Water Resources Management for Sustainable Development, New Delhi, India (ed. R. Mehrotra, B. Soni and K.K.S. Bhatia), pp. 33-50.

Turton, C., Coulter, J., Shah, A. and Farrington, J. (eds.) (1998), *Watershed Development in India: Impact of the 1994 Guidelines*. A report prepared for GoI and DFID (New Delhi), London: ODI.

PART IV

RAIN WATER MANAGEMENT

29

Rain Water Management

S.P. Mittal

"Durlabham Salilam Tata Visheshena Paratra Vai"
(Water is scarce, hard to get, rare, particularly so on other planets)
(Dana-dharma-patva in Mahabharata)

Oceans cover about three-fourths of the earth's surface and nearly 97.3 per cent of the earth's water is in the oceans and seas. Fresh water constitutes a very small fraction (2.7 per cent). Of this fresh water 75.2 per cent lies frozen in the polar-regions and a further 22.6 per cent is present as groundwater. A very tiny portion of the planet's fresh water is available in lakes, rivers, atmosphere, soil and vegetation. What is effectively available for consumption and other uses is a small portion of the quantity present in rivers, lakes and underground aquifers. India which has 2.4 per cent of the world's land resources, has roughly 4 per cent of the world's fresh water resources and supports 16 per cent of the world's population.

The average rainfall of the country is 1170 mm concentrated to about 51 days of monsoon months (June to September). The country receives a total precipitation of about 400 million hectares. Out of this more than three-fourths is lost due to evaporation, going back to the sea and deep percolation. With the remaining water, the country has been able to create irrigation facility for about 40 per cent of the 142 million hectares of cultivated land. The remaining 60 per cent

Reprinted with permission, *Kurukshetra*, September 2005, pp. 16-19.

cultivated land continues to be rainfed. Occurrence of long dry spells between two rainfall events, late onset or early withdrawal of monsoon, are common features. Winter rains are quite uncertain and scanty.

Problems of Dry Land Agriculture

Although great strides have been made in agricultural production in the country, particularly in areas that have assured irrigation facilities, it is estimated that even after exploiting full irrigation potential through conventional sources, about 50 per cent of the cultivated area will continue to remain rainfed and subjected to the vagaries of nature.

In spite of best technologies available for dry land agriculture, the average production from this region has remained low. This region contributes about 42 per cent foodgrains to the national pool. Skewed pattern of rainfall is primarily responsible for this malady. There have been years when farmers did not harvest grain equal to even the amount of seed sown. Deficiency of moisture at the grain formation stage of kharif crops and at the time of sowing of rabi crops, is the single ubiquitous factor affecting crop yields in the rainfed region. The kharif crops may mature to some extent due to monsoon rains, but the fate of rabi crops is particularly precarious because there is hardly any moisture left in the soil for germination after the harvest of kharif crops. The scanty and undependable winter rains play havoc in most of the years. As per records, there is hardly any rain between October and December that can help sowing and germination of rabi crops. This long dry spell leaves a trail of miseries. That is why most of the farmers are sceptical to sow rabi crops.

The only alternative for sustainable crop production in such regions, is therefore, "runoff farming," i.e., harvesting surplus rainwater during monsoon and using it for providing supplemental irrigation as and when needed. This approach has given a new direction to the management of natural resources for the benefit of rainfed farmers as well as the agro-ecosystem.

Runoff Potential

Runoff has been defined as that portion of the precipitation (rainfall) in a drainage area that is discharged from the area in a stream channel.

It can be surface runoff, sub-surface flow or seepage. The average rainfall of the Shivalik region is 1100 mm. Out of this, about 873 mm. is received during the kharif season and 177 mm. during the rabi season with a CV of 28 per cent and 57 per cent respectively. Wide variation in the rainfall during the rabi season clearly indicates the need for supplemental irrigation for the success of the crops.

Rainwater Harvesting

Rainwater harvesting is the collection and storage of rainfall runoff from any catchment or watershed, for subsequent use for irrigation or any other beneficial use. Water harvesting can often mean the difference between crop and no crop in the rainfed areas. In the Shivalik region, where there is no possibility of developing any other source of irrigation due to topographical reasons, rainwater harvesting has proved to be a panacea.

Rainwater harvesting largely depends on quantity and distribution of rainfall and will, therefore, be more successful in areas where rainfall is sufficient. Besides, rainwater harvesting depends on several other factors including topography, soil type and depth, slope and vegetative cover in the catchment areas. For the rainwater harvesting programmes to be successful, it is essential that moderately large catchments and sufficient storage facilities are available in the vicinity of the villages. The rainfall distribution of this region as mentioned above is such that about 80 per cent of the total annual rainfall of 1100 mm is received during the south-west monsoon (June end to mid-September). This offers distinct possibilities of rainwater harvesting during monsoon for its later use for post-rainy season crops.

Rain water harvesting structures (RWHS), besides providing irrigation, can meet the multiple needs of society such as drinking and domestic water requirements, livestock, fish production, etc. It is imperative that the RWHS should have sufficient catchment area and the capacity to achieve the purposes for which these are constructed.

Supplemental Irrigation

Water resource development by constructing RWHS is primarily for supplemental irrigation during stress periods of crop growth or when there is a long gap between two rainfall events. A pre-sowing irrigation is a must for rabi crops because in most of the situations the soil moisture is at critically low levels. In the event of early withdrawal of monsoon in kharif season, one irrigation can be provided from the harvested rain water to maize. Based on the earlier experience of the RWHS constructed in the Shivalik region, generally two or a maximum of three irrigations are sufficient for wheat, mustard and gram.

Water Conveyance System

Since the water in the dams is available in limited quantity every effort must be made to reduce conveyance losses. For delivering water from the dam to the fields, a pipe outlet through the body of the dam is connected to an underground pipeline that carries water to the fields in the command area. This system is most economical and reduces conveyance losses to the minimum. Riser/outlets are provided at appropriate places in the command area. The water from these points is then carried through open channels to the individual fields.

With the success of the Sukhomajri project began the era of constructing small water harvesting dams in the Shivaliks in the Eighties. Consequently, more than 200 such rainwater harvesting dams have already been constructed in the states of Haryana, Punjab and Himachal Pradesh by the Forest, Agriculture and Soil Conservation departments. The World Bank aided Integrated Watershed Development Project, implemented in the above mentioned states, has given a fillip to this programme in a big way. In recent years 7 RWHS have been constructed in Panchkula and Yamunanagar districts of Haryana under the Haryana Union (HU) Forestry Project which is being supported by the European Community. The height of these dams varies from 6 to 16 metres, with the catchments up to 190 hectares, storage capacity up to 60 hectares and the command area varying from 4 to 240 hectares. The harvested rainwater is conveyed to the agricultural fields through underground pipelines by gravity. Thus, there is no need for electricity or diesel engines.

Impact of Irrigation

Farmers usually grow wheat in this belt. However, efforts were made to persuade the farmers to go in for mustard and gram also as these crops not only fetch higher price but require much less water as compared to wheat. Depending on the availability of water, two to three irrigations could be provided to the rabi crops. The studies carried out on farmers' fields with limited irrigation, at critical growth stages of rabi crops, use of optimum dose of fertilizer and improved varieties of seeds, resulted in two to three times increase in yield of wheat, gram and mustard as is evident from the following table:

In addition to food crops almost all the farmers getting irrigation have also started growing berseem *(Trifolium alaxandrinum)* for green fodder. The average yield of this crop is more than 300 q/ha. The green fodder is used as a supplement by milch cattle.

Particulars	*Wheat*	*Gram*	*Mustard*
Yield before project (q/ha)	8.0	3.9	2.0
Yield after project (q/ha)	27.0	102	6.3
Increase in yield (%)	237	161	215

Note: The yields are the averages from farmers' fields.

Community Participation

The dire need of irrigation water for the parched agricultural fields which lead to manifold increase in crop yields, worked as a 'catalyst' in bringing about a change in the attitude of villagers towards the hilly catchments. Meetings were held with the villagers where RWHS have been constructed, where it was emphasized that they must protect the hilly catchments from grazing and illicit cutting of trees if they wanted water in their dams otherwise these would be silted up and they will not get water for their fields. The villagers heeded this advice and stopped grazing and illicit cutting of vegetation from the catchment areas. Consequently, the vegetation started coming up in the denuded hilly catchments and the bare hill slopes were covered with grasses and trees in due course of time. It was probably for the first time in the history of the forests of the Shivalik region that the villagers have themselves started protecting the forests. This new approach of protection of the forest areas by the people, was termed as "Social Fencing."

The experience of executing a number of projects in this region strongly suggests technical economic and social viability of constructing small earthen dams by adopting participatory approach for water resource development and rehabilitation of degraded eco-systems of the Shivaliks. The availability of irrigation water played a pivotal role in binding the people in to a coherent society. To ensure continued peoples' participation, the entire management of the projects has been handed over to village-based societies christened as Hill Resource Management Society (HRMS) or Water Users' Society, which have been registered under the Society's Registration Act, 1860. These societies have been assigned the following responsibilities:

(i) Protection of hilly catchments from grazing and illicit cutting of trees, i.e. *Social Fencing.*
(ii) Distribution of irrigation water from dams among all its members at the rate to be fixed from time to time.
(iii) Maintenance of dams, water conveyance systems and other assets.
(iv) Utilization of society's funds for welfare activities in the village.

The availability of irrigation water has had a spin effect on the socio-economic condition of thousands of families living in this region. The landholders have taken agriculture in a big way, converting the degraded and waste lands into lush green fields. The landless have got jobs as farm labourers and they need not go to far-off places in search of jobs.

Boost to Dairy Sector

The availability of more fodder from the agricultural fields as well as green fodder from berseem and grass from the forest area, has given a fillip to the dairy sector in the villages. For instance, in one village the number of buffaloes has increased from 79 in 1975 to about 300 at present. The daily total milk production in the village has gone up from 160 litres to about 1200 litres. Milk has become the main source of income for the villagers.

With the increase in the income, both from the farm and dairy sectors, the economy of the villagers has recorded an unprecedented upward trend. The villagers are now spending part of their income in constructing new houses and part in acquiring assets and modern electronic gadgets. A recent survey of Sukhomajri village revealed that in 110 households there are 40 telephone connections, 70 TV sets, 45 scooters/motor cycles, 30 fridges, 40 LPG connections, 4 tubewells, 6 tractors, and 4 trucks. These items were never heard of or seen by the villagers before the project. Besides, the villagers are constructing separate sheds for the cattle in a large number.

Other Benefits

Rainwater harvesting and its utilization for crop production has resulted in tangible benefits like ecological, social and economic benefits besides employment generation. The construction of dams in conjunction with treatment of hilly catchments with appropriate soil conservation measures has helped in checking soil erosion, widening of choes/drains, damage to agricultural fields and communication systems. Some of the common lands have been reclaimed and put under cultivation.

The experience of rainwater harvesting in the Shivalik region has translated into reality the Guiding Principle No. 2 of the International Conference on Water and Environment (ICWE) held in January 1992 in Dublin and endorsed by Agenda 21 of the Earth Summit held in Rio de Janeiro in June 1992, which is "Water resource development and management should be based on a participatory approach involving users, planners and policy-makers at all levels." In the true spirit of this principle and to ensure efficient and judicious utilization of the limited water resource, the local community was involved in planning, implementing and subsequent management of the projects and maintenance of its assets.

Lessons Learnt

Some very important lessons have been learnt from these projects that have to be kept in mind while implementing such projects. These are:

- People's participation must be ensured right from the inception of the project.
- Peoples' participation is difficult to be achieved unless they are first convinced that they can derive direct and visible benefits from the project.
- The needs and the problems of the people must be identified at the outset.
- Unless a project is aimed at meeting their needs, solving their problems and mitigating their hardship, it may not succeed.

- There must be flexibility right from the planning stage to the implementing stage, i.e., the implementing agency should have the option to modify/revise the components of the project if required by the villagers.
- The project should have a short gestation period. The benefits should be available to the people in the shortest possible time.
- The emphasis should be on sustainability and equity.
- Constitution of a village society must be a prerequisite.
- Once the benefits from the project start accruing, the people are willing to take up the responsibility of protecting the forests (social fencing), manage the project and maintain its assets.

These projects are an experience of our shift from merely 'thinking about sustainability' to practising sustainable action. These projects represent a change in our concern from development solely for the present generation to the development for all, including ours and many more future generations. The projects have adopted a strong sustainable approach because here the stress was on the complementary nature of man-made and natural resources. The projects envisage not merely renewability of material resources but also concerns itself with human resource development. Be that as it may, the indigenous approach in these projects, with a history of two and a half decades, has established its functional prominence as a model of participatory sustainable management of natural resources which has ultimately resulted in rehabilitation of degraded ecosystems and socio-economic upliftment of the community.

30

Water Harvesting for Drinking Water Security

Dinesh Chand

The population of the country is over 1 billion and is expected to reach 1.64 billion by the year 2050. Towns and villages are expanding rapidly; new habitations are coming up—all requiring and demanding drinking water for sustainance of life. An estimation of demand suggests that the drinking water requirement of rural habitations alone would be 29 billion cubic metres (BCM) in 2050 against the present requirement of about 10 BCM. Meeting the demand of safe drinking water for all is a challenging task with lakhs of villages/habitations spread over high hills and mountain slopes, deep forest valleys, barren deserts, degraded lands and ravines, along saline coastal belts, denuded rocky plateaus and other inaccessible remote areas.

Ground water, the major source of rural water supply is depleting fast in many areas due to large-scale exploitation for expanding irrigated agriculture. Out of a total of 5156 blocks in 8 states (viz., Andhra Pradesh, Gujarat, Haryana, Punjab, Rajasthan, Karnakata, Tamil Nadu and Uttar Pradesh), 247 blocks are declared as over-exploited with groundwater extractions being in excess of net annual recharge and 179 Blocks/Watersheds as Dark as per the report on Ground Water Resources of India (1995). Further, NABARD has also placed 603 blocks/watersheds under the Grey category. Besides, many blocks, presently categorised as "dark" are likely to become "over-exploited."

Reprinted with permission, *Kurukshetra*, August 2006, pp. 4-12.

The fast deteriorating situation of fresh water availability is gradually acquiring an even more dangerous and frightening dimension of worsening water quality. According to the recent findings (1997), arsenic contamination in groundwater is high in about 5029 habitations in West Bengal; fluoride levels above permissible limits in mainly Andhra Pradesh, Gujarat, Rajasthan, Uttar Pradesh, West Bengal, Karnataka, Punjab, Maharashtra, Tamil Nadu and Madhya Pradesh affecting about 16 million people in 31,306 habitations; excess iron in habitations in north-eastern and eastern states affecting about 12 million people and salinity in 23,495 habitations of Gujarat, Karnataka, Punjab, Andhra Pradesh, West Bengal, Maharashtra, Rajasthan and Tamil Nadu. Besides various natural factors, rapid urbanisation, industrialisation and increased use of fertilizers and pesticides in agriculture have also adversely affected groundwater quality.

This being the situation of water sources today, the prospects of augmenting it almost three fold by 2050 and improving its quality to desired levels warrant drastic changes in our water management strategy as the usual approach of augmenting water availability through major, medium and minor irrigation schemes has its own techno-economic limitations. The main problem is not only that of collecting and storing water in huge quantities but also that of providing it within easy reach of the large rural population spread over 14.22 lakh of rural habitations. Our experience of thousands of years since the dawn of civilisation, has shown that minimum water requirements of every household anywhere can be easily met by the traditional methods of collecting rain water locally in village/ community ponds and large man-made containers, diverting and storing water from local streams/springs and tapping sub-surface water below river/stream beds. These basic techniques have been successfully applied in many different ways by the people in different parts of the country depending upon the local climate, soils and rocks, both above and below the land surface and the nature of land forms viz., plains, hill slopes, hill tops, valleys, plateaus, etc. These traditional methods are modern "Water Harvesting," and are environment-friendly and which the villagers themselves can easily adopt at affordable costs.

Factors Responsible for Water Crisis

The over drawals of groundwater in the country has led to an alarming decline in the groundwater level in some areas and consequent stress on groundwater resources resulting in a great threat to groundwater sources sustainability. There are many factors responsible for groundwater sources becoming defunct and dry, viz.,

1. Competing demand of groundwater for irrigation, industrial and other purposes,
2. Excessive drawals of groundwater without considering the recharge,
3. No or low electricity tariff for agricultural and industrial use,
4. Lack of scientific input and management of groundwater,
5. Lack of awareness among the masses about the need of groundwater recharge,
6. Misuse of precious water treating it as a free and ever lasting commodity, and
7. Lack of sustainability principle applications in drawals of groundwater, etc.

Hydrological Aspects

Hydrological processes are important to understand for harvesting rainwater through various techniques. The groundwater interacts both with surface water and streams throughout all types of landscapes from mountains to the sea.

(a) Interaction of Groundwater and Surface Water

Groundwater moves along flow paths of varying lengths in transmitting water from the area of recharge or discharge. The small-scale geologic features in the bed of surface water bodies and lakes affect recharge patterns. The size, shape and orientation of sediments and grain sizes in surface waterbeds affect seepage pattern. Often the surface waterbed consists of sand; the inflow seepage is greatest at the shoreline and decreases away from it. The geology of land units of varying permeability also affects water seepage in surface waterbeds.

The groundwater seepage to surface water is greatest near the shore. Infiltrating rain water passes rapidly through a thin unsaturated zone adjacent to the shoreline which produces a mound of water table adjacent to surface water body as "focused recharge," which results in increased groundwater inflow to surface water bodies.

The groundwater recharge therefore can be focused initially where the unsaturated zone is relatively thin at the edges of surface water bodies and beneath depressions in the land surface.

(b) Interaction of Groundwater and Stream

The streams lose water to groundwater by outflow through the stream bed. For surface water to seep into groundwater, the altitude of water table in the vicinity of the stream should be lower than the altitude of stream water surface. The interaction between groundwater and streams takes place in nearly all streams. Depending upon the magnitude, intensity and frequency of stream flow and increase in stream stage, some streams and adjacent aquifers are in continuous interaction. If the level of water in streams is more than its bank, the floodwater recharges groundwater throughout the flooded area.

The reservoirs behind check dams are designed primarily to control flow and proper distribution of surface water. Like streams, such reservoirs (lakes) also have fluctuating water levels and also lose water-to-water table to recharge groundwater.

Harvesting Techniques

There are two main techniques of rainwater harvesting: (a) Rainwater storage on surface for future use, and (b) Recharge to sub-surface/groundwater.

The storage of rainwater on the surface is a traditional technique and structures used are underground tanks, check dams, weirs, etc. Recharge to groundwater is a new concept of rainwater harvesting and the structures generally used are pits and shafts, trenches, hand pumps, recharge boreholes and wells, lateral shafts with bore wells, spreading techniques, nalla bunding, contour bunding, contour trench, gully plugging, check-dams, basin/percolation tanks, groundwater dams, injection wells, connector wells, dug well recharge, de-silting of tanks, rooftop harvesting, inter-watershed transfer, gabian structure, village tanks, stream augmentation, aquifer modification, ditch and furrow, jacket well technique, trench-*cum*-filter bore well, rainwater recharged bore well technique, etc.

The details of these structures are available in standard books on the subject and manuals on rainwater harvesting published by the Department of Drinking Water Supply, Ministry of Rural Development.

Recommended Water Harvesting Options for Different Agro-climatic Zones

India being a vast and diverse country, it is very difficult to prescribe a single type of RWH structure for sustainability of sources. Moreover, agro-climatic conditions, hydrogeology of the regions, local traditions and customs vary. However, some broad principles can be followed while planning and implementing RWH structures for sustainability.

The country has been demarcated into 15 agro-climatic regions based on the requirements of agricultural development. However, for promoting rainwater harvesting with particular reference to augmenting drinking water availability in rural areas, these regions need to be slightly modified and an "Himalayan foot hills" zone may be added. Broad features and the recommended water harvesting measures for each region are tabulated as follows:

Diversion of Urban Runoff into Existing Surface Water

The huge construction activities within and around cities and reclamation of these tanks for conversion into plots for housing purposes are resulting in the drying up of water bodies. Free flow of run-off into these tanks and water bodies must be ensured. The storm run-off may be diverted into the nearest tanks or depression, which will recharge the groundwater. The methods of artificial recharge, viz., water spreading, recharge through pits, trenches, wells, shafts, roof-top collection of rainwater, induced recharge from surface water bodies, etc., are suitable for urban areas.

Selection and Implementation of RWH Structures

1. The following factors should be taken into consideration while selecting a RWH structure:

    (i) Water availability and rainfall pattern of the area.
    (ii) Favourable topography.
    (iii) Physiography and hydro-geological set-up.

S. No.	*Agro-Climatic Zones*	*Regions*	*Characteristics*	*Recommended Water Harvesting*
1.	Humid north-western Himalayas	Hilly areas of Jammu & Kashmir (J&K), Himachal Pradesh (HP) and Uttaranchal	Skeletal soils, podsolic soils, mountain meadow soils and hilly brown soils, highly undulating terrain with steep slopes. The soils are generally silty loam and are prone to erosion. Landslides are common in denuded hill slopes especially with excessive human settlements with good network of roads and hill tracks.	(i) Roof water harvesting (ii) Diversion of perennial springs and stream water in storage structures (iii) Village ponds/tanks (iv) Collection from hill slopes
2.	Himalayan foothills	Foothill areas of J&K, HP, Punjab and Uttaranchal in the west and parts of West Bengal, Assam and Arunachal Pradesh in the east.	Slope-wash material comprising loose soil deposits underlain by boulders and pebbles having moderate to high percolation rates where the soil cover is thin. In topographic lows the thick soil cover provides scope for dug ponds with fairly good water retention capacity. Often, the groundwater gradient is steep which is conducive to quick ground-water drainage into nearby streams.	(i) Collection from hill slopes (ii) Village ponds (iii) Contour trenching
3.	Humid high rainfall north-eastern zone	Large areas of Sikkim, Darjeeling-hills, Arunachal Pradesh, Meghalaya, Nagaland, Manipur, Tripura, Mizoram, Assam, Jalpaiguri and Cooch Behar districts of West Bengal	Complex geological formations with rocks exposed either on surface or under moderately thick soil cover generally fragile and prone to severe erosion. High rainfall areas with high surface runoff. Because of adverse topography and hydro-geological conditions, groundwater development may not be techno-economically viable.	(i) Roof top harvesting (ii) Diversion of perennial springs and streams in storage structures (tanks)

4.	Humid Assam-Bengal plains	West Bengal, Assam	Parts of the lower Gangetic plains comprising alluvium with diverse mix of sand, silt and clay. The main topographic features of the region are the fluvial plains, and lower and upper alluvial terraces. The fluvial plains are characterized by abandoned river channels, ox-bow lakes and the land surface carved by numerous perennial and seasonal streams. Though the region receives good rainfall, there is often drought-like situations due to long gaps between successive spells of rainfall especially in areas drained by small seasonal streams.	(i) Tanks (ii) Check dams/ Anicuts (iii) Gully plugging (iv) Contour bunding
5.	Sub-humid and humid Sutlej-Ganga alluvial zone	Parts of Punjab, Haryana, UP and Bihar and served by middle reaches of the Sutlej basin and the lower and middle reaches of the Ganga basin. The eastern part of the region covering plains of Bihar and eastern UP.	Receives good rainfall but due to its uneven distribution in space and time, some areas face sub-humid conditions and even drought like conditions in the years of below-normal rainfall. The southern part of the Sutlej basin has sub-humid climate. During the last 5 decades the region has seen large-scale development of groundwater for irrigation. This has resulted in lowering of groundwater table in many areas. The problem of drinking water supply is, however, mainly because of non-sustainability of the water sources for various socio-economic reasons.	(i) Ponds (ii) Check dams (iii) Gully plugging (iv) Contour bunding

(Contd.)

S. No.	*Agro-Climatic Zones*	*Regions*	*Characteristics*	*Recommended Water Harvesting*
6.	North-western semi-arid and arid zone	Western Rajasthan	Areas characterized by hot sandy desert, erratic & low rainfall, high evaporation, absence of any perennial rivers and scanty vegetation, negligible natural groundwater recharge. The groundwater table in most places is at considerable depth. At a few locations, potable groundwater at reasonable depths is found.	(i) Nadi/Talab (ii) Tanka (iii) Khadin (iv) Percolation tanks (v) Anicuts (vi) Gully plugging (vii) Contour bunding
7.	Central semi-arid Vindhyan zone	South-eastern districts of Rajasthan, southern districts of UP and central parts of Madhya Pradesh (MP). The area has diverse topography with ravines in some parts of Narmada Valley and hills in others. Nearly one-third of the land is not suitable for cultivation. Irrigation and cropping intensities are low.	Rainfall in areas lying in MP is as good as 900 mm and low as 350 mm in the areas falling in Rajasthan and UP. Because of the predominantly hilly terrain, high monsoon run-off causes extensive soil loss from hill slopes and erosion of riverbanks. Ground water movement from higher levels to lower levels is significant and resulting in the depletion of water levels in wells and hand pumps especially those along stream banks.	(i) Ponds (ii) Check dams (iii) Contour bunding (iv) Gully plugging (v) Sub-surface dykes
8.	High rainfall high runoff Chhota-nagpur plateau	Jharkhand state and adjoining hilly areas of Bihar, West Bengal and Orissa.	Area having soils of medium to shallow depths and undulating topography. Because of steep slopes, high rainfall intensities and long rainy spells resulting in high surface runoff causing extensive soil loss due to rill and gully formations and stream bank erosion. The problem is further compounded by unscientific agricultural practices. Because of adverse topography and pattern of human settlements in the hilly terrain, potential groundwater sources are not within convenient reach of all the rural population.	Improvement of water-sheds and local rainwater collection and storage are necessary to improve water availability. The following structures may be adopted: (i) Tanks/Ponds (ii) Check dams/Anicuts (iii) Gully plugging (iv) Contour bunding

9.	Malwa plateau & Narmada basin	Major part of peninsular India with an annual rainfall of about 900 mm.	Predominantly deep black soil with low permeability. Thus, the natural groundwater recharge is mainly through fissures and joints in exposed rock strata and through streambeds.	(i) Ponds (ii) Check dams (iii) Sub-surface dams
10.	South-central Deccan plateau zone	Parts of Andhra Pradesh (AP), Tamil Nadu, Karnataka and Maharashtra are typically semi-arid.	Area having highly diverse geological setting with predominance of hard basaltic rocks and variable rainfall. Surface strata and soil types are by and large conducive to natural ground-water recharge. Groundwater occurs under varying conditions in shallow and deep aquifers.	(i) Ponds (ii) Check dams (iii) Percolation tanks (iv) Bandhara (v) Gully plugging (vi) Sub-surface dams (vii) Contour bunding
11.	Chhattisgarh plateau zone	Chhattisgarh state and south-western Orissa hills.	Geological and geo-morphological characteristics of the region are more or less similar to those in South-Central Deccan plateau zone even though rainfall in the region is relatively higher.	Same as in S. No. 10
12.	South-eastern brown/red soil zone	Pachamalai and Kadavur hills and pediplain areas of Tamil Nadu and Veligond hills and part of the plains (excluding the 4-5 km wide coastal belt) of AP	The rainfall in the region varies from about 818 mm in Perambalur district of Tamil Nadu of 1148 mm in Nellore district of AP. Runoff coefficient varies from 6.64 to 10.67 per cent in plains and from 20 to 45 per cent in plateau and foothill areas.	(i) Traditional ponds/tanks/percolation tanks (ii) Sub-surface dams in the vicinity of water sources like dug wells, hand pumps and tube wells.

(Contd.)

S. No.	*Agro-Climatic Zones*	*Regions*	*Characteristics*	*Recommended Water Harvesting*
13.	Southern variable rainfall, mixed soil zone	Southern parts of Maharashtra and west-central parts of Tamil Nadu	Highly undulating and dissected landform with an elaborate natural drainage system. Distribution of rainfall is highly uneven. The land surface is diverse in composition, the main features being sandy or younger alluvial plains and rocky gravel pediments. The soils are friable and prone to erosion and prone to gully formation.	(i) Ponds/Tanks/ Kunta (ii) Percolation tanks (iii) Nadi (iv) Check dams (v) Sub-surface dams (vi) Gully plugging
14.	Southern bi-modal rainfall zone	Southern-most parts of Kerala, Karnataka and Tamil Nadu	Prominent physio-graphic features are the southern plateau & hills, east coast plains & hills and west coast plains & hills.	(i) Ponds/Tanks (ii) Percolation tanks (iii) Check dams (iv) Gully plugging (v) Contour bunding
15.	Eastern Coromandel	Entire eastern coastal belt of Orissa, Andhra Pradesh and West Bengal	Favourable for water harvesting, groundwater recharge and watershed development.	(i) Ponds/Tanks/Kunta (ii) Percolation tanks (iii) Nadi (iv) Check dams (v) Sub-surface dams (vi) Gully plugging
16.	Western Malabar	Western Malabar area of Kerala and coastal areas of southern Karnataka	Favourable for water harvesting, ground-water recharge and watershed development.	(i) Ponds/Tanks/Kunta (ii) Percolation tanks (iii) K.T. Weirs (iv) Bandhara (v) Check dams (vi) Sub-surface dams (vii) Contour bunding

Advantages and Disadvantages

Advantages	*Disadvantages*
• A water harvesting system collects and stores water within users' reach. • Assures a more continuous and reliable access to water. • Surface water storage structures improve the yield of hand pumps and wells. • Provides an alternative source of good quality water in the areas where ground-water or surface water is chemically contaminated. • Easy to construct with locally available materials, labour, environment-friendly and operated and community managed. • Investments, construction, operations are low. • Rainwater harvesting promotes self-sufficiency and fosters an appreciation for water as a resource. It also promotes water conservation. • Rainwater harvesting also conserves energy as the energy input needed to operate a centralized water system is bypassed. Many systems require only a small pump to create water pressure in household pipes. • Local erosion and flooding from impervious cover associated with buildings is lessened as a portion of local rainfall is diverted into collection tanks. • Rainwater is one of the purest sources of water available and does not get polluted. As rainwater is soft, it can significantly reduce the quantity of detergents and soap needed for cleaning. Water heaters and pipes are free of the deposits, if rainwater is used. • It provides an essential reserve in times of emergency and/or breakdown of public water supply systems, particularly during natural disasters.	• The success of rain harvesting depends upon the quantity and frequency of rainfall. Thus, it may fail during dry weather or prolonged drought. • Low storage capacities limit rainwater-harvesting benefits and large storage capacities may not be economically affordable. • Leakage from cisterns can cause the deterioration of load bearing slopes. • Cisterns/storage tanks can be a breeding ground for mosquitoes or unsafe for small children, if proper access protection is not provided. • Dirty catchment surfaces, animal wastes, bird droppings and vegetable matter may contaminate stored water. Rainfall in areas where heavy industry or crop dusting is prevalent may not have the same purity as rain falling in other areas. • Where treatment of the water prior to potable use is infrequent, lack of adequate resources or knowledge, health risks may result. • Domestic RWH systems increase construction cost of a building (by 30% to 40%) and may have an adverse effect on home ownership. • Rain water harvesting systems may reduce revenues to public utilities hampering their operation & maintenance due to shortage of funds.

(iv) Infiltration and percolation characteristics of vadose zone.
(v) Hydrologic characteristics of the aquifers such as capacity to store, transmit and yield water.
(vi) Techno-economic feasibility, etc.

2. Implementation of RWH structures shall follow the following steps:
    - Basic surveys including contour survey, hydro-geological, hydrological surveys, remote sensing surveys, soil classification and land capability analysis.
    - Monitoring, using satellite imagery at regular intervals to evaluate impact of recharge structures on the overall sustainability of source.
    - Specific design analysis of resolution of specific technical problems through research/action/operational research assignments.
    - Such other technical inputs as well help to achieve better results for all or any of the activities mentioned above.

Implementation Strategy Based on Community/PRIs/NGOs Participation

In fact, individuals cannot take up water harvesting and recharging of groundwater except roof top water harvesting work of small roof catchments. The water harvesting and artificial recharge systems would require group action by committees, societies and community with financial assistance from government and financial institutions. Implementation may be done in the following manner:

1. GPs under PRI System can be entrusted with implementation work having technical support of independent experts authenticated by nodal programme agency. Implementation should best be done by Watershed Management Approach through specially set-up various watershed committees for initial decision-making, planning, designing, construction, supervision, operation and maintenance, monitoring and evaluation of systems so constructed.
2. Build upon participatory process within each Zila Parishad/ Panchayat to engage civil society, government, NGOs and user groups.

3. The CGWB, SGWBs, NGRI like institutions be associated to provide advice on scientific and technical issues including issue of designs of water harvesting and recharging systems and registering experienced NGOs and VOS groups to involve them at local levels in system constructions. The two processes could work parallel and in tandem. Institutions like CGWB, SGWBs/ NGRI could be entrusted with the following activities:

Preparation of detailed National and Regional Perspective Plans and Master Plans to assist the State agencies including revision of such plans, National Guidelines/area-wise problems specific guidelines and Manuals for use by State Govt./PRIs/NGOs, etc. and Annual Review of efforts through evaluation, success stories, etc.

The strategy for participatory implementation and monitoring, largely, may have the following components:

1. Generation of mass awareness among the people and functionaries.
2. Formulation of women groups/Self-Help Groups, micro-watershed management committees, etc.
3. Capacity building through central/state groundwater agencies and rural/agriculture universities/water technology centres.
4. Preparation of area specific modules for training in different regional languages for (distribution to group and individuals) group and individual distribution.
5. Strengthening of PRI for implementation of water harvesting and recharge measures and their monitoring.

Monitoring and Evaluation

Water harvesting and recharge structures taken up for sustainability of sources are generally aimed at local source augmentation for sustained yield and increasing the life span of the source. Operation and maintenance (O&M) is of critical importance for efficient functioning of any water harvesting and recharge system. The post-implementation monitoring and evaluation is a must to determine the efficiency of water harvesting systems and thus, the benefits accrue to the community in the area. The overall monitoring and evaluation may cover the following aspects:

1. Monitoring of post-construction rise in groundwater levels due to enhancement in surface/groundwater storages.
2. Additional area benefited and population served.
3. Monitoring the improvement in water quality caused by recharged water.
4. Periodic O&M of water harvesting and recharging structures.
5. Monitoring and evaluation activities shall both be inbuilt in the schemes as well as concurrent system through independent agencies with rich experience of the subject.
6. Appropriate harvesting technology should be chosen as per local area and culture and thoroughly assessed both before and after implementation and corrections made where necessary with people's involvement.

Strategy

Policy Intervention

1. Treating water as an 'economic resource' instead of a 'free commodity' and ensuring participation of the local community in planning, development and implementation of projects/schemes relating to water supply.
2. Encouraging States/UTs to adopt and implement Model Bill for regulation and control of pollution and development of groundwater especially in water stressed areas.
3. Planning and implementation of water supply and groundwater management projects based on the principle of sustainability. Making water recharge compulsory in groundwater-based water supply schemes and withdrawal of water quantity may be restricted to only replenishable amount of groundwater. Concept of water auditing on the lines of natural resource auditing should be introduced in water supply projects.
4. Gradual withdrawal of all subsidies relating to water supplies to industry, irrigation and agricultural sector.
5. Promotion of use of dual water supply in critical areas by reserving fresh/treated water exclusively for drinking and cooking.

Activities Intervention

6. Intensive awareness generation on the necessity of conservation of water and encouraging adoption of self-regulation by community through extensive capacity development/ Information, Education & Communication (IEC) programmes.
7. Revitalisation of traditional system of water harvesting involving community/NGOs, civil society, Panchayati Raj Institutions (PRIs).
8. Institutionalising implementation and maintenance of community-based water-harvesting structures like check-dams, percolation ponds, etc.
9. Monitoring of groundwater level twice a year (pre- and post-monsoon period) to understand seasonal and long-term fluctuation/trend of water level for planning appropriate remedial measures in identified pockets.
10. According priority to watershed development and management and promoting conservation of forests as it accelerates groundwater recharge.

Benefits

(a) *To Private:* Recharges private wells, reduces crack formation in walls and structures, reduces main water consumption, improves water supply security, improves groundwater quality.

(b) *To Public*: Rainwater harvesting replenishes the groundwater table and enables dug wells and bore wells to yield in a sustained manner, reduce water supply infrastructure costs, reduce requirements for new or bigger dams, improve asset protection (e.g., lawns, gardens and motor vehicles), improve storm water quality, reduce storm water volume and peak storm water discharges which control flooding low lying areas and roads to a large extent and improve performance of water sensitive urban design measures.

Conclusion

Relatively cheap and simple water conservation devices, such as spray taps and simple rainwater butts, can offer short payback periods and should be considered before high-tech rainwater harvesting or recycling of greywater. On June 18, 2001, Hansard Records, the

Tanzanian Parliament rightly said, "We must do away with the notion that droughts we face from time to time in many parts of the country are caused by shortage of rainfall. With a good programme of harvesting rainwater we can avoid droughts even in times or places considered to have low rainfall."

Although, rainwater harvesting techniques appear to be simple but the full benefit could only be gained by adopting a scientific approach of implementation together with community awareness, their involvement and legislative measures for protection of groundwater from over exploitation.

31

Need for Rainwater Harvesting in Agriculture

Dr. Harender, Raj Gautam and Rohtashav Kumar

The earth is the only planet of the solar system that is supporting life for ages because of the presence of water. Fresh water is a precious resource. Only 2.5 per cent of the world's water is not salty and out of that two-thirds is locked up in ice-caps and glaciers. The population explosion witnessed in the latter half of the last century and the rising demand in various sectors of consumption of fresh water to improve the quality of life are putting a severe strain on the limited fresh water resources of the world. India has 16 per cent of the total population of the world. But the country has only 4 per cent of the water resources present on the earth. India gets approximately 4000 billion cubic metres (BCM) of water every year from all natural resources. Out of this 700 BCM are lost in evaporation and another 700 BCM are lost during the flow on ground. Also, 1500 BCM of water flows into the sea due to floods. Thus, the remaining available water is only 1100 BCM. Out of this groundwater recharge accounts for 430 BCM per year and the present utilized surface water is 370 BCM. The balanced utilized water which can be harnessed is 300 BCM. Further, the country has only 2.5 per cent of the area, out of the total geographical area of the world. We receive approximately 1100 millimetre average rainfall annually, that too irregularly and only during a limited period of two to three months. Two-thirds of all the

Reprinted with permission, *Kurukshetra*, September 2007, pp. 12-15.

water abstracted from the environment goes to irrigate crops. This use of water is massively unsustainable. Today, more than 21 million Indian farmers tap underground reserves to water their fields, and two-thirds of India's crops are irrigated with underground water. This water is running out and unlike the rivers, it will not be quickly replaced. The International Water Management Institute, part of a worldwide network of agricultural research centres funded by the World Bank, recently estimated that about 250 cubic kilometres of water are abstracted for irrigation each year. This is at least 100 cubic kilometres more than the rains put back. It feeds India. But as every year passes, the aquifers get emptied. Out of a total potential of 1869 billion cubic metres (BCM), only 1122 BCM are from surface water and 432 BCM are from groundwater. The rest flows into the sea. Per capita availability of water has declined in the last five decades from 5200 cubic metres in 1951 to 1820 cubic metres in 2001 and it is expected to decline to 1140 cubic metres by 2050 if urgent corrective measures are not taken.

According to an estimate of the Central Ground Water Board, if we continue to exploit our groundwater indiscriminately, then in the next 20 years, 15 states of the country may face acute shortage of underground water. In our country, out of 40 crores hectare metres of rainfall and snowfall received in a year, only 17 crores and 8 lakh hectare metres of water is properly tapped by the soil due to land topography and other problems. In the document on India Water Vision 2025, the vision for development for the country in 2025 is projected taking into account the various water resources and the present rate of consumption. The vision was developed to ensure food security, livelihood security, health security and ecological security. The total estimated demand for water for 2025 has been estimated at 1027 BCM. In order to meet these demands water availability of 520 BCM (1997) will have to increase to more than 1000 BCM in 2025. This would require an investment estimated at Rs. 5000 billion during the coming 25 years. In the vision exercise the water demands in the year 2025 has been estimated at 730 BCM for irrigation, 70 BCM for water supply, 77 BCM for ecological requirements, 12 BCM for industrial requirements, 30 BCM for energy purposes and the rest for miscellaneous requirements. The vision also provides, with a view to meet the gap between availability and future demand.

To bridge this gap, actions such as reconsideration of lifestyles, development paradigms and attitudes to consumption, rainwater harvesting for improving soil moisture content, measures for optimum production of crops and its sustainability, watershed development, improving water-use efficiency for appropriate technology in irrigation, households and industries are needed. Further recycling and reuse of treated water needs to resorted.

Fifty years ago, farmers in northern Gujarat used bullocks driving leather buckets lifting water from open wells dug to about 10 metres. Now tube wells are sunk to 400 metres and they still run dry. Half the traditional hand-dug wells and millions of tube wells have dried up across western India. In Tamil Nadu, two-thirds of the hand-dug wells have failed already and only half as much land is irrigated as a decade ago. In Punjab also, more than 70 per cent of irrigation water is supplied through tube wells and this has resulted in continuous decline in the water table. In 2004, more than 20 per cent of the centrifugal pumps went dysfunctional. In some areas, even submersible pumps had to be lowered more than 10 feet. This strongly points to the fact that the present crop production system is not sustainable if withdrawal of underground water is not tapped with the natural water recharge. In a Water Symposium held at Stockholm in Sweden, in August 2004, the world's leading water scientists warned that this crises could cause widespread famines in the decades to come.

India has a pump revolution in the last four decades and farmers have drilled approximately 21 million tube wells into the saturated strata beneath their fields. Every year, farmers bring another million wells into service, most of them outside the control of the State irrigation authorities. Indian farmers have invested some $ 12 billion in the new pumps but they constantly have to drill deeper to keep pace with the falling water table. As in the majority of the States farmers get electricity at subsidized rates, water is pumped day and night to irrigate thirsty crops like rice, sugarcane and alfalfa.

The problem is severe and keeping in view the fact that agriculture is the backbone of our economy, the question that now arises is what are the ways to come out of these crises. Some states are placing thousands of small dams across riverbeds in a bid to replenish groundwater by infiltration. The Central Government has recognized water harvesting as a thrust area and some centrally sponsored schemes are already in operation. The Central Government has accelerated continuous higher budgetary support in recent years to rainwater harvesting and watershed schemes to recharge our underground water sources. The Ministry of Agriculture under the Horticulture Mission Programme being implemented in different states is also giving incentives to farmers for making water storage tanks to save water for their crops.

Rainwater Harvesting

Rainwater harvesting is of course a focus area for sustainable agricultural production but attention should also be paid for efficient management of available water resources. Even if 5 per cent of annual rainfall were harvested properly, that will produce a substantial quantum of water to the tune of 900 million litres. There are two main practices of rainwater harvesting. In the traditional method, storage of rainwater is done on the surface for future use in the form of underground tanks, ponds, check dams, weirs, etc. Another method is a new concept of rainwater harvesting where different types of structures like pits, trenches, dug wells, hand pumps, recharge wells, recharge shafts, lateral shafts with bore wells and spreading techniques are generally used. Rainwater harvesting saves water, improves soil moisture, improves the quality of water, allows drought-proofing, prevents flooding, saves energy required to lift water, reduces soil erosion and above all it is an ideal solution of water problem in areas having inadequate water resources. There is need to encourage modern methods of irrigation like drip irrigation. Micro-management is also needed for efficient use of irrigation water. Farmers should avoid one time flood irrigation in their fields and instead should give more number of irrigations at intervals for higher output. Weeds should be managed effectively in annual and perennial crops. Moisture conservation techniques like mulching should also be used in crops. Waste water of kitchens and toilets can also be recycled and channeled for farming or charging of the underground water resources.

Until the early 19th century, much of India was irrigated by shallow mud-walled reservoirs in valley bottoms that captured the monsoon rains each summer. These structures were called in some parts of India as tanka, a word adopted into English as tanks. Some individual success stories of rainwater harvesting with remarkable results are really showing the way and Rajsamadhiya is one such unique village in Gujarat. News about this remarkable village has spread around India and beyond. One foreign scientist arrived in Rajsamadhiya with satellite images of the village that showed hidden cracks in the geology through which water flowed. In this village one individual Haradevsinh Hadeja has redesigned the village's drainage system to slow the passage of monsoon rain long enough for it to collect in specially dug ponds. The water passes from one pond to the next in a slow cascade. The villagers do not use the water directly from the ponds, but allow it to percolate into the soil to refill underground reserves and replenish their wells. As a result, the village has twice as much water as before; and wells find water at only 7 metres down, where once the water had to be hauled up more than 30 metres. In Bangalore, the city authorities are trying to boost the aquifers by rehabilitating the city's 60 ancient tanks. In parts of Delhi also, where old tanks and ponds have been cleared of garbage and refilled with water, the water tables are rising. By some estimates, 20,000 villages in India are now harvesting their rain.

The Union Ministry of Water Resources constituted a standing sub-committee for assessment of availability and requirement of water. It has put forward a multi-pronged approach highlighting the need for completion of storage dams, interlinking of rivers, recycling of domestic water and of industrial used water, desalination of sea water and artificial recharge of groundwater. It takes a good monsoon to highlight the need for better storage and conservation of rain. The Bharat Nirman Programme envisages creation of 10 million hectares additional assured irrigation during the 4-year period of 2005-09. To achieve this, the pace of potential creation will be doubled. Various national-level bodies have been constituted to bunch together disparate schemes, ministries and missions for water. An omnibus National Rainwater Authority has been set up. A committee on Artificial Recharge of Groundwater has also been constituted. In the National Rural Employment Guarantee Programme also top priority has been given to works related to restoration of old water harvesting structures and construction of new ones.

Flood management is another key area to work on so that we can create irrigation potential, reduce the losses caused by floods and also generate hydro power. Floods normally affect 8 major river valleys spread over 40 million hectares of area in the entire country affecting nearly 260 million people. Similarly drought affects 86 million people who are spread in 14 states covering a total of 116 districts. If we have to prevent the damage due to floods and reduce the severity of drought, we have to harness 1500 BCM of water lost due to floods and distribute it to drought affected areas. Proper management of floods will result in recharging of groundwater aquifers and also result in deposit of fertile silt on the soil. If we succeed in doing all these, it is estimated that it will save the loss arising out of the damage caused to crops, property and people by the floods to the extent of Rs. 2400 crore on an average per year, we will also save the recurring expenditure of Rs. 1200 crore incurred by different agencies as relief measures. There is a lot of discussion these days for linking of the existing rivers to create a kind of national water grid but the cost of such a scheme is estimated to be as much as Rs. 4,44,331.2 crore and expected to take nearly 35-40 years. Inter-Linking of Rivers (ILR) is expected to take-off soon. While the government has approved the terms of reference for the preparation of a detailed project report for inter-linking of Ken and Betwa between Uttar Pradesh and Madhya Pradesh, four other projects, including the Parbati-Kalisindh-Chambal link between Madhya Pradesh and Rajasthan, are under high priority consideration. Ken-Betwa project is likely to begin in as early as 2008.

The regulatory mechanism by the State governments is also necessary to check the blatant and unscientific use of this resource. Excess digging of wells should be avoided or restricted in severely affected areas. Permission for digging of wells should be linked with construction of water harvesting structures. In urban areas, harvesting of rainwater should be made mandatory so that the water stored could be used for other than drinking purposes. Of course, there is no more water than before, but local harvesting does seem to be a key to using it more efficiently and on a sustainable basis. We have to keep in mind that we can not make more rain, so we have to manage water better. It might just rescue us from hydrological anarchy and also sustain the desired higher growth in agriculture.

32

Harvested Rooftop Rainwater in Rural Areas

Neelima Sinwal and Dr. Neeta Lodha

The study was conducted in five villages of district Udaipur, Rajasthan, to assess the microbial quality of harvested rainwater. The harvested water from both types of the systems was within the permissible limits as suggested by WHO and BIS for chemical quality.

Introduction

Water harvesting refers to the collection and storage of rainwater and also other activities aimed at harvesting surface and groundwater, prevention of losses through evaporation and seepage. Rain is a primary source of water for all of us. There are two main techniques of rainwater harvesting (www.eng.warwick.ac.uk):

(1) Storage of rainwater on the surface for future use.
(2) Recharge to groundwater.

A research study by the International Center for Diarrhoeal Disease Research, Bangladesh (ICDDR, 2004), confirms that rainwater can be a safe drinking water resource. Rainwater has very low dissolved minerals and as such relatively corrosive and free from any contaminants. The contamination occurs due to catchment areas. The purity of rainwater makes it an attractive option in areas with uniform high arsenic levels in other water resources. The chemical quality of water used for domestic purposes is of vital importance. Within the

Reprinted with permission, *Kurukshetra*, September 2007, pp. 16-19.

normal pH ranges available in drinking water, the pH does not appear to affect human health adversely (Vyas, 1996). As the pH of rainwater can vary with location and roof material and may be aggressive towards concrete, plastic storage cisterns are usually recommended. The dissolved solids give a particular taste to the water at high concentration and reduces its palatability. Hardness in the water is the sum of the concentrations of alkaline earth metal cations (e.g., Ca++, Mg++). In most natural water nearly all the hardness is due to calcium and magnesium. The high concentration of chloride is considered to be the indicator of pollution, which is due to organic wastes of animal origin or industrial effluents (Vyas *et al.*, 1996).

Fecal coliform and E. coli are bacteria whose presence indicates that the water may be contaminated with human or animal wastes. Disease-causing microbes (pathogens) in these wastes can cause diarrhoea, cramps, nausea, headaches, or other symptoms. These pathogens may pose a special health risk for infants, young children, and people with severely compromised immune systems. It is an indication of the microbiological quality of water and indicates the presence of bacteria in the water sample. Standards require potable water to be completely free of Total Coliform Bacteria (Rajput, 2001). The quality of rainwater used for domestic supply is of particular importance because in most cases, it is used for drinking untreated. The issue of water quality is a complex and sometimes controversial one. Several studies indicate that rainwater supplies often do not meet WHO and other national drinking water standards especially with respect to bacteriological water quality (Haebler *et al.*, 1989). Hence, the study aims to assess the quality of harvested rooftop rainwater.

Methodology

The study was conducted in five villages selected randomly from two blocks of Udaipur district, Rajasthan. A purposive random sample of 30 households having rooftop rainwater harvesting systems was selected. To study the chemical and microbiological quality of harvested rainwater samples were collected for laboratory experiments twice at an interval of one month. The data was compared with the drinking water permissible limits determined by BIS and WHO.

Results and Discussion

To find out that harvested rainwater was of potable status with regard to chemical and microbiological quality the data was compared with the standards of BIS and WHO.

Chemical Aspects

The data presented in Table 1 clearly depicts that the overall mean value of pH in water samples collected from the flat rooftop rainwater harvesting system's cistern (7.58) was lower as compared to the kellu rooftop rainwater harvesting system (7.82). The overall mean value of chloride in stored rainwater samples collected from the kellu rooftop rainwater harvesting system's cistern (39.55 mg/litre) was higher as compared to the flat rooftop rainwater harvesting system (39.142 mg/litre). The total dissolved solids, hardness and electrical conductivity levels in the stored rainwater has been presented in the table which clearly depicts that the overall mean value was 250.69 mg/litre, 93.94 mg/litre and 0.39 respectively for flat rooftop rainwater harvesting systems which was higher than that of kellu rooftop rainwater harvesting system. These values for pH, total dissolved solids, chloride and hardness were within the limits of WHO and BIS determinants for drinking water.

Table 1: Chemical Aspects of Stored Rainwater

Chemical Aspects	*Flat Rooftop Rainwater Harvesting System*	*Kellu Rooftop Rainwater Harvesting System*	*WHO Standards*	*Drinking Water Permissible Unit BIS: 10500-1991*
	Overall Mean Values n=15	*Overall Mean Values n=15*		
pH	7.58	7.82	6.5-7.5	6.5-8.5
Electrical Conductivity (mS/cm)	0.39	0.38	NSS*	NSS*
Hardness (mg/l)	93.94	86.94	500	600
Chloride (mg/l)	39.142	39.55	250	1000
Total Dissolved Solids (mg/l)	250.69	242.56	1000	2000

*NSS—No Standards Set.

Table 2: Microbiological Aspects of Stored Rainwater

Microbiological Aspects	*Flat Rooftop Rainwater Harvesting System*	*Kellu Rooftop Rainwater Harvesting System*	*WHO Standards*	*Drinking Water Permissible Limit BIS: 10500-1991*
	Overall Mean Values n=15	*Overall Mean Values n=15*		
Total Coliform (MPN/100 ml)	510	791	10	10
Fecal Coliform (MPN/100 ml)	6	7	0	0

Microbiological Aspects

Data as can be seen from Table 2 depict that the overall mean value of total and fecal coliform in stored rainwater from flat rooftop rainwater harvesting systems was lower than the kellu rooftop rainwater harvesting systems. The water quality of domestic rainwater harvesting systems has often been in question, particularly when the water is used for drinking. Standards set by the WHO, 1997, suggest microbiological standards of zero E. Coli per 100 ml, which is appropriate for treated water supply systems. Roof water does occasionally meet these standards but the water quality is time dependent, strongly following the rainfall pattern. Generally, roof water appears as good or better than rural water sources but (as expected) not as good as chlorinated urban sources. It is apparent that the water improves with time after the rain, mainly due to sedimentation and bacteria die-off. It takes an average of 3.5 to 4 days to achieve a 90 per cent reduction in E. Coli numbers (Martinson *et al.*, 2003).

The water quality of domestic rainwater harvesting systems has often been in question, particularly when the water is used for drinking. Standards set by the WHO, 1997, suggest microbiological standards of zero E. Coli per 100 ml, which is appropriate for treated water supply systems. Roof water does occasionally meet these standards but the water quality is time dependent, strongly following the rainfall pattern. Generally, roof water appears as good or better than rural water sources but (as expected) not as good as chlorinated urban sources. It is apparent that the water improves with time after the rain, mainly due to sedimentation and bacteria die-off. It takes an average of 3.5 to 4 days to achieve a 90 per cent reduction in E. Coli numbers (Martinson *et al.*, 2003).

The data in the table shows that none of the samples came in zero and high-risk grades. The majority (90 per cent) and one-fifth of the water samples fall in the low and medium risk categories respectively. The majority of the water samples from flat rooftop rainwater harvesting systems and sixty-seven per cent from kellu rooftop rainwater harvesting systems are in the low risk category. Only one-fifth of water samples from flat rooftop rainwater harvesting systems and 33 per cent from kellu rooftop rainwater harvesting systems fall in the low risk category. According to the drinking water guidelines of WHO, 1984, there should be no faecal coliform in drinking water. This shows that the harvested rainwater is of non-potable status.

Table 3: Percentage of Samples at WHO Risk Grades

S. No.	*Risk Category*	*Flat Rooftop Rainwater Harvesting System n=15*		*Kellu Rooftop Rainwater Harvesting System n=15*		*Total n=30*	
		F	*%*	*F*	*%*	*F*	*%*
1.	Low risk (1-10 FCs/100 ml)	12	80	10	67	22	90
2.	Medium risk (11-100 FCs/100 ml)	03	20	05	33	08	10

Conclusion

The harvested rooftop rainwater was found to be of potable status as per the chemical quality but not the microbiological quality. Thus it can be summarized that numerous studies have shown that due to contamination following contact with the catchment surface, stored rainwater often does not meet WHO guideline standards for drinking water especially with respect to microbiological quality criteria. This does not in itself mean that rainwater is unsafe to drink. Millions of people in rural areas around the world depend on rainwater for drinking and other domestic purposes and a very few number of cases have been reported of serious health problems related to rainwater supplies.

33

Rainwater Harvesting: A Panacea for Water Woes

V.P. Rajvedi

Rain is the first form of water in the hydrological cycle. Rainwater offers advantages in water quality both for irrigation and domestic use. Rainwater is naturally soft (unlike well water), contains almost no dissolved minerals or salts, is free of chemical treatment and is relatively a reliable source of water for households. Rainwater collected and used on site can supplement or replace other modern sources of household water. Generally, the conservation/harvesting of water refers to collection and storage of rainwater and other allied activities aimed at prevention of losses through drain off, evaporation, seepage, etc. Rainwater conservation makes droughts less severe, rivers will have water throughout the year and the soil holds a greater level of moisture and consequently, there is increase in agricultural yield and thus economic conditions of the rural poor is appreciably improved. All this leads to regeneration of vegetation and forests and thus overall environment of the region is positively impacted.

Water Harvesting in Ancient Times

In ancient times, people in different parts of the world knew the importance of different methods of conservation of rainwater. There is evidence that, even during the Harappan period, there was a very good system of water management. People used to manage water resources considering it as part of nature which is essential for their survival. This could be seen from the rainwater harvesting structures in the low rainfall areas of Rajasthan, harvesting springs in hilly areas and mountainous regions and percolation ponds and tanks in southern India. In Tamil Nadu, the ancient people stored rainwater in public places separately for drinking purposes and bathing and domestic purposes. They also formed percolation tanks or ponds for the purpose of recharging irrigation or domestic wells. They would periodically clean the waterways so as to get clean water throughout the year.

An extensive rainwater harvesting apparatus existed 4000 years ago in the Negev Desert. In ancient Rome, residences were built with individual cisterns and paved courtyards to capture rainwater to augment water. On small islands with no significant river systems, rainwater is the only source of water. The Island of Gibraltar has one of the largest rainwater collection systems in existence.

Present Water Crisis

It is common knowledge that fresh water sources which are finite and fragile are becoming scarce day-by-day. More than 1.5 billion people worldwide depend on groundwater, and many more rely on agricultural products grown with groundwater. The global water scenario is so grim that more than one-third of the world's population is already living in countries with moderate to high water stress. According to a report of Global Environment Outlook, the global fresh water consumption has risen six-fold between 1900 and 1995 which is roughly twice the rate of population increase. This problem is assuming serious proportions in Africa and West Asia. Roughly 20 per cent of the world population lacks access to safe drinking water. Excessive withdrawal of groundwater, more than recharge, has become widespread in many parts of the Arabian Peninsula, China, India, Mexico, former Soviet Union and the United States resulting in appreciable fall in the water level. With rapid industrialization during the last century, excessive use of fresh water for different purposes is mainly responsible for the present scenario. Over-extraction of groundwater has also affected its quality leading to saline ingress in coastal areas as in the case of Oman, Bahrain and India. Biological contamination in the form of faecal coliform count, chemical fertilizer and pesticide residue in Asia's rivers is 50 times higher than the WHO guidelines making the local population vulnerable to high risk level. The problem is not widely recognized because it is going underground. However, in many places the situation has already reached a crisis level and may be economically irreversible.

The water resources scenario in India is more or less a replica of the global picture. India, though blessed with a fairly high annual rainfall averaging about 1100 mm, the distribution pattern and duration of the monsoon is not uniform resulting in the bulk of the rainfall escaping as run-off. It is estimated that approximately only 25 per cent of the annual distribution of rainfall is being utilized at present. The groundwater level in India's western states of Punjab and Haryana—the nation's principal breadbaskets—has dropped precipitously because of overuse. Poor farmers once had to drill a well just 33 feet to get water, now they have to go down as much as 330 feet or more which increases the cost of drawing water many times more.

Indian NGOs' Experiences

Some non-governmental organizations have been doing pioneering work in the area of rainwater harvesting in India. Shri Rajendra Singh's Tarun Bharat Sangh in Rajasthan and Shree Padre's work in Western Karnataka stand out as shining examples among them. These organizations, which are working without any help whatsoever from the government, are showing how community participation can change the destiny of the local populace.

What started as a humble effort to repair a damaged *Johad* at Gopalpura in the State of Rajasthan soon became a mass movement of sorts by Rajinder Singh's Tarun Bharat Sangh. This 426 metre long *Johad* was renovated which took the villagers almost a year to complete. More than 600 *bighas* of land became suitable for agriculture. To everyone's surprise, there was water in the Gopalpura wells. At a time when the entire region was stricken with drought, Rajinder Singh's efforts came as welcome news. Ever since that day, the word spread to more villages and so Tarun Bharat Sangh started helping villages build water harvest structures.

So far, 4500 *Johads* have been built in 850 villages covering 6500 sq. km in the last 15 years in Rajasthan alone. The increase in groundwater level in these villages has done wonders for agriculture. The output per acre has doubled and farmers are able to grow two to three crops a year. Four rivers, which turn into drains during the monsoon season, have now turned into perennial rivers. Among these are the *Arvari, Ruparel, Bhagvari* and *Jahajwali.* Further, the number of trees in the Sariska Tiger Reserve have increased. According to the Deputy Director (Forest), Sariska, the forest cover has risen from a mere 7 per cent to 40 per cent in the past 18 years.

Shree Padre's workshops on water conservation have been transforming the lives of millions of rural people in Karnataka. He makes slide presentation on Rainwater Harvesting success stories. "I always stumble upon a farmer or a householder who has devised a novel method," says Padre. They are often simple but suited to the situation. There is palpable enthusiasm across 5 districts of Karnataka. People seem involved in trapping every drop of water that falls on their property. Padre's workshops are very popular and draw a large number of people. Village groups cheerfully subscribe and pay the cost of Padre's travel and incidental expenses. Everywhere people are hunting water. In Karnataka, Padre and others are turning it into a widespread, serious and competitive business.

Similarly, the Rajiv Gandhi Watershed Management Mission is doing some exciting work in Madhya Pradesh. Simple do-it-yourself methods are both for on-farm and community-level water harvesting. During the Gram Sampark Abhiyan, 2001, the frontline functionaries trained in disseminating information fanned out into all 51,806 villages of the State. The response they received from the people was beyond the wildest expectations. It was an agenda people seemed to have been waiting for. The simple message "Khet ka Pani Khet Mein and Gaon ka Pani Gaon Mein" has done the trick and assumed the level of a people's movement. The Pani Roko Abhiyan saw several water warriors emerging and taking leadership. The Mission funds to support this programme from Rural Development Schemes like Employment Assurance Scheme, Jawahar Gram Swarojgar Yojana and from other national and international agencies. The people of Madhya Pradesh have been able to create additional water impounding capacity of 14,387 lakh cubic metres under the Pani Roko Abhiyan. More than twenty thousand tanks have been constructed and more than twenty-five thousand tanks were renovated. Several lessons have been learnt from the Pani Roko Abhiyan. Most important of them is that people, waiting to take charge of the agenda of development, can dream big and do big.

International Initiatives

Similarly, other countries are also reviving these old methods of water harvesting, including more technically advanced countries:

- Some exciting work on bringing back traditional rainwater harvesting technologies is being done by individuals and small groups in the United States. Several variations involve capturing and storing rainwater in a tank and using the water with or without treatment. The University of Texas built a system of three cascading ponds to support aquatic life for its biology laboratory, fed by harvested rainwater.
- The user association that manages the Hermosillio aquifer in Mexico has managed the extraordinary feat of getting 50 per cent reductions in pumping of groundwater, so that withdrawals of water now equal aquifer recharge. Water users, mainly farmers, voluntarily cut their rights for water withdrawals in half. Whoever needs additional water has to buy it.
- In South Africa, a non-native weed has supplanted a native one, becoming a major threat to groundwater. Some 25 million acres of land in South Africa became infested by an alien weed that uses almost 7 per cent more of the country's total run-off than the indigenous plants it replaced. A special long-term programme by the South African Government's Department of Water Affairs and Forestry, called 'Working for Water', employs 42,000 people at peak times every year to remove these weeds.
- A small but growing worldwide movement is underway to promote the cultivation of vetiver grass hedgerows as a powerful way of reducing the velocity of rainwater run-off and recharging groundwater in Denmark. The vetiver network is supported by the World Bank, the Danish Government and several global NGOs. Rainwater run-off is reduced by 70 per cent when vetiver hedgerows are planted across the slope, by slowing down and spreading out the run-off over larger areas.

The strong roots of this grass can also penetrate hard earth and improve infiltration.

- One major problem is trans-boundary aquifers, which run beneath the borders of two or more countries. A South American project is just getting underway to protect one of the world's great aquifers, the Guarani Aquifer, that runs under Brazil, Uruguay, Argentina and Paraguay. The project, supported by the Global Environmental Facility and the World Bank, is aimed at the management of the aquifer's resources to prevent its pollution and overuse.

Some Interesting Facts

Water by its very nature flows downwards—from upper regions to low regions—whether it flows on the surface or under it. For example, one of the largest freshwater sources in Israel and Palestine is the Mountain Aquifer, a well protected resource that provides about 50 per cent of Israel's drinking water. The geology of this mainly limestone aquifer is complex—water flows in several directions and quite rapidly for an aquifer. But the flow is from east to west which means that the sources are in Palestine and the outlets in Israel. Ninety per cent of the catchments lie under Palestine and sixty to seventy per cent of the storage lie under Israel. Similarly, in India, the Indira Gandhi Canal in Rajasthan has immensely benefited Rajasthan. But, more than Rajasthan, it has indirectly benefited the border areas of Pakistan as water which seeps into the earth gets stored in the low lying areas of Pakistan.

Israel has done a lot of work in this area. They have drawn maps of underground waterways. India can also be profited if such studies are undertaken here also. It ensures use of water twice. While farmers can take advantage of water flowing on the surface, in times of scarcity, these well-known underground water reserves can be utilized to everyone's advantage in rain deficient years.

In the sandier tracts, the villagers of the Thar Desert had evolved an ingenious system of rainwater harvesting known as kunds or kundis. Kund, the local name given to a covered underground tank, was developed primarily for tackling drinking water problems. Usually constructed with locally available, inexpensive material, kunds are more prevalent in the areas where groundwater is moderately to highly saline. The first known construction of a kund in Western Rajasthan was during 1607 AD.

Large Irrigation Projects vs. Small Rain Water Harvesting Structures

The 20th century saw a phenomenal increase in mega irrigation projects, dams and reservoirs. Billions and billions of dollars were spent in their construction and maintenance during the last century. A huge number of local people were displaced, and thousands of acres of forests were submerged causing irreparable damage to wild life and the fragile eco-system of the region. Cost effective studies of these mega projects all around the globe have seldom been done and whenever they were done they were not given any publicity whatsoever. The problem of water availability has only worsened. There is also the problem of silting reducing the water holding capacity of reservoirs. In the event of an earthquake, they have the potential to wreck havoc. As per a study, if Tehri dam is damaged due to seismic activity, the area upto Haridwar will be submerged.

Concerns are being expressed all around the world almost daily over the paucity of drinking water, level of contamination and presence of heavy minerals in groundwater sources. Scores of conferences, seminars and workshops are being organized to discuss this problem. Thousands of crores of rupees are being spent on tackling droughts and floods and providing relief to those affected. Greedy multi-national companies are eyeing the huge water market of developed and developing countries. Votaries of such measures are advancing the argument that the option of all cheap and easy methods to tackle the problem has been exhausted. Contrary to such prevalent misconceptions, cheap and easy options have hardly been looked into. According to a 400 page report by the Centre for Science and Environment (CSE) entitled, "Dying Wisdom: Rise, Fall and Potential of India's Traditional Water Harvesting Systems," which documents the diversity of traditional water harvesting systems across the country, if the Gujarat Government had diverted the money spent on advertisements for Sardar Sarovar Project for cleaning up traditional water harvesting systems, the water problem of Gujarat would not be of such a nature.

Modern man has caused enormous damage to the environment and now he is becoming victim of his own greed. It is time to go back to our roots, taking refuge in simple, traditional ways of solving problems. A simple and cheap method like saving of rainwater displaces none to achieve impressive benefits. Unlike big dams, the *Johads,* check dams, bunds, etc. do not destroy any river or submerge huge tracts of land and forest areas wiping-off several species of plants and animals. Instead they create forests, rivers and rejuvenate many forms of vegetation. They do not require any complex technical know-how neither do they require huge investment for which loans from multilateral international agencies with many strings attached need to be arranged. There is minimal scope for corruption in such methods with no role for greedy contractors and the bureaucracy. With community participation and adopting locally available techniques, such water conserving structures can transform the lives of millions. *Bundhs,* small *check* dams, ponds and *jhods,* etc. not only increase groundwater level but also result in the saving of thousands of mandays which are wasted in bringing water from far flung areas and thus can be more productively used. It not only has the potential to solve the water problems of the thirsty millions, but is also environment-friendly. With a little governmental support, the problems of famine, flood, deforestation, etc. can easily be tackled.

34

Rainwater Harvesting

Farook Nimbal

The UN report, published ahead of the third world water forum in Kyoto, Japan, March 16-23, 2003, says world water reserves are drying up fast and booming populations, pollution and global warming will combine to cut the average person's water supply by a third in the next 20 years.

The report also ranked 122 countries on the quality of their water provision. Belgium was at the bottom of the league, below developing countries including India and Rwanda. By 2050, water scarcity will affect between two billion and seven billion people out of a projected total of 9.3 billion, depending in part on what measures are taken to tackle the crisis, the report elaborates.

Optimal sustainable development, maintenance of quality and efficient use of the country's water resources to match the growing demands on this precious natural resource with the active involvement of all in order to achieve accelerated, equitable economic development of the country.

It is common knowledge that water resources hold the key for the socio-economic development of any country. This is true for India also with a predominant agrarian economy. It is a fact that water, a fragile and finite resource, is fast becoming scarce day by day. A recent study by the World Bank indicates that the per capita availability of water in India, which was in the order of 5000 cubic metres per year at the time of independence, has drastically come down to 2000

Reprinted with permission, *Yojana*, June 2005, pp. 27-30.

cubic metres per year at present. The average annual rainfall of 1100 mm in the country, though fairly high, is marked by wide variations, both spatial and temporal. The total water resources, comprising surface water (1953 bcm) and groundwater (423 bcm) are not uniformly distributed, in the sense, roughly 67 per cent of the resources are reported to be available in the Indo-Gangetic alluvial basins covering 33 per cent of the geographical area of the country as against 33 per cent of the potential in the hard rock regions occupying 67 per cent of the geographical area. The bulk of the utilizable part of surface water resources has more or less been harnessed already by a number of major and medium storage reservoirs. During the last two decades, focus was only on development of groundwater rather than its management. Management aspects like water conservation, recharging, efficiency in water-use, water recycling, self-regulation and ecosystem sustainability were not paid adequate attention. A 85 per cent of rural water supply is sustained by groundwater though the rural water supply sector as such uses around 5 per cent of the resource. On the other hand, the irrigation sector, utilizing nearly 85 per cent, is the largest consumer of groundwater.

The frequent failure of the monsoons in some region or the other, results in drought conditions causing acute drinking water scarcity especially in 1174 blocks in 204 Drought Prone Area Programme (DPAP) and Desert Development Programme (DDP) districts. The ever increasing mismatch between the supply-demand scenario is precipitated by a combination of factors including population explosion, ever increasing desire for higher levels of supply, gross mismanagement of water resources and negligence of the environment that have further aggravated the situation in the form of falling water levels, degradation of water quality and concomitant break out of water-borne diseases.

Water Consumption

(In per cent)

	World	*India*
Agriculture	69.0	90.0
Domestic	8.0	4.0
Industry	23.0	6.0

India's water consumption is approximately 20.1 per cent of the world consumption with a per capita consumption of 297.7 cubic metres. It is more than the world average per capita consumption of 287.3 cubic metres.

Against this backdrop, it becomes necessary to examine various options for meeting the basic requirements of safe drinking water to the community. In this regard, the one option that is technically feasible, socially desirable and economically viable is rainwater harvesting, which is a simple cost effective and easily adaptable approach. It has proved to be a dependable management tool for supplementing the domestic water requirements.

Water in the 21st Century

Challenges

- Groundwater depletion
- Water quality deterioration
- Low water-use efficiency
- Expensive new water sources
- Resource degradation
- Water and health
- Massive subsidies and distorted incentives
- Development of new water

Strategies

- Rainwater harvesting
- Comprehensive water policy reform and demand management
- Secure water rights
- User management of irrigation systems
- Reformed price incentives
- Appropriate technology
- Environment protection
- Tradable water rights
- International co-operation

Rainwater Harvesting

It is well known that rainwater is biologically pure, soft in nature and free from organic matter. Rainwater harvesting has today proved itself to be an effective technique of conserving water by guiding the rainwater that falls on rooftops to storage tanks or underground sumps for future usage. Groundwater recharging, on the other hand, is undertaken by guiding water through pipes to wells, bore wells or recharge pits to ensure recharging water in the underground aquifers, for later use, whenever the need arises.

The principle of collecting and strong precipitation from a catchment surface is referred to as rainwater harvesting. Water harvesting also includes activities aimed at harvesting surface and groundwater, prevention of losses through evaporation and seepage and other techniques aimed at conservation and efficient utilization of limited water endowment. In general, water harvesting is the activity of direct collection of rainwater. The collected water can be stored for direct use or can be used to recharge the groundwater.

Rainwater is the primary source of fresh water. Rivers, lakes, and groundwater are all secondary sources of fresh water, as they are all stores and channels of rainwater. Water harvesting is aimed at understanding the value of rain and to make optimum use of rain water at the place where it falls. We have lot of rain, yet we do not have water. This is because we have rainfall in short spells of high intensity. Due to this intensity and short duration of heavy rain, most of the rain falling on the surface tends to flow away rapidly, leaving very little for the recharge of groundwater.

Quantum of harvested rainwater depends upon

(a) Frequency duration and intensity of rainfall
(b) Nature of catchments
(c) Run-off characteristics

Even if 5 per cent of the annual rainfall were harvested properly, it would produce a substantial quantum of water to the tune of 900 million litres.

Rainwater harvesting saves water and . . .

- Improves soil moisture
- Increases groundwater level
- Improves the quality of water
- Allows drought-proofing
- Prevents flooding of storm water drains

- Saves energy required to lift water
- Reduces flooding of roads
- Reduces soil erosion
- Is an ideal solution of water problem in areas having inadequate water resources.

Need for Rainwater Harvesting

- To improve the groundwater quality in aquifers.
- To raise the water in wells and bore wells that are drying up.
- Surface water is inadequate to meet our demand and we have to depend on groundwater.
- Due to rapid urbanization, infiltration of rainwater into the sub soil has decreased drastically and recharging of groundwater has diminished.
- Over-exploitation of groundwater resources has resulted in decline in water level in most parts of the country.
- To enhance availability of groundwater of specific place and time.
- To arrest seawater ingress.
- To reduce power consumption.
- To improve the vegetation cover.
- To avoid flooding of storm water drains.

Rainwater Harvesting Practices

There are two main practices of rainwater harvesting:

1. Storage of rainwater on the surface for future use.—It is a traditional practice and structures used are underground tanks, ponds, check dams, weirs, etc.
2. Recharge of groundwater—It is a new concept of rain water harvesting and the structures generally used are:

   (a) Pits—Recharge pits are constructed for recharging shallow aquifers.

   (b) Trenches—These are constructed when permeable strata is available at shallow depths.

   (c) Dug wells—Drainpipes to a filtration tank, from which it flows into the dug well, diverts rainwater that is collected on the rooftop of buildings.

(d) Hand pumps—The existing hand pumps may be used for recharging shallow/deep aquifers, if the availability of water is limited.

(e) Recharge wells—Recharge wells are generally constructed for recharging the deeper aquifer and water is passed through filter media to avoid choking of recharge wells.

(f) Recharge shafts—For recharging shallow aquifers, which are, located below clayey surfaces.

(g) Lateral shafts with bore wells—For recharging the upper as well as lengths. Deeper aquifers lateral shafts of 1.5 to 2-mt widths and 10 to 30-mt.

(h) Spreading techniques—When permeable strata start from the top then this technique is used. Water is spread in stream/nalas by making check dams, cement plugs, gabion structures or a percolation pond may be constructed.

The world's thirst for water is likely to become one of the most pressing resource issues of the 21st century. Global water consumption rose six-fold between 1990-95, more than double the rate of population growth and continues to grow rapidly as agricultural, industrial, and domestic needs increase. In some areas, water withdrawals are so high relative to supply that surface water supplies are literally shrinking and groundwater reserves are being depleted faster than they can be replenished by precipitation. Agriculture is by far the biggest user of water, accounting for over 70 per cent of water withdrawals in low-income countries. Irrigation remains a prime engine of agricultural growth. Irrigation is done by both surface and groundwater. The supply of water is diminishingly low; on the other hand, demand for water is increasingly more. It has certainly become a serious concern and is most likely to aggravate further in the years to come. Reform of water policy is urgently needed to avert severe national, regional, and local water scarcities that will depress agricultural production and water-related health problems.

Two sites, [Research farm Mansadevi and Johranpur, Solan (H.P)] were selected to develop models of rainwater harvesting and recycling on sub-mountainous regions under NATP (National Agricultural Technology Project). Before the project, most of the runoff was going to choes through fields, causing soil erosion. Conservation measures and utilization of stored water in the watersheds resulted in significant improvement. Constituting watershed society named as KRISHIVIKAS SANGH to take decisions on watershed development ensured peoples' participation, water distribution, water charges and all other project-related matters. Improved varieties with complete package of practices and INM (Integrated Nutrient Management) were introduced in the watershed to enhance the yield. Various horticultural (fruits/ vegetables) species were introduced. About 28 per cent of total beneficiaries established mango orchards. A bumper crop of ginger yielded 350q/ha and farmers earned about Rs. 3.33 lakh/ha. A tomato variety *manisha* was introduced which yielded 187 to 301q/ha to earn Rs. 1.25 to 2.45 lakh/ha under rainfed conditions through proper rainwater management.

Major Initiatives

- Since sustainability of the drinking water source is of paramount importance for the smooth functioning of rural water supply, 25 per cent out of 20 per cent of the allocation under Accelerated Rural Water Supply Programme (ARWSP) has been earmarked exclusively for water harvesting schemes to make implementation of such schemes mandatory.
- Similarly, 25 per cent out of the allocation under the Prime Minister's Gramodaya Yojana has also been earmarked for funding schemes under submission on sustainability.
- MPs are requested to utilize Local Area Development Fund in their respective constituencies to take up water harvesting schemes.
- Besides feasibility studies, consultancy services for preparation of pilot projects on rainwater harvesting in select states have already been taken.
- Further, preparation of a user-friendly atlas type of document on traditional water harvesting structures in various parts of the country has been initiated for popularizing the concept of water harvesting amongst all concerned including the community.

There is an urgent need for propagating water harvesting, conservation and recharging on a large scale. Based on "Best practices" of water harvesting with active community participation by select individuals and institutions, prospects for large scale advocacy of this people-oriented programme for ensuring sustainability of the source are bright. In this regard, the efforts by the government alone may not be adequate. Prominent, voluntary and non-government organizations have a major and crucial role to play for keeping liaison between the state and the community to educate, moderate and transform water harvesting into a mass movement. In this context, the allocation earmarked by GOI for planting and implementing water-harvesting schemes would be of some help in realizing these objectives.

Studies to develop a base-line data for better understanding of the existing and merging situations need to be undertaken. Recycling of water and water conservation will be critical components of our daily lives in the coming millennium. As far as possible, the technologies should be indigenously developed so as to make them socio-economically relevant.

PART V

INTERLINKING OF RIVERS: NEED OF THE HOUR

35

Inter-Linking of Rivers: Vision and Issues

Arabinda Ghose

It is not unlikely that many among us have not heard of a district in Rajasthan called Barmer. Or, even though we might have heard about it, atleast in the context of the "Barmeri Print" of various textile items, we may not be aware where it is situated. Well, it is the westernmost district of Rajasthan and most probably of India itself and is known more for acute shortage of drinking water, it being situated in an inhospitable region of Thar desert which receives very little rain.

Wonder of wonders, this town got full 127 millimetres (mm) of rainfall in early July this year and the floods resulting from this rain killed three people. At a place where drinking water shortage might be the reason for death, it was excess rainfall, beyond the draining capacity of the area which killed these three unfortunate people.

However, it is quite possible that during the next monsoon period in 2004 or later, Barmer might not prove to be so lucky. One cannot rule out the return of drought to Banner then. Does that mean that the people of this district will have to suffer— like the generations which preceded them—perpetural drought-flood syndrome? Well, the answer is obviously a big No.

Within two to three years, water from the Narmada River will commence flowing into Barmer district, which will not only enable the people drink water when thirsty and not milk or butter-milk, but will also enable them to take up irrigation in over 75,000 hectares of land. So, before the decade is out, Barmer might become the granary of Rajasthan, at least of western Rajasthan, growing not only jowar, sorghum, bajra (pearl-millet), cotton, wheat and fodder such as bersem, but also rice, not a traditional crop in these parts.

How will that be possible? Because, consequent to the completion of the Sardar Sarovar Dam on the Madhya Pradesh-Gujarat border in about two to three years time, the Narmada main canal of 460 kilometres, will deliver a certain amount of water at the Rajasthan border, to be taken up by the Rajasthan Government's Irrigation Department through a network of main canals and their tributaries for irrigating these 75,000 hectares of land. The Narmada main canal is now complete over a length upwards of 200 kilometres from the Dam and it will be a couple of years or so, till the main canal is complete.

We are not discussing here the Sardar Sarovar (Narmada) Project. What is aimed at is explaining what is meant by inter-basin transfer of river waters, from the Narmada basin to the Luni Basin in western Rajasthan, from a basin which has surplus water to one that is chronically short of water. So, instead of the surplus waters of the Narmada going waste to the Arabian Sea, a portion of it is being transferred to the arid Barmer district of Rajasthan.

This inter-basin transfer of river waters, conveying water otherwise going waste to the seas after meeting the needs of their basins and after maintaining a steady, perennial flow through their lengths, is being called inter-linking of rivers. The basic concept of this proposal is to transfer surplus waters (after meeting the needs of the basins) of the rivers to the deficit ones, and not to link all rivers of India with one another for just the heck of it. One feels that the nomenclature of the concept should be inter-basin transfer of river waters and not inter-linking of rivers.

The former Irrigation Minister, Dr. K.L. Rao envisaged in his "Ganga-to-Cauvery" link, the transfer of about 65,000 cusecs (cubic foot per second) of flood flow in the river (it goes up to 27 lakh cusecs during the months of June to October) from the Ganga near Patna down to the Cauvery through a network of canals joining the various rivers en route (the Sone, the Narmada, the Wainganga, the Pranhita, the Godavari, the Krishna and the Pennar). Since the project sought to link two of the holiest rivers of India, people became emotionally attached to the concept. So much so, even 23 years after this concept was discarded by the Ministry of Water Resources (Irrigation at that time) in 1980, people still refer to the new proposal as "Ganga to Cauvery" link. In fact, the correct position today is that you can at best call it the Mahanadi to Cauvery link extended further southwards to the Vaigai via the Gundar. The Garland Canal scheme proposed by an Indian Airlines pilot Capt. Dastur, too was rejected, it was a more romantic idea than a practicable one.

What happened in 1980 was that the Ministry for Water Resources evolved the National Perspective for Water Resources Development encompassing the entire country and not merely the north-south linkage. For the sake of convenience, the perspective was divided into the Peninsular river development scheme and the Himalayan river development concept. There were about 30 such links proposed then. The Ministry set-up a separate special purpose vehicle in 1982, called the National Water Development Agency (NWDA), a society under the Registration of Societies Act, 1860.

It is this agency which carried out surveys and pre-feasibility surveys for all these 30 links and feasibility surveys for about eight of them. This work was carried out for 20 long years, with dedication, often against the wishes of the States, that were not interested in inter-linking. This is a remarkable engineering feat and NWDA deserves all praise for conducting these surveys. The wealth of information the Agency gathered during this period would go a long way in implementing the inter-basin transfer of water when it is undertaken.

The severe drought that affected India in July 2002 and continued thereafter in several States, revived the demand for the "Ganga-Cauvery link" by several political leaders and even the President, Dr. A.P.J. Abdul Kalam asked for the implementation of the inter-basin transfer proposal. At around the same time, a public interest litigation was filed in the Supreme Court demanding the early implementation of the concept.

The Supreme Court, in its turn, not only made sympathetic observations, but also asked the Government to implement the interlinking project within ten years. Around the same time, even a little earlier, Prime Minister Atal Bihari Vajpayee announced in the Lok Sabha that the Government would take up this scheme. His announcement was also warmly welcomed by the opposition. The Supreme Court has asked the Government to set-up a Task Force for preparing the project report and other details of the proposed linking projects.

Accordingly, a Task Force on Inter-Linking of Rivers (TFILR) was set-up on December 13 with former Union Energy Minister, Sh. Suresh Prabhu as its Chairman. The Vice-Chairman is Dr. C.C. Patel, former Secretary, Irrigation, Government of India, and the former Chairman of the Sardar Sarovar Narmada Nigam Limited (SSNNL), and the member Secretary, Dr. C.D. Thatte, former Secretary, Ministry of Water Resources and now Secretary General of the International Commission on Irrigation and Drainage (ICID). Subsequently, a number of other members of the Task Force have been appointed representing various disciplines and States which have 'surplus' waters or States which are "deficit" ones. A former diplomat, Chandrashekar Das Gupta, too has been appointed as a member. So also has been Dr. R.K. Pachauri. The former will look after negotiations with neighbouring countries such as Bhutan, Nepal and Bangladesh with respect to rivers in the Ganga-Brahmaputra-Meghana (GBM) basin which encompasses India, Bhutan, Nepal and Bangladesh and is one of the richest, in terms of water resources, in the entire world. Dr. Pachauri will take care of the environmental aspects of the entire project.

At this stage, let us discuss the cost aspect. The NWDA had estimated that the cost of interlinking would be a total of Rs. 5,60,000 crore. This is not the final figure which will be known only after Detailed Project Reports (DPRs) of each of the thirty links, give or take one or two, are completed.

Does this tentative amount appear to be too formidable? Let us first consider the fact that all this money is not being spent in one year. It will take at least one decade to complete the inter-linking projects after they are taken up. So, this quantum of money is not being spent in just one year. Secondly, the size of the Indian economy has grown so much that this amount may not prove to be a very large one in a few years' time. The expenditure budget of the Government of India for the year 2003-04 is Rs. 4,65,741 crore (plan and non-plan taken together). So, in a few years' time India will be able to finance this project on her own.

However, at this stage, what appears likely is that a Special Purpose Vehicle (SPV) will be set-up on the lines of the National Highway Authority of India (NHAI) or the Delhi Metro Rail Corporation (DMRC) for implementation, including raising funds. In any case, the matter of finance is being looked into by the ICICI Bank now.

Then environment. Dr. Pachauri will look after this aspect. One can add here that there is no proposal to block the entire flow of water in the rivers which will be inter-linked. A constant flow is necessary in order to look after plant, animal and microorganism life downstream of dams. Secondly, the uninterrupted flows cleanse the cities, towns and villages through or by the side of which the rivers flow. These "rubbish" materials flushed by the rivers will prove to be food for fish and other aquatic life. Thirdly, slow release of stored water will not only produce hydro-electricity, but also help large-scale plantation of trees on canal banks, which would compensate by several times the loss of trees during the construction phase. In any case, NEERI, Nagpur and other institutes are looking into this aspect.

The benefits would be an additional 35 million hectares of land under irrigation and production of 40,000 megawatts (of installed capacity) of hydro-electric power. Imagine what would have been the cost of these two items if they were taken up separately.

However, it is not as if the construction work is being taken up immediately. There are two options. One is to take up the entire work of linking simultaneously after all the DPRs are prepared and the total cost computed. There is another option of starting work on the smaller links in which two or three states are involved, which may agree on the construction of these links. One must state here that one of the mandates of the task force is to evolve a consensus among the States involved for construction of the dams, canals and hydro-electric units.

There appears to be an urge to start work on such links as the Damanganga-Pinjal and Par-Tapi Narmada, both involving only Gujarat and Maharashtra. The first link will benefit Maharashtra by providing additional drinking water for the Mumbai metropolis. The second will generally help Gujarat alone as the additional waters from the Par and the Tapi to the Narmada will help not only Gujarat for coverage of additional command areas from the Narmada waters, but will also help it transfer excess waters in the Narmada to Rajasthan, as stated at the beginning of this article. The third is the Ken-Betwa involving Madhya Pradesh and Uttar Pradesh and the fourth is the Parbati-Kailisindh-Chambal link involving Rajasthan too. Apart from irrigation, these small links will help augment drinking water supply in villages and towns and small hydro-electric plants are also to be built at dam sites.

Let us now describe in greater detail some of the links. The southern grid begins from a place called Manibhadra in Cuttack district in Orissa where a dam is proposed to be built for storage and diversion of excess water in the Mahanadi during the flood season. From this place, a 900-km long canal is to be constructed for taking surplus waters to the Godavari at Dowlaiswaram barrage near Rajamundry in Andhra Pradesh. Water for irrigation en route will also be provided for.

From Dowlaiswaram, the excess waters of both the Mahanadi and the Godavari will be taken to the Prakasham Barrage across the Krishna river near Vijayawada in Andhra Pradesh. Provision has also been made to transfer Godavari waters to the Krishna from the proposed Inchampally project upstream of Rajamundry.

There is also a proposal to take Godavari waters from Polavaram on its bank to the Krishna.

From the Krishna, a canal will take the water from this river, its flow augmented by the transfer of surplus waters from the Mahanadi and the Godavari, to the Pennar river. Another canal from the Almati Dam across the Krishna in Karnataka to the Somasila Dam across Pennar has also been proposed. From Pennar, a canal will take water to the Grand Anicut to the Cauvery. However, this is not the ultimate destination of the waters from the Mahanadi and the Godavari. From the Cauvery waters will flow to Gundar and the Vaigai further south.

The eastern links begin from the Manas and Sankosh rivers flowing southwards from Bhutan. These waters will be taken to the Teesta and then on to the Ganga at Farakka. There is a proposal to build a canal from Farakka which will take some water (a couple of small rivers might also be used as conduits) to the Subarnarekha which drains West Bengal, Bihar, and Orissa. From there, another canal will take this water to the Brahmani and then on to the Mahanadi. Thus, Mahanadi will be compensated for its contribution to the main southern link from Manibhadra.

The third ambitious link is the one proposed to connect the Yamuna with the Rajasthan Canal (Indira Gandhi Nahar Pariyojana) and extend that remarkable canal towards Barmer district at first and then on to the Sabarmati river in Gujarat on the banks of which the city of Ahmedabad is situated.

Lastly, the Ganga. This sacred river has no surplus waters "above" Allahabad. However, thereafter, a large number of rivers originating in Nepal join it, such as the Ghaghra, the Gandak, the Kosi and the Mechi to name a few. Surplus waters of these three rivers will be taken towards the west to join the Yamuna and a part of this supply will be provided for the Rajasthan-Gujarat link.

Obviously, these links, the dams and the reservoirs, will result in displacement of a large number of people. The Task Force is engaged in evolving a rehabilitation package which will then be presented to the people and the authorities concerned for their comments. In any case, the Project will take full care of the PAPs (Project Affected People).

Bangladesh is unlikely to be affected because the proposal now is not to divert water from the Brahmaputra (Jogighopa-Teesta-Farakka). Instead, the Mansas-Sankosh-Teesta-Ganga link has been proposed. In this case too, perhaps both Assam and Arunachal Pradesh in India and Bangladesh might as well have same surplus waters taken away elsewhere so that the flood fury in those areas is lessened.

There are other issues too for resolution. For example, a number of State Governments are not yet convinced about the utility of the project. Kerala, which was opposed to the implementation of the Pamba-Achankovil-Vaippar link, that proposes to transfer waters from Kerala to Tamil Nadu, has now agreed to hold discussions on this issue. Bihar is supposed to be opposed to it and reportedly averse to providing waters of the Ganga to the proposed scheme. However, the main problem of Bihar is the stagnation of rain and flood waters in north Bihar which prevents any agricultural operations to take place during the Kharif season. If this accumulated water is drained-off to the Ganga, this state can have a good Kharif crop too in North Bihar along with winter maize and wheat during the Rabi season.

There are other issues involved too. However, the most important among these is the fact that the Constitution of India provides (Seventh Schedule, List II, Entry 17) water as a subject to the States. As such, the States have more or less the final say in matters connected with irrigation, dam construction or hydro-electricity generation. As such, the consensus among the States with the Centre is of vital importance to this concept becoming a mega project, the underlying idea behind which, as a priority, is producing 450 million tonnes of foodgrains a year from about 2025.

36

Inter Linking of Rivers

Radhakant Bharati

The discussion on the concept of inter-basin transfer of water started long back about 50 years ago, on the initiatives of Dr. K.L. Rao, former Union Minister of Irrigation and Power in preparing proposals for a National Water Grid, followed by Garland Canal, through Capt. Dastur. After several years the Government of India had set up an organization called National Water Development Agency (NWDA) in 1982, which has in the last 20 years done extensive studies of the various possible links for inter-basin water transfers.

The concept is rational and can solve a lot of problems. But it has also thrown open several delicate issues—the constitutional provisions, the existing legal provisions, water ownership, political support, willingness of participating states, etc. Various proposals involving inter-basin transfers within India on a large scale have been and are being studied for about the last 50 years. In the 1970s, Dr. K.L. Rao prepared proposals for the National Water Grid. His proposals better known as the Ganga-Kaveri Link consisted of 2640 km link from Ganga near Patna to transfer the Ganga waters during high flow to the south. The proposal also envisaged the Brahmaputra-Ganga Link and Western Link. Another proposal which received considerable publicity was that of Captain Dastur. This proposal better known as the Garland Canal consisted of a 4200 km long Himalayan Canal, a 9300 km long Southern Garland Canal and a connection between the two systems

Reprinted with permission, *Yojana*, June 2005, pp. 21-24.

through pipelines near Delhi and Patna. After intensive study of these proposals, the Ministry of Irrigation and the Central Water Commission in 1980, prepared a National Perspective Plan comprising of two components namely: (i) The Himalayan River Component, and (ii) The Peninsula River Component. The outline of the National Perspective Plan was widely discussed at the political level and a decision was taken by the then Prime Minister Smt. Indira Gandhi to start immediately.

Accordingly, the National Water Development Agency was set up in July 1982 by the Government of India. This Agency is charged with the detailed planning of the link proposals and preparing the feasibility reports of the various components. By now, the NWDA has completed all water balance studies and pre-feasibility studies. It has completed six feasibility level studies and is engaged in 18 other feasibility studies. Meanwhile, the concept of inter-basin water transfers again came into focus and the Government of India, in December, 2002 set-up a Task Force.

The Task Force has responsibility to suggest modalities for implementing the programme on inter-linking rivers of India. This follows from the National Perspective Plan for water resources development of the country. The Task Force needs to work towards achieving following four objectives, which, by all accounts are over ambitious at this stage:

- To augment irrigation potential by 35 million hectare (from 140 mha to 175 mha) which would increase the production of food for our growing population;
- To fulfil the growing need of water for the people (the domestic and industrial needs of water is expected to grow steeply by 300 per cent to 400 per cent in the coming decades);
- To generate about 34,000 MW of additional power through hydro-electricity to meet the increasing need of energy in the country; and
- To facilitate transportation in the country through inland waterways.

The project would insure the country against water stress and create a greener India. Needless to say, the successful implementation of the programme will result in the creation of a large number of jobs

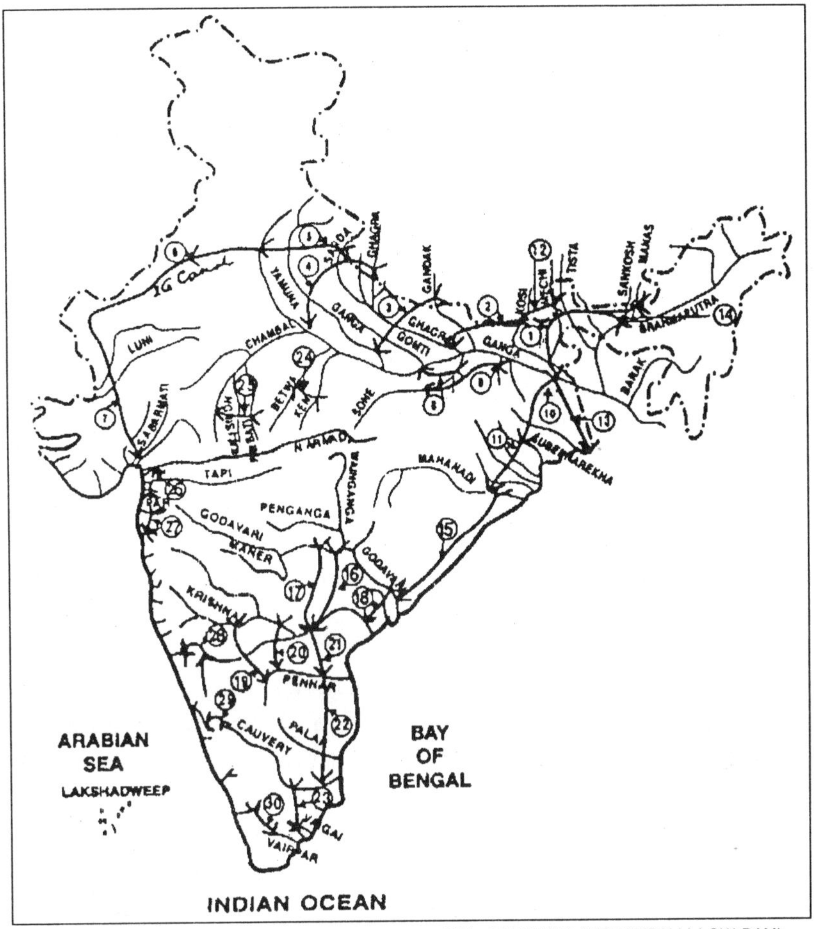

HIMALAYAN COMPONENT

NAME OF THE LINKS

(1) BRAHMAPUTRA-GANGA (MSTG)
(2) KOSI-GHAGRA
(3) GANDAK-GANGA
(4) GHAGRA-YAMUNA
(5) SARDA-YAMUNA
(6) YAMUNA-RAJASTHAN
(7) RAJASTHAN-SABARMATI
(8) CHUNAR-SONE BARRAGE
(9) SONE DAM—SOUTHERN TRIBUTARIES OF GANGA
(10) GANGA DAMODAR-SUBERNAREKHA
(11) SUBERNAREKHA-MAHANADI
(12) KOSI-MECHI
(13) FARAKKA-SUNDERBANS
(14) JOGIGOPA-TISTA-FARAKHA (Alternative to Sl.No.6 above)

PENINSULAR COMPONENT

NAME OF THE LINKS

(15) MAHANADI (MANI BHADRA)-GODAVARI (DOWLAISWARAM)
(16) GODAVARI (INCHAMPALLI LOW DAM)-KRISHNA (NAGARJUNASAGAR TAIL POND/ PULICHINTALA)
(17) GODAVARI (INCHAMPALLI)-KRISHNA (NAGARJUNASAGAR)
(18) GODAVARI (POLAVARAM)-KRISHNA (VIJAYAWADA)
(19) KRISHNA (ALMATTI)-PENNAR
(20) KRISHNA (SRISAILAM)-PENNAR
(21) KRISHNA (NAGARJUNASAGAR)-PENNAR (SOMASILA)
(22) PENNAR (SOMASILA)-CAUVERY (GRAND ANICUT)
(23) CAUVERY (KATTALAI)-VAIGAI-GUNDAR
(24) KEN-BETWA
(25) PARBATI-KALISINDH-CHAMBAL
(26) PAR-TAPI-NARMADA
(27) DAMANGANGA-PINJAL
(28) BEDTI-VARDA
(29) NETRAVATI-HEMAVATI
(30) PAMBA-ACHANKOVIL-VAIPPAR

NATIONAL WATER DEVELOPMENT AGENCY

and will be a positive step toward national integration and all round progress in agricultural India.

As desired, the Task Force started work on the National Prespective Plan which comprises of two components, namely: Himalayan Rivers Development and Peninsular Rivers Development.

Himalayan Rivers Component

The Himalayan Rivers Component envisages construction of storages on the main Ganga and Brahmaputra rivers and their principal tributaries in India and Nepal, so as to conserve monsoon flows for flood control, hydropower generation and irrigation. Interlinking canal systems will be provided to transfer surplus flows of the Kosi, Gandak and Ghagra to the west. In addition, Brahmaputra-Ganga Link will be constructed for augmenting dry weather flows of the Ganga. Surplus flows available on account of interlinking of Ganga and Yamuna are proposed to be transferred to the drought prone areas of Haryana, Rajasthan and Gujarat.

The scheme will also enable large areas in South Uttar Pradesh and south Bihar to obtain irrigation benefits from the Ganga with a moderate lift of less than 30 m. Further, all lands in the Terai area of Nepal would also get irrigation apart from generation of about 30 million kw of hydropower in Nepal and India. It will also provide flood moderation in the Ganga-Brahmaputra system. With this proposal, about 140 BCM of additional water would be available from these river systems for irrigating an estimated 22 million ha. in the Ganga-Brahmaputra plains, apart from Haryana, Punjab, Rajasthan and Gujarat. It would also provide 1120 cumecs (40,000 cusecs) to Kolkata Port and would provide navigation facilities across the country. The scheme will benefit not only parts of India but also neighbouring countries of Nepal and Bangladesh (NWDA Report, 1998).

Link Proposals for Peninsular Rivers

The link proposals formulated by NWDA under the Peninsular Component are:

The Mahanadi-Godavari-Krishna-Pennar-Kaveri-Vaigai link running through the eastern region of peninsular India and inter-connecting all the major east-flowing rivers of southern India is the main link of the peninsular rivers component. This link system has been divided into several parts as follows:

- Mahanadi to Godavari
- Manibhadra-Dowlaiswaram Link
- Godavari to Krishna
- Inchampalli-Nagarjunasagar Link
- Inchampalli-Pulichintala Link
- Polavaram-Vijayawada Link
- Krishna to Pennar
- Almatti-Pennar Link
- Srisailam-Pennar Link
- Nagarjunasagar-Somasila Link
- Pennarto Cauvery
- Somasila-Grand Anicut Link
- Cauvery to Vaigai
- Kattalai Regulator-Vaigai-Gundar Link
- Par-Tapi-Narmada and Damanganga-Pinjal links under the component of interlinking of small west-flowing rivers along the west-coast south of Tapi and north of Mumbai.
- Ken-Betwa and Kalisindh-Chambal links for inter-connecting the southern tributaries of Yamuna.
- Pamba-Achankovil-Vaippar, Netravati-Hemavati and Bedthi-Varada links for the diversion of surplus waters of the west-flowing rivers of Kerala and Karnataka to the east.

Link Proposals for Himalayan Rivers

The Himalayan Rivers Development Component comprises water balance studies at 19 diversion points, 16 toposheet and storages capacity studies of reservoirs, 19 toposheet studies of links and 14 pre-feasibility studies of links. NWDA has completed all these studies.

Based on NWDA studies, the interbasin Water Transfer links under the Himalayan Component for which feasibility reports are to be prepared by NWDA are as follows:

- Brahmaputra-Ganga link (Manas-Sankosh-Teesta-Ganga)
- Kosi-Ghagra link
- Gandak-Ganga link
- Ghagra-Yamuna link
- Sarda-Yamuna link
- Yamuna-Rajasthan link

- Rajasthan-Sabarmati link
- Chunar-Sone Barrage link
- Sone Dam-southern tributaries of Ganga link
- Ganga-Damodar-Subernarekha link
- Subernarekha-Mahanadi link
- Kosi-Mechi link
- Farakka-Sunderbans link
- Brahmaputra-Ganga link (Jogigopa-Teesta-Farakka)

Field surveys and investigations for preparing feasibility reports of links are in progress.

Main Issues

The current proposals for inter-basin transfer prepared by the National Water Development Agency, and the objectives which it could have filled, can be distinguished. In short the distinguishing features are:

- These transfers by their nature are inter-basin and these seem to violate the basic premise of 'basin' as a hydrologic unit for water development and management.
- These transfers allow the diversion of waters to the 'non co-basin' states or provinces of India which are rather uncommon.
- Inter-basin transfers in particular, long distance transfers are perceived as somewhat unusual.
- Conformity of these proposals with the existing legal system (international law, the Constitution of India and the relevant laws within India) needs special examination.
- Before embarking on such large proposals, the available alternatives require careful consideration.
- The methods and practice in the inter-basin transfer proposals need to be reconsidered and if necessary modifications need to be worked out.
- These transfers being rather large, can have serious social, ecological and environmental impacts which could perhaps be larger than and different from those of the conventional in-basin developments.

On this gigantic project, discussions are going on at various levels. The concerned authorities say that the project will bring the desired prosperity to the Indian people. But some expressed their doubts regarding the implementation of the inter-linking proposals. Important among them are Dr. K.C. Thomas (former Chairman, CWPC), Dr. M.S. Reddy (Ex-secretary, Ministry of Water Resources), Dr. Bharat Singh, Prof. Kanta Prasad and Chief Engineer R.C. Jha. In his recent book Prof. Ramaswamy R. Iyer opined, "Even more serious is the funding problem. Plan outlays are barely adequate even for completion of projects already undertaken. The amounts needed for completing spillover projects is Rs. 70,000 crore in the Tenth and Rs. 1,10,000 crore in the Eleventh Plan. That leaves no scope for new major projects and necessitates a severe selectivity even in regard to the continuance of what are called ongoing projects. Against this background there seems to be little likelihood of funding the massive resources needed for a major river-linking undertaking. The rough figure mentioned in the Supreme Court (by the Government of India) in this context was Rs. 5,60,000 crore!"

Under these circumstances, one can agree with Prof. Ramaswamy when he says, "We must hope that the Task Force set up as directed by the Supreme Court will consider not merely the "modalities" of the "linking of rivers" but also the soundness and wisdom of the idea. Any headlong rush in the pursuit of this will be disastrous."

37

Linking Forests and Rivers

Pandurang Hegde

The political leaders ruling the country as well as the bureaucrats are planning to link rivers in the country from north to south, with the sole objective of solving the recurring water problem. It is claimed that with this expensive mega linking project the country will be able to solve the problem of water supply, both for irrigation as well as for growing food to meet the needs of hungry people. This noble idea is well intentioned, but the facts that are emerging, of late, point to a different story altogether.

One of the main hypothesis of river linking is that the rivers in North India are perennial as they originate from the snow clad peaks or glaciers in the Himalayas.

The recent report of the WWF (World Wildlife Fund for Nature), an international organisation, has come out with the fact that "Himalayan glaciers are among the fastest receding in the world due to global warming and this will eventually lead to the drying up of glacier-fed rivers and causing water shortage in the Indian subcontinent." Obviously, with such a drastic prediction, the project to interlink rivers in India loses its rationale.

The rivers in India originate either from the glaciers in the Himalayas or from the forests in the hill regions. As Chipko leader and noted environmentalist Sunderlal Bahuguna says, "The forests are the mothers of rivers." The forests are the catchment areas of most of the rivers in our country. The mighty Ganga originates in the

Reprinted with permission, *Yojana*, June 2005, pp. 25-26.

Himalayas whereas the Cauvery and Krishna originate in the forest region of the Western Ghats.

These catchment forests serve the basic function of absorbing moisture from rainfall and assist in recharging the streams, which feed our rivers. Essentially, the natural forests perform these functions effectively. Realising this primary function of the catchment forests and also to conserve these fragile forest ecosystems, people from time immemorial have made the sources of rivers as "sacred" and converted them into pilgrimage centres.

Thus, the Gangotri, (the origin of the Ganga) or Tala Cauvery (the origin of the Cauvery) are pilgrimage spots for us. The reverence to the origin, to the rivers and to the catchment forests is in-built with the purpose of conserving these resources. Before our bureacracy coined the term "watershed development," the theme of conservation of the origin of rivers had already evolved in our culture.

Nevertheless, at present, we have jettisoned the culture of conservation of river catchments and have adopted an approach which has not only destroyed the forests but also created a trail of destruction of water resources (our rivers and streams). In most parts of the country, the natural forests in the catchments of rivers are clearly felled to make way for monoculture plantations. In the Himalayas, the natural broad leaf oak trees are felled to make way for pine monoculture plantations. In Central India and Eastern regions, we have felled sal forests to replace it with teak monocultures.

Finally, in south India, in the Western Ghats, we have felled the most bio-diverse tropical forests to plant teak and eucalyptus plantations. Recently, the group that walked along the River Sharavati in Karnataka found that almost eighty per cent of the catchment forests are planted with exotic acacia plantations.

This large-scale conversion of natural forests into monoculture plantations has had a drastic impact on the river ecosystems as well as on the hydrology of the region.

These plantations are not in a position to perform the role of water conservation or in recharging the river streams. Most often, their water requirement is more and it leads to drying of streams and water sources. This has a cumulative effect on the river basins, accelerating water shortage on a large scale.

The present water crisis as well as the forecast of an impending water shortage in the coming years, is the result of the narrow policies followed by the government as well as our leaders and bureaucrats. They have ignored the links between forests and water as well as rivers. If the catchment forests are intact, then the rivers and streams are healthy. This is a globally accepted norm.

Timber Mines

But, we have ignored this wisdom and created thousands of hectares of plantations, which can be ideally called "Timber Mines" serving the function of mining timber and ignoring roles of other forms of water conservation.

Consequently, we see that most of the rivers that flow during the monsoon months, are red with the silt of the hilly region. This is an indicator of dead river. Coupled with this is the fact that most rivers are polluted and the water is not fit for human or animal consumption. The National Forest Policy recognises the fact that forests need to be conserved for meeting the ecological functions and conservation of water resources in the country. The National Water Policy of the government does not even mention the link of forests to water resources. It takes for granted the availability of water that needs to be supplied to various stake-holders. These crucial policy papers are devoid of looking at the important issues in a holistic manner.

The need of the hour is to re-establish the links between forests and water, to evolve the holistic approach to the water crisis. It is essential and priority ought to be given to conservation of the natural catchment forests instead of converting them into monoculture plantations. In order to get assured perennial water supply in our rivers and streams, it is essential to go back to the wisdom of conserving our sources of water and rivers, the forests.

In our national anthem, we say *sujalam* and *suphalam*, meaning the abundance of water for our countrymen. In reality, the country is facing one of the worst water crisis.

While celebrating World Water Day, let us commit ourselves to conserving the watersheds of rivers and not pollute them. Similarly, while celebrating World Forestry Day, let us not look at the forests as the resource that provides us timber, but consider it as nature's factory that provides soil and water.

It is no wonder that the Chipko women have coined this slogan: 'What do the forests give? soil, water and pure air'. Soil, water and pure air are the basis of life. It is only the link of forests and rivers that can really lead to an abundance of water in the country.

(Courtesy: Deccan Herald)

38

Transferring River Water

A. Ravinder

Water is the most important natural resource and is vital for all life on earth. The well-being and development of any society is dependent on the availability of water.

According to Hindu mythology, the whole universe is made up of five elements. They are Vayu (Air), Jal (Water), Bhoomi (Earth), Agni (Fire) and Akasha (Sky). These elements are to be duly respected and considered in planning the progress of any country to avoid disasters. Water is the prime element in the socio-economic development of any nation.

Water in the Indian rivers is basically derived from rainfall and a portion from snow. The rainfall during the monsoon season, June to September, is responsible for the availability of water in the rivers. The annual rainfall in India varies from as high as over 1000 cm at Cherrapunji in Meghalaya to as low as 10 cm in the western districts of Rajasthan. The distribution of rainfall is highly erratic both with respect to space and time.

The water inflow in the major rivers of India, as estimated by the Central Water Commission is provided in Table 1.

The water resources availability of India provides ample opportunity for utilization. The following data gives an insight into the utilisation of resources:

(a) Annual rainfall: 400 m.ha.m.

Table 1: Basin-wise Surface Water Potential of India

S. No.	*Name of the River Basin Average*	*Annual Potential in River (Cubic Km/Year)*
1.	Indus (up to border)	73.31
	(a) Ganga	525.02
	(b) Brahmaputra Barak and others	585.60
2.	Godavari	110.5
3.	Krishna	78.12
4.	Cauvery	21.36
5.	Pennar	6.32
6.	East flowing rivers between Mahanadi and Pennar	22.52
7.	East flowing rivers between Pennar and Kanyakumari	16.46
8.	Mahanadi	66.88
9.	Brahmani and Baitarni	28.48
10.	Subernarekha	12.37
11.	Sabarmati	3.81
12.	Mahi	11.02
13.	West flowing rivers of Kutch, Sabarmati including Luni	15.10
14.	Narmada	45.64
15.	Tapi	14.88
16.	West flowing rivers from Tapi to Tadri	87.41
17.	West flowing rivers from Tadri to Kanyakumari	113.53
18.	Area of inland drainage in Rajasthan desert	NEG.
19.	Minor river basins drainage into Bangladesh and Myanmar	31.00
	Total	186.33

(b) Annual available surface water flow in rivers: 187 m.ha.m (47 per cent of rainfall).

(c) Annual utilizable surface water: 69 m.ha.m (37 per cent of available water).

(d) Utilizable groundwater: 45 m.ha.m.

(e) The utilizable surface and groundwater after development of water resources: 114 m.ha.m (28 per cent annual rainfall).

As it can be seen, the percentage of utilizable surface water is likely to be only 37 per cent of available water as the country does not have adequate storage sites. If all the probable sites are developed, the position will be as follows:

(1) Ultimate storage capacity: 41 m.ha.m (major, medium and minor).
(2) Capacity already utilized through 2900 major dams and 2 lakh minor dams: 174 m.ha.m.
(3) Capacity of major dams under construction: 75 m.ha.m.
(4) Capacity of proposed dams: 13.2 m.ha.m.

Though the country has the capability to utilize 20.7 m.ha.m, the fullest utilization may not be possible, as all the projects may not pass all the investigations. Therefore, the total utilizable capacity can be estimated to be about 25-30 m.ha.m.

The present population of India is about 1000 million. The projected water demand for the various purposes is shown in Table 2.

Table 2

	2020 AD	*2025 AD*	*2050 AD*
Irrigation	688	910	1072
Drinking	56	73	102
Industrial	12	23	63
Energy	5	15	130
Others	52	72	80
Total	813	1093	1447

Figures in billion cu.m.

To meet the requirements, it is necessary to tap the resources available. The utilisation can be at macro or micro-level. To utilize the resources in a big way a project would involve interlinking of major rivers of India.

This concept had been proposed during the British regime by Sir Arthur Cotton with respect to transportation. Instead of railway network, he had proposed to connect the nation through interlinking canals with navigation facilities.

It was almost a century, before a similar scheme was proposed again in the late 1960s by K.L. Rao, Union Minister.

A similar proposal was made by Captain Dastur in 1977 which became popular as the Garland canal project. The committees comprising experts from the CWG, state governments and professors

PROPOSED INTER BASIN WATER TRANSFER LINKS

HIMALAYAN COMPONENT
NAME OF THE LINKS

(1) BRAHMAPUTRA-GANGA (MSTG)
(2) KOSI-GHAGRA
(3) GANDAK-GANGA
(4) GHAGRA-YAMUNA

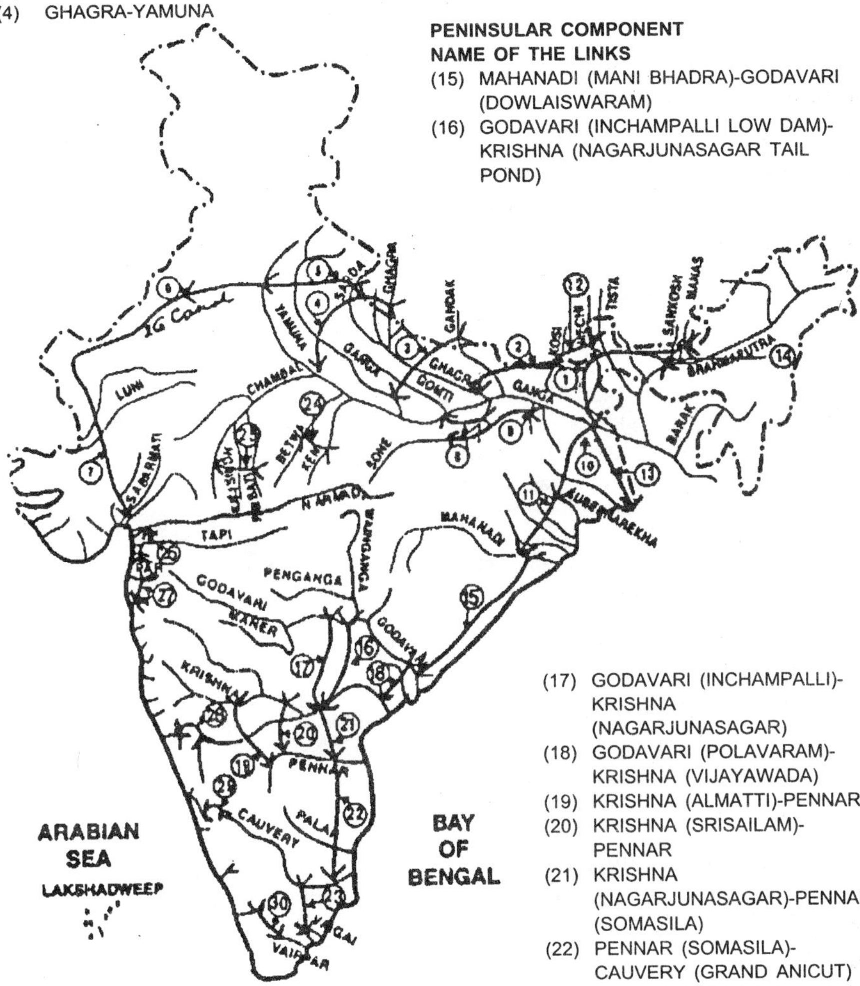

(5) SARDA-YAMUNA
(6) YAMUNA-RAJASTHAN
(7) RAJASTHAN-SABARMATI
(8) CHUNAR-SONE BARRAGE
(9) SONE DAM—SOUTHERN TRIBUTARIES OF GANGA
(10) GANGA DAMODAR-SUBERNAREKHA
(11) SUBERNAREKHA-MAHANADI
(12) KOSI-MECHI
(13) FARAKKA-SUNDERBANS
(14) BRAHMAPUTRA GANGA (JTF) (ALT)

PENINSULAR COMPONENT
NAME OF THE LINKS

(15) MAHANADI (MANI BHADRA)-GODAVARI (DOWLAISWARAM)
(16) GODAVARI (INCHAMPALLI LOW DAM)-KRISHNA (NAGARJUNASAGAR TAIL POND)
(17) GODAVARI (INCHAMPALLI)-KRISHNA (NAGARJUNASAGAR)
(18) GODAVARI (POLAVARAM)-KRISHNA (VIJAYAWADA)
(19) KRISHNA (ALMATTI)-PENNAR
(20) KRISHNA (SRISAILAM)-PENNAR
(21) KRISHNA (NAGARJUNASAGAR)-PENNAR (SOMASILA)
(22) PENNAR (SOMASILA)-CAUVERY (GRAND ANICUT)
(23) CAUVERY (KATTALAI)-VAIGAI-GUNDAR
(24) KEN-BETWA
(25) PARBATI-KALISINDH-CHAMBAL
(26) PAR-TAPI-NARMADA
(27) DAMANGANGA-PINJAL
(28) BEDTI-VARDA
(29) NETRAVATI-HEMAVATI
(30) PAMBA-ACHANKOVIL-VAIPPAR

of IITs and University of Roorkee, examined this proposal and decided that it were technically unsound and economically prohibitive.

The proposals were taken seriously and created a lot of interest at the intellectual level to look for a viable solution for tackling droughts and floods.

The Government of India formed the National Water Development Agency (NWDA) in 1982 to identify river links for a national grid, to prepare feasibility studies and execute detailed project reports on these. The NWDA has identified 30 river links which would connect every major river and has proposed feasibility reports on six of these. The NWDA estimates that the cost of the entire project would be Rs. 5.6 lakh crore and it would take 30 years to execute.

Table 3: Time Table for Interlinking of Rivers

Notification of the Task Force	*16.12.2002*
Preparation of action plan-1, giving an outline of the time schedules for the completion of the feasibility studies, detailed project reports, estimated cost, implementation of the schedule, concrete benefits and advantages of the project	30.04.2003
Preparation of action plan 2, giving alternative options for funding and execution of the project as also the suggested methods for cost recovery	31.07.2003
Meeting with the chief ministers to deliberate over the project and to elicit their cooperation	May/June, 2003
Completion of feasibility studies (already in progress)	31.12.2005
Completion of Detailed Project Reports	31.12.2006
Implementation of the project (10 years)	31.12.2016

NWDA was geared up in 1982 to carry out indepth studies in order to implement the proposals of NPPP.

According to the studies, the water availability status of major rivers is as given in Table 4.

Based on the water balance studies of various river basins/sub-basins/the proposals identified for preparations of feasibility reports by NWDA are:

The implementation of national river linking will have to necessarily be carried out in phases. There are two components:

Table 4: Water Availability Status of Major Rivers

S. No.	*Basin*	*Water Availability (BCM)*	*Water Requirement (BCM)*	*Balance (BCM)*
1.	Mahanadi	66.29	54.71	11.58
2.	Godavari	77.64	62.62	15.02
3.	Krishna	66.00	69.24	3.240
4.	Pennar	5.32	9.14	3.82 (–)
5.	Cauvery	19.13	22.05	2.92 (–)
6.	Vaigai	1.60	2.26	0.65 (–)

(1) Himalayan river component.
(2) Peninsular river component.

The phase-wise implementation plan is as follows:

Phase-I: Linking of major peninsular rivers—Mahanadi, Godavari, Krishna and Cauvery.

Phase-II: Other links in the peninsular system such as Keri-Betwa, Par-Tapi, etc.

Phase-III: Linking of tributaries of the Ganga and Brahmaputra-Tanger link.

Peninsular Component

(1) Mahanadi (Manibhadra)-Godavari (Dowlarswaran link)
(2) Godavari (Inchamapalli Low/Dam)-Krishna (Nagarjuna Sagar Tail Pond/Pulichintala) Link
(3) Godavari (Inchampalli)-Krishna (Nagarjuna Sagar) Link
(4) Godavari (Polavaram)-Krishna (Nagarjuna Sagar) Link
(5) Krishna (Almatti)-Pennar Link
(6) Krishna (Srisailam)-Pennar Link
(7) Krishna (Nagarjuna Sagar)-Pennar (Somasila) Link
(8) Pennar (Somasila)-Cauvery (Grand Anicut) Link
(9) Cauvery (Kattalai)-Vaigai-Gundar Link
(10) Ken-Betwa Link
(11) Parbati-Kalisindh-Chambal Link
(12) Par-Tapi-Narmada Link
(13) Damangana-Pinjal Link
(14) Bedti-Varada Link
(15) Netravati-Hemavati Link

(16) Pamba-Achankovil-Vaippar Link

Himalayan Component

(1) Manas-Sankosh-Teesta Link
(2) Kosi-Ghagra Link
(3) Gandak-Ganga Link
(4) Ghagra-Yamuna Link
(5) Sarda-Yamuna Link
(6) Yamuna-Rajasthan Link
(7) Rajasthan-Sabarmati Link
(8) Chunar-Sone Barrage Link
(9) Sone Dam-southern tributaries of Ganga Link
(10) Ganga-Damodar-Subernarekha Link
(11) Subernarekha-Mahanadi Link
(12) Kosi-Mechi Link
(13) Farakka-Sunderbans Link
(14) Jogigopa-Teesta-Farakka Link

A brief description of some of the linkings benefiting Andhra Pradesh is given below:

Mahanadi-Godavari Link

In this link 11,176 m.cu.m. of water is proposed for diversion through the link taking-off at Manibhadra reservoir (proposed) to Dowlaiswaram Barrage on Godavari.

This link will provide en route irrigation benefits to the tune of 4.54 lakh hectares, of which 1.02 lakh hectares will be in Andhra Pradesh and 3.52 lakh hectares will be in Orissa. In this process it will utilize 3854 m.cu.m. of water. Transmission losses will be 822 m cu m. The balance 6500 m.cu.m of water is proposed to be transferred further south. The total length of this link will be 932 km including 6.3 km long tunnel. Canal capacity will be 627 cu.m./sec. There is provision for generation of 966 MW of hydro-power at Manibhadra dam. Manibhadra reservoir will submerge 45,000 ha of land including 4881 ha of forest. 90,582 persons are likely to be affected.

Godavari (Inchampalli)-Krishna (Nagarjuna Sagar) Link

21,520 cu.m. of water including 6500 m.cu.m. of water from Mahanadi is planned for diversion to the Krishna basin through three links. The Inchampalli dam (proposed)-Nagarjuna Sagar link will transfer 16,426 m.cu.m of water through a 299 km link including a 9 km long canal. The canal will have a capacity of 1219 cu.m./sec. and will be operated for a period of 195 days a year. En route irrigation is of the tune of 3.19 lakh ha. utilizing 1850 m.cu.m. Transmission losses are estimated to be 376 m.cu.m. The link will require a total lift of 116 m utilizing 1705 MW of power. There is a provision of 975 MW of peaking power at Inchampalli reservoir which will be 92,555 ha. of which 21,734 ha. is reserved forests. About one lakh population will be affected.

Godavari (Inchampalli Low Dam)-Krishna (Nagarjuna Sagar Tail Pond/ Pulichintala) Link

This link envisages transfer of 521 m.cu.m. of water through a 419 km canal of which 13 km will be through a tunnel section. En route irrigation will be 2.97 m.ha. utilizing 1757 m.cu.m. of water and delivering 3213 m.cu.m. of water at the tail pond after meeting transmission losses of 248 m.cu.m. The proposal involves an initial lift of 21 m. requiring 147 MW of power. Two dams are proposed, namely, Inchampalli on Godavari and Nagarjuna Sagar Tail Pond on Krishna with gross live storage of 976 m.cu.m. and 901 m.cu.m. respectively. The submerged area under Inchampalli Low Dam will be 17,900 ha, which is confined to the river portion only.

Godavari (Polavaram)-Krishna (Vijayawada) Link

The link will take-off from the proposed Polavaram reservoir and divert 5325 m.cu.m. of water over a length of 174 km. The link canal is proposed to be operated throughout the year and the design discharge is 405.12 cu.m./sec. This link will provide irrigation benefits to about 5.82 lakh ha. in Andhra Pradesh. The link will transfer 2265 m.cu.m. of additional water for stabilization of the Krishna delta. The Polavaram reservoir will submerge an area of 63,691 ha comprising 60,063 ha. in Andhra Pradesh, 2398 ha in Chhattisgarh and 1230 ha. in Orissa. Out of the total submergence 30,650 ha. is under cultivation and 3705 ha. is under forests. Population affected will be 1.45 lakhs in 250 villages.

Krishna (Almatti)-Pennar Link

For interlinking Krishna with Pennar, three links are envisaged. The Almatti Pennar link will divert 1980 m cu m of water and will provide en route irrigation to 2.35 lakh ha (1.61 lakh ha in Andhra Pradesh and 0.74 lakh ha in Karnataka).

Krishna (Srisailam)-Pennar Link

This link envisages transfer of 2310 m.cu.m. of water to Pennar which will be picked up at Somasila for onward transmission further south. No en route irrigation is proposed. The link canal will be 204 km long and it is proposed to generate 17 MW en route utilizing natural falls of the streams.

Krishna (Nagarjuna Sagar)-Pennar (Somasila) Link

This link envisages diversion of 12,146 m cu m of water from the Nagarjuna Sagar to Pennar. Total length of the link canal is about 393 km. The en route irrigation proposed is 5.81 lakh ha. entirely in Andhra Pradesh by utilizing 3264 m.cu.m. of water. 124 m.cu.m. of water is provided for drinking water supply needs and 332 m.cu.m. will be the transmission losses. Balance 8426 m.cu.m. is available at Somasila for further diversion to Cauvery and Vaigai.

In the final analysis, the advantages and disadvantages of interlinking of the rivers in India can be put forth as follows:

Advantages

The National Perspective Plan would give additional benefits of 25 million ha of irrigation from surface waters, 10 million ha. by increased use of groundwater, raising the ultimate irrigation potential from 113 million ha to 148-150 million ha and generation of 34 million KW of power, apart from the benefits of flood control, navigation, water supply, fisheries, salinity and pollution control, etc.

Disadvantages

- The Himalayan and the Peninsular plans have flood flows estimated at 30,000 to 60,000 cubic metres of water per second (cusec) during a few days in the monsoon season. But finer analysis reveals that only 4500 cusecs is to be lifted from a total flood flow of 60,000 cusecs. Quite obviously lifting such small proportions will not mitigate the country's flood problems.

- Interlinking is hardly justified as the solution for this problem. Moreover, it will be almost impossible to take the water to all the habitations without huge investments in a centralized distribution network.
- The World Bank estimates the health costs of water pollution in India to be equivalent to three per cent of the country's gross domestic product with Indian rivers being severely polluted; interlinking them may actually increase these costs. Also, with the widely recognized failure of the Ganga Action Plan, there is a danger that contaminants from the Ganga basin might enter other basins and destroy their natural cleansing processes. The new areas that will be river-fed after the introduction of the scheme may experience crop failures or routing due to alien compounds carried into their streams from the polluted Ganga.
- The costs of interlinking is estimated to be about Rs. 5,60,000 crore. But this is a conservative figure.
- The government suggested that it can raise money through loans, taxes and user charges. This means that local users will have to bear the enormous costs of sustaining the project. Interlinking rivers might thus end up creating illusions of water security, while in reality it will create conditions where privatisation becomes the only alternative.
- The Himalaya and the Peninsula projects have flood flow estimates at 30,000 to 60,000 cubic metres of water per second during a few days in the monsoon season.
- The plan envisions tapping these flows, storing them in reservoirs and finally draining them over thousands.
- But finer analysis reveals that 4500 cusecs is to be lifted from a total flood flow of 60,000 cusecs.
- Quite obviously lifting such small proportions will not mitigate the country's flood problems.
- Transferring water might end up creating rancour between the states.

Index